PSYCHOLOGY OF ETHICS

The Foundations of Human Nature (Longmans, Green and Co., 1935).

Living Consciously, with Walter H. Seegers (Detroit: Wayne State University Press, 1959).

The Growth of Self Insight (Detroit: Wayne State University Press, 1960).

The Jefferson-Dunglison Letters (Charlottesville, Va.: University of Virginia Press, 1960).

Illness or Allness (Detroit: Wayne State University Press, 1965).

American Government, Conscious Self Sovereignty (Detroit: Center for Health Education, 1969).

Psychology of Emotion (Detroit: Center for Health Education, 1971).

Psychology of Language (Detroit: Center for Health Education, 1971).

Psychology of Political Science (Detroit: Center for Health Education, 1973).

Monographs

Some Considerations of the Psychoanalytical Principle and Religious Living (Indian Psycho-analytical Society, 1954).

Science of Sanity (Detroit: Center for Health Education, 1954).

Living Education (Michigan Education Journal. April and May 1957).

A Psychoanalytic Appreciation of American Government (The American Imago, 1961).

Discovering My World of My Mind, A Conscious Way of Life (Detroit: Center for Health Education, 1965).

ii

PSYCHOLOGY OF ETHICS

John M. Dorsey, M.D., LL.D.

Published by
Center for Health Education
4421 Woodward Avenue
Detroit, Michigan   48201

BJ
1012
. D58

Printed by Edwards Brothers, Inc.

iii

Whoever feels any love or skill for ethical studies may safely lay out all his strength and genius in working this mine.

Ralph Waldo Emerson

CONTENTS

PREFACE

When Shakespeare is charged with debts to his au-
thors, Landor replies: "Yes, he was more original than his
originals." He breathed upon dead bodies and brought
them to life.

Ralph Waldo Emerson

July 30, 1932, under the auspices of the International Institute of Intellectual Co-operation, Albert Einstein wrote to Sigmund Freud about the need of his world for peace, for educative methods to deliver mankind from the menace of war, of psychosis of hate and destructiveness.[1]

September, 1932, Professor Freud replied with his characteristic genius for thoroughness describing the ethicality of most important discoveries in his psychoanalytic research.

December 3, 1932, Dr. Einstein wrote his appreciation for Professor Freud's "gratifying gift to the League of Nations. . . . You have earned my gratitude and the gratitude of all men for having devoted all your strength to the search for truth and for having shown the rarest courage in professing your convictions all your life. . . ."

It is specifically in keeping with the profundity of this magnificent effort for the all-worthy cause of world peace that I present this work. It is fitting to this cause that I quote Jan Christian Smuts:

[1]*Einstein on Peace*, Preface by Bertrand Russell, edited by Otto Nathan and Heinz Norden (New York: Simon and Shuster, 1960).

> ... the concept of Freedom is rooted in that of the whole ... the external is absorbed and transformed by the subtle mechanism of the whole into something of itself; otherness becomes selfness ... and as the series of wholes progresses the element of Freedom increases in the universe, until finally at the human stage Freedom takes conscious control of itself and begins to create the free ethical world of the spirit. ... The ethical message of Holism to man is summed up in two words: Freedom and Purity. And ... it is clear that these two grand ethical ideals are at bottom identical.[2]

Daily I live my fellow student protesting his inability to call his living his own and his all his living. He believes he cries "out" (instead of *in*):

"How can I further the likelihood of living my self so that I can simultaneously appreciate *that* is what I am doing (just living myself), particularly when everything I do (except when I am acknowledging that my doing *is* my being) distracts me from this sanifying truth? How can I learn that my *practice* of noticing myself in my living is my lifesaving life-lesson? How can I make sure to feature the fact that I am creating (in and of myself) everything that has any meaning at all for me? I can see that I take myself for granted nearly all of the time, except for rather frequent (mostly vague) stirrings of specific self consciousness. I see also that it must seem easier for me to carry my feelings of guilt for my self disregard than my feelings of responsibility for my self recognition, in nearly all of my behavior. Can I be immoral! My divinity is not immoral!

"Surely my mind itself is all that I *can* be experiencing in any and all of *my* mental activity and often I have told myself to appreciate that observation by making it more frequently, — but I just go on forgetting myself as usual most of the time. For example, how can

[2]*Holism and Evolution* (New York: The Viking Press, Inc., 1961), pp. 120, 314.

I learn to realize that there can be nothing but my own life's creation to please or displease me? And, most of all, how can I get over expecting somebody else (not *my* somebody else) to help me? For example, how can I convince myself that my seeming to be able to interrogate (my) you, is preventing my seeing that I can only make self inquiry, and that my *acknowledged* self questioning is a sign of my readiness to grow self experience revealing the answer covered by my question?

"It is most difficult for me to see that my sensation or perception is nothing but my self production; that my fellowman is nothing but some of my own being; that what I eat or drink is nothing but my original self growth; that I must first create my parent or spouse or offspring or nourishment before I can be aware for the existence of either in my living; that *my* "objective" world exists all and only as some of my *subjective* existence.

"Please, in (my) your words, grow your science of ethics or ethics of science, and compose it in the form of exposition, so that I can ultimately and convincingly author it my self. But please *keep it short, sir.* I must believe my time is valuable even if I cannot see that all so-called time seems to take over the meaning of life itself, surreptitiously of course."

The following observation on my *ethic* is acknowledged self observation. My reason for any of it is no different from my reason for being. I find all of it helpful for clearing my view of the integrity of my individuality and thus for enhancing my appreciation for my living. *The mission of the hero is to lead himself well.* It is hardly necessary to point out that the preservation of health, the first and fundamental obligation of personal responsibility, cannot be safely disposed of as an unearned blessing of life.

Each meaningful organ or system of my constitution is my mind's frontier, immediately dependent upon my mental condition for the exercise of its own wisdom. A mind divided against itself by dissociation into revered and repudiated elements finds expression in organic embarrassment and compensation known as "signs and symptoms of impaired health." The physician himself is the first one to observe of his science of medicine as it now exists: What is presently known in it is very little indeed considered against the background of what remains to be learned. Man could well do without the most of his health ordeals, and endure the others kindly, if he could develop sufficient understanding of how to use his mind according to the law of its being. I am my only lifebearing love and truth.

My life work has consisted of medical research in this particular interest and I have constructed a powerful *novum organum* for myself in a science of health built upon self insight utilizing the self helpfulness provided by my own nature. The idea of my goal is clear. The road leading to it is open. That goal is the acknowledgment of perfection everywhere; that road is the study of the fact perfectly accounting for whatever is. A conscious self confrontation is necessary before I can qualify as this scientist of health; I must make myself grow to see that the *only* possible control of nature by science is the control of his own human nature by the given scientist.

My modern "science of nature" is not at all sufficiently supplemented by a modern science of human individuality. Indeed, the more one spends his life in "the study of nature" the less he may devote his attention to appreciating that very life itself. Rarest of all is the scientist of the inviolable wholeness of his own individuality, although each and every other scientist cherishes the highest opinion of the practical value of whatever science he may be paying for with his life.

Utility largely determines my scientist's value of science, and a form of his mind consciousness he calls "observation" constitutes his scientific method, but the utility of his one and only possible scientific method, namely *self observation,* may remain largely unexplored. As in nearly all so-called peaceful human enterprise, my scientist, military fashion, may dull his appreciation for his individuality, seeing himself largely as organized into a vast "army" of collaborators "fighting" ignorance or disease or some other hostile force.

The individual's own idea that "the rational State" scientifically ordered would adequately guard the welfare of each of its citizens is a cherished delusion diametrically opposed to Thomas Jefferson's "expression of the American mind," namely: the best government is self sovereignty. Little wonder Rousseau's assertion that "culture" and "civilization" do not make man appreciate his excellence. *Only I, acting as my own acknowledged agent, can teach my self any of my own greatness.* My current scientific literature, psychological often included, seems to illustrate extreme mental need in author and reader by the consistency with which it records impossible impersonality and impersonation as if possible.

My only real scientific control of nature must be a form of my self control. Furthermore, my claiming irresponsibility over that which I cannot recognize as my own living, results in my accruing loss of recognizable self control producing augmenting health compensation popularly known as health impairment. Therefore, whatever I am not ready to experience as entirely and only my self development is the specific kind of living to avoid if possible, until I can succeed in cultivating the self tolerance (self love) enabling me to sense my personal identity in it. The recklessness with which "knowledge for control and use of nature" has proceeded (and continues to be planned as a presumably wise educational goal) stands in shocking contrast to one's prudent searching and planning for the self control which only can provide "unimpaired" health.

The good-and-bad dichotomy is deeply entrenched as the seeming ethic operative in my day-to-day living. My fellowman stands ready to defend it with his life. It represents nostalgic guardian helpfulness from his earliest efforts to go straight. It is integral to his idiolect, speaking a language steeped in love. What is more to his liking, it favors his presenting self concept, his thus far acknowledgeable personal identity, indispensable for his personally caring what kind of living he experiences, indeed for his personally caring whether he lives or dies. He may even have no way of using purposefully his unhappy self experience which therefore he has consciously disowned as life-unworthy. He cannot detect as such the inevitable sign and symptom always created by his rejected personal living. In short, he has no way of telling himself how dangerously he is managing his life. He realizes that he helps himself quickly and evidently by classifying much of *his living* as bad, undesirable, but he does not realize at what grievous cost in terms of life duration he maintains this emotional judgment of what seems good for him and what seems bad for him.

Many an issue may be raised. How does it happen that human longevity is greater than before? Is that due to the discoveries of the medical scientist? Is it my idea that the age span attributed to biblical man resulted from his disciplining his mind with self awareness? Or, do I mean that modern man would live even longer than he can now if he would devote himself strictly to appre-

xiv

ciation for the indescribable greatness of his living? Or, am I referring to the conscious meaning, not the duration, of human living? Am I indicating that the beginning of my conscious living is the birth of my due life appreciation? Or, do I merely uphold conscious living positively as the symptom-free way of life? Each such leading question helps to clarify the truth that I must die in the way I live. As far as my every possible self experience is concerned, it is my choice either to succeed in living it or end my life with it. Every hardship tests the remaining strength of my will to live.

It helps me to account fully for my perseverance in honoring whatever meaning there is in my mind that I name God or Divinity. One purpose in this insistence is my clearly realizing that *whatever living of my mind that I deny or reject in any way immediately becomes the only specific source of the sign or symptom I call mental disorder.*

My potential mental trouble intrinsic in localizing my God anywhere but everywhere arises from the depressing conscious self belittlement that results from it. Therefore my life worthy aim for safeguarding my mental health (evident self wholeness) is to ascribe divine perfection to my every experience. In the total interest of my whole self I make my ethic a fact-finding rather than a fault-finding one. Any of my experience from which I withhold this whole measure of its perfect truth troubles my mind, fortunately, in one way or another, thus providing me with my motivation to honor my own divine order.

I consider how much helpful but costly confusion I have created in my own inviolable individuality by taking for granted a kingdom of God versus a worldly kingdom, as though any so-called kingdom of God would not be all-inclusive. Similarly I consider the helpful costly chaos I have made of my own one-mind-

xv

edness by resorting to such softly and secretly con-
venient "dualities" as: singular and plural, individual
and society, great and small, strong and weak, sacred
and secular, holy and profane, young and old, divine
and human, God and devil, love and hate, life and
death, affirmative and negative, whole and part, God
and man, black and white, man and woman, spirit and
flesh, internal and external, heaven and hell, heaven and
earth, freedom and slavery, subjective and objective,
truth and falsehood, fact and fancy, wise and foolish,—seemingly without end. I observe just how each of
these conciliating concessions to my momentary limit of
conscious self love is further supported by the fascinating fallacies of grammar with its so-called "parts" of
speech seemingly favoring every which kind of permanent mental diremption.

I painstakingly notice how the little coordinate con-
junction "and" consistently begs the question of the
allness of individuality (including its every individuation). Whatever is, all is. The innocent appearing
word "and" would simply undo any full appreciation for
the allness of oneness. The indefinite article "the" may
be used to facilitate vagueness and irresponsibility. Every plural may be used to deny the truth of individuality. Every tense but the present may be used to
negate the inevitable *nowness* of all existence. Every
preposition may be used to belie the omnipresence of
here. Similarly each of my *parts* of speech, as the rest of
my grammar, may lend itself to vain efforts to qualify
and quantify the identical oneness of my individuality.

True, it is perfectly difficult and often perfectly impossible for me to be able to acknowledge the perfection ever present in my perfect suffering. One of the
most powerful uses of my acknowledged mind is to
protect my self from overwhelming my self with mental
tension that I am not yet prepared to value as self

helpful. Accumulation of such "disagreeable" but perfect personal identification in my recognized individuality could lead me to consider my life as not worth living. Such fixed attitude of rejection towards my own existence favors my dying rather than my living and is incompatible with my conscious interest in self preservation. Therefore I possess the mental power to decide which of my experiences I shall accept as desirable for constituting my freely and fully acknowledged life worthy self and which I shall reject as "undesirable," as not seeming worth living.

My requiring my self to evaluate all of my living as perfect would prevent my barring any of it from my conscious self conception on the basis of its being undesirable. I need the negative evaluation "imperfection" to be able to apply it to my own negated living (to my unconscious perfection). Any of my living that I consider undesirable thereby enters into my realm of my unconscious (consciously negated) living.

"Perfection" of any or all conduct is all about itself and cannot be altered by any feeling of perfect pain or perfect unhappiness which may happen to be present. Neither is perfection of all conduct a product of my pleasure. What makes perfection perfect is the fact that it is wholly and sufficiently whatever it should be or ought to be, whatever its nature or constitution or make-up requires its being, whatever it is ideally essential for it to be. Nothing *can* be unless it is really ideally perfect. Nothing *can* be until every fact required to make it perfect is present. To be possible is to be perfect.

Marcus Aurelius sagely recorded, "He is injured who abides in his error and ignorance." As the guardian of my life I am constantly on duty. My perfect motivation is always present with which I may instigate development in my self favoring my consciously enjoying all of my living. My human constitution cannot passively tolerate its undoing through misprision of the wonderfulness of living, and is always revealing exactly where and how I am leading my self astray from honoring the necessities of my marvelous nature. Learning how to treat my self kindly through interpreting the language of my organs accurately, comes as naturally as learning to take a new posture when the present one becomes uncomfortable. I soon learn the benefit to my self in disciplining myself as to how to see, hear, sit, stand, walk, as well as otherwise use my mind to serve my life-giving rather than life-taking interests.

Living my life as wholly perfect does not rid me of any of my zest for growing my self experience to be able to discover my world of self. I may continue to enjoy the perfection of *all* of my living (including all of my suffering) without losing any of its spirit. Recognizing perfection as all that is possible can merely lift my whole being to fuller appreciation for itself. All that I *can* mean by "living in the service of God" is living in the service of the all-pervading soul of my self. As Hippocrates ethicized, all is divine and all is human. This truth grows strong with exercise.

The singular "plurality" implicit in the very term "ethics" may serve to obscure the ethical essence: full appreciation for all of individuality. Reasoning in terms of duality (or other plurality) distracts from observing in terms of oneness and is thus responsible for much ado of the ethicist to restore the unanimity possible only in that oneness. Witness Schleiermacher's logical exertion, or Schopenhauer's brilliant negation in the name of goodness. Schiller believed the moral in an act to be no mere "part of a beautiful soul" but rather an expression of its wholeness. The ultimate ground of every moral distinction is the same as that of every other distinction of the human individual, namely the whole person's conscious or unconscious self interest based upon his wish (will) to live.

However, there is undeniable helpfulness in my being able to identify my dislikes with what I call "bad," and my likes with what I call "good." Thus, simply by allowing my pleasure and pain to divide my world into good and bad respectively, I can conduct my life instinctively upon an emotional plane, thereby sparing my self the hard mental work involved even in reasoning, not to mention in scientific self-observing. "Scientific self-observing" calls my attention to my subjectivity as my disciplined truth of my reality. It provides me with the motivation to temper the role of my emotion in my sensing and perceiving, by conducting my observational power without exciting my feeling dominatively.

Nevertheless, sufficient fact always accounts fully for every so-called "bad" or "evil" behavior, thereby disclosing it as good, desirable, and in every respect helpful. The very conduct I repudiate as "bad" is really quite as essentially good as the behavior I freely honor as noble or beneficial. Who would ever suspect that hatred is all and only inhibited love! So-called "unethical misconduct," sufficiently studied, turns out to be as noble and honorable as possible. Thus on and on I can adduce fact completely explaining that gloriously simple ethic, As you do unto the least of these my brethren you do unto me.

Once I give birth to the negative conception "imperfect" or "fault" I may let my self in for no end of trouble traceable to my consequent belief in my first "lie," such as falsehood, error, deception, sickness, deformity, death, and every troublesome imagining characterizing my new found delusional kingdom of evil. Once I let my self be carried away by countless imaginings traceable to my mind's need to help itself, through its lifesaving power of negation or denial of the ubiquity of its perfection, then it is truly difficult for me to restore my mental equilibrium to become capable of balancing all of its perfect vitality nicely as the recognizable perfection it really is.

Without realizing it, I can develop a habit of dividing my living into good and bad. Custom tends to make any way of living easy. Furthermore, I can never do anything at all until I see to it that I have to do it, until I make it a necessity for my self. Certainly I never intended my first lie (namely, "What I am living is not I") to make me an habitual liar. My intention was merely to assert "It is I" of all of my then *consciously* livable and lovable self. It served my self preservation to maintain whatever extent of my evident personal identity I possibly could. I could not serve my self preservation by losing track of my remaining personal identity, by so-to-speak "going to pieces," in my efforts to acknowledge mental excitement I could not then moblilize as life worthy self interest.

My early psychic creation of each member of my family was attended by inordinate excitement requiring repudiation as being my own origination, once I achieved any unity in which I could claim my self identity. An ethic requiring the duplicity self-and-not-self seems to be a necessity for everyone's turbulent living of his early parental or sibling experience. This ethic of convenience is then re-enforced by practice as well as by continuing incontinence of recognizable self consciousness for extreme tension.

Even though my constitution may be sending out sign and symptom of my recklessness constantly endangering my existence, I may be, and usually am, incapable of associating such unconscious alarm with anything so seemingly inconsequential as my current way of using my mind. Nevertheless, except by my arranging for the presence of every factor essential for bringing a desired event about, I cannot make it occur. That means I must devote my attention to the study of the wisdom expressed in my every sign and symptom and learn to prize my pain and unhappiness of every kind as expertly counselling me to choose a way of living that does not run counter to the very nature of my present being.

However, I need never frustrate my self with regard to living in any conceivable way, for I can consciously *imagine* any kind of abandonment with impunity. Indeed I am daily imagining just such wantonness freely as I scan my newspaper account of undisciplined, unrestrained excess of every description. I may or may not hold my self strictly responsible for this reading-of-the-newspaper living of mine, but it *is* all and only mine and all and only about me. *My* psychical living is all that I can ever know anything about. All of my consciousness is all and only *self* consciousness, whether I am able to acknowledge that truth or not.

I know of no more basic foundation of my nature than my power to wish (to will). Its first expression is in my wish to live. From the start it extends throughout all of my being. All of my experience is an exciting of my wishing. My every wish is also its own fulfillment, an unrecognized finding of that for which it searches,— quite as an accurate question contains its own answer. Recognizable fulfillment of a wish is the evident form for its realizing itself, quite as self fulfillment continues to be self activity. Right after satisfying my hunger I can use my imagination to excite my wish to be hungry and conceive my self even as starving for food. My joy of living arises from my pleasure in my capacity to wish my self living whatever way I can, hero or coward, law-maker or law-breaker, saint or sinner, and so on.

Cowardly living is heroic living in the making. Sinning provides for the renunciation of the saint. Law-breaking is the making of another law.

The human mind, sole scene of all of every man's unique genius, is constantly self helpful. Whatever of it appears otherwise, upon further study proves ideally self devoted. The mind, ever the arena of epic effort of its heroic adventurer, lends itself to useful effort of every kind although most of its power is seldom consciously exercised, instead remaining unconsciously active. To illustrate, my unconscious mind can freely experience its several elements juxtaposed, however opposite to or exclusive of each other, without any sense of conflict, incompatibility, opposition. This is a most desirable faculty respecting the fact that each element is all and only about itself, and therefore uninvolved with any other one.

I find it practical to notice how each of these unconsciously exercised mental powers, technically unified by unique Sigmund Freud as the "primary process" (so-called timeless and spaceless displacement and condensation, omnipotence, unrecognized order, unbridled imagination and so on) may be helpfully and regularly employed consciously throughout my life,—not left largely as the exclusive prerogative of the artist, or seemingly pre-empted by developing "common sense" virtues. Also technically unified by Professor Freud is the "secondary process" (judgment, reasoning, personal temporal and spatial orientation, limitation, dissociation, insightlessness, externality illusion and delusion). I help my self indispensably by practicing my self consciousness with the same naturalness with which I formerly practiced only my self unconsciousness. I distinctify this lifesaving process, of making all of my meaning observable as self consciousness, with the term *tertiary process*.

Living fully my human life, most difficult of all conceivable achievement, properly requires my use of *all* of my resources, including those deeply founded in the truth of my divinity. For example, not only is it lifesaving for an infant or child to use his mind for enjoying his day dream, fairy tale, or so-called "wild" imagining, but also, as long as I live, such vital and vitalizing reach of my soul holds essential store of worthy self experience, absolutely necessary for cultivating my due self esteem. Most popular TV plays "for the masses" attest the factuality of this assertion (e.g., "Superman" or "Batman"). It is such volitional self use that can help a person to stay alive and spare his *involuntary* withdrawal into his sovereign realm of lifesaving mental freedom where he can honor all of his truth (however fanciful) as his solid reality.

As may my every fellowman, I take proper pride in my mind's observing every meaning of my whole universe where it really is, within my mind; heeding that its own is the only power or glory or perfection my mind can even consider; seeing that it is its own universe of innumerable universes, infinity of infinities, eternity of eternities; recognizing that it can enable me to juggle the planets, raise the dead, or whatever; acknowledging itself as divine god of its all. I need admirable courage to honor my belief that my conscious greatness consists of my conscious self understanding. I cannot but obscure the acknowledgeable value of my soul to the extent that I seem able to uphold any other value.

That mind is strong that can equally consider *each* of its (only) apparently conflicting views; that can grow additional understanding without feeling forced to take leave of previously limited appreciation; that can develop its strength not at the cost of depreciating its previous strength level as weakness; that can grow itself without judging its previous growth as immature; that

xxiii

can imagine anything and everything with appreciation for its helpfulness as psychic reality (its only reality); and so on and on depicting *conscious* freedom of mind (the only possible conscious freedom). This self service known as full *living* is its own reward. Despite contradictory seeming it consists basically of the godly endowment: Providence.

All of my government is either conscious or unconscious *self* government.[3] It is only my *whole* self that governs. Quite as it governs the constitution of my body nucleus of my mind, my so-called body ego, so it determines my attitude towards the constitution of my government of my country, as of all organization in my world of my own creating. Hence it is most helpful to discover as much as possible of my wholeness in order to be able to realize just how I am conducting my life.

The kind of deepening understanding of man always most urgently needed, certainly now, is that of individual human being potentially capable of cultivating appreciation for the divinity constituting all of his nature. The key to my world peace is in my own mind's whole-making self consciousness. My only possible liberation is my mind liberation. This book is a stage for my enlightenment about my own divinity to manifest itself to itself. Its Glossary is fairly full for my purpose.

All evidence is present self evidence,—none of it can be magically "presented" in a so-called past or future tense. Inductive, systematic (scientific) research becomes possible from each scientist's faith in the evidence of his senses as providing his mind with its senso-

---

[3]See my *American Government* (Detroit: Center for Health Education, 1969), *passim*. Attempting to originate the originality of my esteemed one is my sincerest form of veneration. I am wholly grateful in using for my book *American Government* a meaningful jacket styled after a choice one used by my Professor Julian P. Boyd for his great *The Declaration of Independence: The Evolution of the Text* (Princeton, N.J.: Princeton University Press, 1945).

ry self knowledge, also termed life experience. Man alone is capable of discovering and believing that all of his observation is self observation. Not only all Knowing but also all Doing is Being, and that truth must be perfectly honored if every man is to become consciously glorified as the perfectly whole one that he is.

My Ralph Waldo Emerson discerned the oneness in (so-called) oriental subjectivity and occidental objectivity, "the human form is a pledge of wholeness, suggests to our imagination the perfection of truth or goodness, and exposes by contrast any halfness or imperfection."

My Persian poet, Jelaleddin, relates the following fable set forth in Salaman and Absal illustrating the meaning of self identity as associated with conscious love:

> One knocked at the Beloved's door; and a voice asked from within, "Who is there?" and he answered, "It is I." Then the voice said, "This house will not hold me and thee." And the door was not opened. Then went the lover into the desert, and fasted and prayed in solitude. And after a year he returned, and knocked again at the door. And again the voice asked, "Who is there?" and he said, "It is thyself!" — and the door was opened to him.

ACKNOWLEDGEMENTS

The author wishes to thank the following for permission to quote from the works listed: Roy P. Basler for *A Touchstone for Greatness,* 1973; Harcourt Brace Jovanovich, Inc., for *Christianity and Evolution* by Pierre Teilhard de Chardin, 1969; Dumas Malone for "Mr. Jefferson and the Living Generation"; Otto Nathan for *Einstein On Peace,* 1960; The Philosophical Library, Inc. for *The Creative Mind* by Henri Bergson, 1946.

I also thank Barbara Woodward for her most valuable editorial work and Dorothy Maskal for her very valuable assistance in editing and typing.

This volume would not be possible were it not for the financial and kind support of each trustee of the Center for Health Education of Detroit: H. Walter Bando, Mrs. William D. Crim, Robert L. DeWitt, Dwight C. Ensign, Mrs. Carl B. Grawn, Robert F. Grindley, Miss Emilie G. Sargent, Walter H. Seegers, and Frank J. Sladen.

My wife, Mary Louise Carson Dorsey, is most helpful, as ever.

INTRODUCTION

Words are, of course, the most powerful drug used by mankind.

Rudyard Kipling

Only I can know or feel the meaning of any word that I use. I am the only one who can speak to my self or hear my self speak. My *Psychology of Language*[1] asserts that all of my language is idiolect, a naming of meaning occurring only in my own mind. *Self* is a word of unique definition for every individual. Usually I find my fellowman showing his life appreciation in the specific way he uses every word, for his every word names some of his existence. Mostly his attitude is that his word *self* does not apply to very much of his individuality, quite as his word *individuality* does not seem to apply to very much of his world. He resists increasing his vocabulary even for his so-called impersonal words.

By my word *self* I mean specifically the whole of my being. My ethic consists in my devotion to the sameness underlying *all* of my selffulness. *Selfishness* is a faultfinding term in ordinary parlance, a so-called pejorative, commonly a name for my depreciating the wonderfulness of some of my own life without realizing it. *Not-self* is a term for designating any or all of my living for which I am unconscious.

Whenever I live any of my external world without seeing and feeling my identity in it, I thereby create

[1] Detroit: Center for Health Education, 1971.

1

potential evidence of the existence of my unconsciousness. Similarly whenever I use my word *soul* or
spirit without seeing and feeling my identity in it, I
thereby create further potential evidence of the existence of my unconsciousness. All of my unconscious
living is merely active mental existence of mine which I
am not yet able to live with conscious responsibility
or control.

My only ethical problem is that of teaching my self
how to do right by my self, how to help my self to obey
the law of my nature ideally. Actual motivation to help
my self as best I can is inherent in my life. When I use
my words to speak or write "ethics of a people" I feel
helpfully confused, for by "people" I can have in mind
only an abstraction consisting merely of my own identity. My own good behavior is my only possible ethical
performance in the interest of my society.

Too much cannot be made over the fact that every
word is a label I create for certain meaning in my living.
Thus, I cannot word any meaning except by living that
word. Therefore, anterior to every meaning of the word
is the immeasurable value and wonderfulness of my life
itself. However, my natural feeling of love of life can be
readily obscured merely by my living any experience,
i.e., any operation of my mind, that I must feel as
painful or unhappy in varying degree on account of my
being unable to recognize that it consists all and only of
the truth that I am living it, and indeed living on account of it.

The growing child's first ability to think or feel in the
first person with the pronoun "I" or "me" indicates a
beginning of conscious authority and responsibility. For
biologically adequate conduct of life, it is necessary that
my seeing and feeling my identity in all of my experience continue as my augmenting estimation concerning
the worth of my life itself. It is my cultivation of my

2

sense of identity that develops awareness for all that I mean by my soul life. I feel my identity firmly in my Emerson declaring, "I cannot find language of sufficient energy to convey my sense of the sacredness of private integrity." It is my thinking of my own unfathomable might that enables me to divine that my will and my God's will are one.

The phantom problem of whether or not I can be capable of free will is traceable entirely to my having divided my mental life into 1) that which I can call my self and 2) that which I must call "somebody else" or "something else." Whenever I live the latter mentality I do not acknowledge my volition in such activity, although certainly that is all that can be present. Only by preserving the extension of my consciousness for my self identity can I preserve the extension of my consciousness for the freedom of my will. I can feel the freedom of my mind itself only to the extent that I am able to be conscious that it is mine. I can realize my lifesaving ideals of love, justice, order, and freedom by discovering the allness and wholeness of my self and thereby recognizing that I am my law unto my self.[2]

This treatise records the lines along which my research has travelled to find that the ethical trend in my living is its directive power activated in my developing my awareness for the whole unity of my living I call my self. All of my life is an integrating process constantly making me into an integrated individual maintaining my unified wholeness in the constant flow of life characteristic of organic being. I feature the provident truth of my wholeness, for that is the only basis of my motivation to discipline my integrating mind with conscious identity, with appreciation that its every experience is a

[2]See my *Illness or Allness* (Detroit: Wayne State University Press, 1965), p. 1.

3

growing of its selfsame nature. My self growth is self begetting selfness.

My Jan Christian Smuts clearly focused attention upon the pervasive functioning of wholeness throughout all of life's organic extent, "The functioning of an organic whole releases it from the domination, the causation of the external, and conduces to its freedom."[3] My living is an incessant growing of new wholeness consisting of nothing but my self identity, for which I may be conscious or unconscious. The issue of which I will to become, self-conscious or self-unconscious, is my *ethical* choice.

Every scientific truth has become a possession of my mind only through my mind's creating it. Whatever I mean by science is as meaningful for my ethical living as is any other meaning I can create. There is a perfect harmony in all of the meaning of my mind. My own interest is all that my mind can live. In this basic sense, my every word voices my conscience.

By *psychism*, I mean my egoism that subsumes all that I can mean by my altruism. By *uselessness*, all I can mean is unconscious usefulness. I find it helpful to consider that my ethic introduces a criterion not only for observing the worth of motives irrespective of the feeling of pleasure and pain, but also irrespective of my momentary feeling of self identity and self non-identity. The purpose of life is to live. The ethical purpose of my life is to live responsibly, that is, with conscious sense of my own identity in the living. The psychology of successful living that includes all other successes is that of attaining reverence for the justice (whole truth) inherent in *all* of my living.

By attaining my conscious self identity I discover the virtue of being my individual self. Goethe, like Aris-

---

[3]*Holism and Evolution,* p. xiv.

totle, defines happiness in terms of virtue. I define virtue as the spiritual treasure of conscious soul life, man's consciously full estate in which the worth of living is never even questioned. The cause of truth of the divinity of man will be served in any case by him, either consciously or unconsciously. With the full realization that truth is, and must be, always on the side of whatever happens there is associated a liberation of lovable justice that may be described as biologically adequate euphoria, the affective foundation upon which all of my ethic rests.

The demonstrable and verifiable fact that nothing can happen unless all of the truth (fact) is present to make it happen always serves as a regulative principle of ethical sanction. Thus, despite all appearance to the contrary, it is never possible to do anything wrong. Sufficient study of all of the fact entering into any event reveals a complete justification of whatever happens. Complete appreciation for this realization, of the omnipresence and omnipotence of truth, gives the love of life its full intensity, unmodified by any indulgence of fault-finding or of depreciation of living in any degree. There is little difficulty in feeling the identity of this biologically adequate appreciation of living with all the descriptions of a hereafter or of a heretofore kind of paradise. Miltonized, the mind can itself a conscious heaven make.

Sustained consciousness for its worth is what my mind requires in order to be quickened and renewed to the extent of my consciously appreciating its divinity, so that I can equate it with all that I can mean by my soul. But, why should I ever overlook my very own tremendous mental power? Apparently, merely on account of its being astounding. My conscious mind, that is, my living of my mind which I can responsibly claim as my own, is able to endure only limited excitement. Whenever my living of excitation exceeds the mental tolerance which is adequate for my current sense of personal identity, I suffer some degree of shock, am stunned "out of my wits," and lose the so-called "presence of mind" which I need for my mind's prizing its worth.

Nevertheless, all of my truth can be realized only in my self. To imagine it as being outside of me, is to imagine it as deprived of its only reality. An insightless notion of "externality" carries all of the intense conviction characteristic of any other delusion, and produces a certainty of mind favorable to rigidity and consistency of obsessive and compulsive action. Such "dead sure" imagining creates a disrelish for the vagueness and uncertainty often essential for appreciating the actual novelty of living.

No self heedlessness is fraught with more cautionary irrationality than is persistent disregard for the amazing providence of my nature. Self-ingratitude for my own plenteous abundance, unfailing helpfulness, and continuous supply of all-giving life itself, is properly the source of admonishing signs of mental neglect. George Bernard Shaw noted, "Life is the force that strives to attain a greater awareness of contemplating itself." My mind's process of realizing its astonishing meaningfulness is my only source for my recognizing the immensity of the nature of my life. Everyone must *unaided* create his own just conception of his true greatness in order to promote his highest welfare; herein is the open secret of the ideal "making of my self."

Everyone must *unassisted* come to his senses sufficiently to see that all that he admires or abjures is his own wonderfulness; this is the most difficult of all of my life-lessons. Each individual, *all and always alone,* must discover that he is all there is, and that this self-insight is his only reliable tie to his fellowman,—such is his highest wisdom revealing the highest

6

purpose of his existence. Every person's most reward-ing life attainment, his *summum bonum,* is his most satisfying answer to the meaning of his life itself, and it must be entirely and only the accomplishment of his own unassisted undertaking. However, that is so trying a truth that it is understandably either completely over-looked, or when fleetingly glimpsed, quickly decried exactly as regularly as it is.

What is it that commends mind consciousness so highly that it must not be ignored? Every person can learn to exercise it and enjoy its benefits. It is every individual's only way to appreciate his life. It is each person's only possible foundation for knowingly making a true success of himself. Only by conscious mental effort can anyone use what lies in him to see and eval-uate his wonderfulness. Consciously keeping himself in sight, everyone will not let his only truth get out of sight. Furthermore, repressed meaning is always symp-tom forming, providently.

Mind-conscious living is elementary, simple, in-dependent of special talents or exclusive faculties. It requires no particular privileges, is free from every so-called "worldly advantage," and is associated with no extravagant educational facilities. A child can culti-vate it without any formal schooling. It is least ex-pensive and most rewarding of all ways of life. It en-ables everyone to appreciate his imagination as being his meaningful stream of life, his source of reflection and research, his peaceful and remedial agent for exercising his naturally excursive mind.

Mind-consciousness resolves all blind jealousy, envy, inequity, or comparison of every kind, in the all-ness-quality of personal identity. It dispels every un-happy mental condition associated with the spell of self-ignorance. It is not school-bred, only self-bred. *It is freely available to the so-called "indigent," formally uneducated, or underprivileged individual.* It cannot safely be overlooked since ignorance strikes the rich or poor, formally educated or uneducated, gifted or ungifted person, alike, closing his mind-springs of joy of living, of interest in his world, of wonder for his own marvelous creation emanating in his every experience.

By attaching exclusive importance to my individuality, mind-consciousness acquaints me with my only reality (my life) and teaches me to heed that all of my reliance, faith, goodness, helpfulness, or meaningfulness of every kind is where it actually belongs, — in my own ongoing being. I turn my attention upon the mental nature of my *every* degree of sensibility whenever possible in order to practice experiencing *consciously* the enlightening and gratifying truth of the exclusive subjectivity of my every meaning.

What happens when I help my self by restricting my range of personal identity to any of my living other than my whole mind-consciousness? Most costly consequence of all can be my creating a feeling of familiarity with my self as *seemingly fixed,* which belies the fact of my ever-present inattention, indifference, carelessness, listlessness, boredom, and similar self-sleepiness of innumerable forms. Unable to find my happiness in enjoying my own conscious worth, I must invent and seek compensatory pleasing values in which I cannot seem to see my self, such as my pursuit of wealth or fame or objective science or entertainment.

That this most important self orientation (conscious mindfulness) is rarely realized in my land of freedom is mainly attributable to everyone's conscious freedom, his most wonderful of all advantages. Everybody's conscious self sovereignty must begin as it does over *his* recognizable range of self, always personally worked up by him alone. His parent cannot begin or extend it for him, nor can his schoolteacher. My everyone is a Prometheus, helping himself as best he can to see that self-help is all there is, and that his conscious self-help is derived from his cultivation of consciousness for his own mind. Finding he is the law unto himself and that he must pay with health trouble for his every infringement of the law of his allness, wholeness, oneness and newness, is his regularly happy discovery of the health meaning of his moral law.

Human consciousness, self consciousness, a term expressing self sentience or individuality-awareness, consists of subjectivity. It serves as self observer witnessing self evidence. Its essence is its self meaningfulness connoting worth for the one-being of one-being. Enlivened life consciousness awakens the nature of meaning (investment of self-love, including its modalities).[4]

All there is for me to be able to observe, or observe with, is my allness or wholeness, for such is all that I consist of. Studied consideration of my individuality always discovers it to be universality. Therefore it is with some feeling of inconsistency that I may view the experience of being aware for all of my self with all of my self as impossible. My illusion of quantification is based upon my illusion of objectivity. It is all of my illusion-making of my wholeness which I cannot consciously observe and with which I cannot consciously observe, thus involving my self in negation-frustration.

My illusions of time, space, and motion support my considering my self as partial rather than whole, so that I can involve my self observation in no end of *illusional* partialities, particularities, and analogous seeming fractionations, which appear to deny my intact wholeness. My arousal of my universality awareness, however, is always my moment of truth.

Caught in the toils of my self deceiving objectiv-

[4]See my *Psychology of Emotion* (Detroit: Center for Health Education, 1971), pp. xiii–xx.

9

ity-illusion, I find it necessary to compensate for my deep-felt longing for my wholeness-consciousness by relying upon my Something-greater-than-myself dependency, thus alienating my own divinity consciousness.

Every question leads always to its own answer, which gives it its sense. A hard question to pose accurately, asks, "Why is selfishness nearly always repudiated as unworthy, particularly since selfishness is all that can possibly exist in any kind of behavior?" Surely all of the earnest objection to so-called selfishness has every right to exist. Surely the strong rejection of egotism must serve a most important purpose. Everyone has felt the hurt traceable to his living his short-sighted self-centered fellowman ignoring everything but his striving to please himself, regardless of the cost of severe pain to anybody else of his world. My reader starts in,

"Is the whole growing up process one of getting rid of the selfishness of one's infanthood? Everyone starts out selfish but usually one grows up to seem to consider somebody besides his self. I can cite innumerable instances of a grown person's acting like a baby and making everybody around him uncomfortable. Certainly my resentment against such infantile manners might be classified as self interest or self defense, but hardly as selfishness. Maybe my selffulness in trying to see to my best interests is a form of enlightened selfishness, but I prefer to make a distinction between the anachronistic selfishness of a twenty- or thirty-year-old baby and the timely self-regard of a tolerant person of any age." And so on.

Yes, selfishness is *all* that is humanly possible. Yes, selfishness of any kind or degree may be rejected by my self (or by my fellowman) depending upon my (or his) degree and range of tolerance for selfishness. Yes, when

I am "all in" I may be ready to resent *any* further self experience, whether it be in the form of my enduring a self tolerant or self intolerant individual in my living. Yes, it seems easier for me to experience my living my forbearing than my overbearing fellowman.

Yes, anyone's earnest (or frivolous) objection to selfishness (or to anything else) has its right to exist. Such rejection of seeming inconsiderateness which one finds intolerable does serve a most important function, even though study of the facts always reveals that the seeming "offender" was momentarily as considerate of as much of himself as he had studied and disciplined himself how to be. I am selfishly justified in trying to save my self from overwhelming my mind with my neighbor's justifiable selfishness.

Everyone wants to grow up, but it is the rare one who is able to learn the fact that he can and must learn exactly *how* to grow up, namely, with painstaking self responsibility. Everyone would like to be a full-grown person, with the least exertion possible.

Why do I find it helpful, even necessary, to deny that I am all-perfect? Why *must* I depreciate my very own excellence? Why do I prefer the view that there is something "wrong" with me when I experience my perfectly-working feeling of pain or unhappiness? Why do I find it *natural* to complain about *my* accident, injury, spouse, loss, or whatever I do not happen to like at the moment? Why does the illusion of the imperfection of this world appeal to me so very strongly? Why does it come natural to me to find fault with my fellowman? Why do I let my conscience bother me as a wrong-doer? Why am I extremely sensitive to criticism of any kind? Why do I let accusations of guilt disturb me, even when I know I am not guilty? Why can it annoy me when my fellowman seems to think he is perfect no matter how he behaves? Why am I dis-

11

satisfied when my fellowman dwells on his imperfections? Is the antithesis between egoism and altruism meaningless? In short, if it is natural for me to be all-perfect, how can it seem perfectly natural for me to feel far from perfect nearly all of the time?

Furthermore, if it is perfect for me to behave in any old way at all, why should I, or how can I, take the trouble to modify, cultivate or model my behavior? And most particularly, if my way of life is already a perfect one, why oh why and how oh how should I *discipline* my self into some other course of being? Being perfectly right now, from where is to come any motivation whatsoever to grow otherwise? In short, how can this view of perfection-everywhere-forever deliver me from a fatalistic view of life that it seems to imply? Am I merely asserting that my unconscious guidance and control are biologically inadequate to guide me in my conduct of my life? What is the evidence of self consciousness on this pained inquiry?

Although I can certainly acknowledge that it is most beneficial for me to know my self, the procedure for operating this principle is hard to understand or accept. The chief difficulty lies in the fact that I am unable to feel my tremendous need for it, except in the form of painful criticism of my doing my best right now. All that I live concerns only the conduct of the individual life of my self, but my sensing this all-important truth, as such, is most perilously lacking. Furthermore, I have come to take my mental condition of sensory illusion for granted, as being quite a normal standard of rightness.

Lacking self understanding, I lack the one criterion for evaluating any method of my fellowman professing to deal with human individuality. To illustrate, only my reader who has laboriously risked his own hard-won conception of his self identity, in order to augment it, can possess the one criterion absolutely required for accurately evaluating his author's recording of the unique helpfulness of his enlarging his self insight. My reader has already seen many a panacea for human suffering come and go,—each one attested by testimony of personal cure or benefit. Furthermore, his disappointing experience may not have taught him that a safe and sound program of self help must prove itself in its exclusive reference to the trying demands it makes specifically upon each individual's mind. Also, it is the rare person who is courageously exerting his own effort to use his mind for the purpose of discovering that his only possession is self possession, his only observation is self observation, his only world is the one he has been creating all along, by and in his living (growing) of his own mind.

In order to justify my ethical procedure as scientific, I must reveal how it is "repeatable." I must make it lend itself to verification by my fellow scientist who is willing to demonstrate it to himself. I unhesitatingly claim that the principle at work in difficultly cultivating self identity by mobilizing conscious self love is scientifically validatory in its consequence, workability and so-called repeatability in and for my fellow scientist's experimentation.

Instead of building up a technical scientific terminology I take pains to show that all language is idiolect only, that every word I use is a name for a meaning in my own mind only. Thus I succeed in developing a new technique for creating new sensory observation as test and evidence of my, including my fellow scientist's, developing scientific self identity. My science of self requires my new meaning of all language: *self* meaning.

My Greek's ethic was oriented around questions of life such as its end or its ideal order; of virtue construed as sanction of moral law. My Jewish and Christian ethics are oriented in the close relation of religion to life

13

also. Ordinarily it is contended that the term *ethics*, like *politics*, is accurately used only in regard to the responsible conduct of man in mutual relations with his fellowman. However, my ethical position is completely contained within my own individuality, formed anew from my own original experience, integral to my own creative vitality.

My ethic consists of my conscious self-command and self-obedience, rather than my unconscious prescription. Except in my imagination, I cannot live "in relation to my fellowman." I *am* all that I can mean by my fellowman. All that can seem to me to be "in relation to" anyone in my living must be occurring completely *within* me. Furthermore, all that can seem to me to be my fellowman's living "in relation to" anyone must be occurring completely *within* my fellowman's individuality.[5] My moral evolution has been my gradual discovery of the full meaning of my conscious wholeness.

I can actually shudder when I imagine my reader's assuming that he is able to know what my writing is about, unless (my) he refers insightfully to his author's necessity to be writing to his self only, and also about his self's meaning merely.

I write without risk of being either understood or misunderstood by my reader whose understanding must consist only of his own self understanding. I now make my life bright by assuming to be all my own the perfection proverbially ascribed to a divinity I could not formerly claim to be mine. I find that anyone who is willing to make the exertion similarly, to call his soul his own and his all his soul, thereby gradually assumes personal responsibility for being all that he formerly ascribed to his depersonalized divinity. Evidence attest-

[5]See diagram of so-called family living in "The Psychology of My Ethic" chapter, p.130.

ing how self-undevout I am is my living proof of my inhibited piety.[6] Devout or undevout, I am God-glad or God-mad. Most devastating disguise of self identity lies in the segregation of God and man.

In his sermon, "Excellency of the Religious," Henry Scougal, bright luminary of his Calvinistic church, preached, "Learn to adore your nature." I am fearfully and wonderfully made. And I can imagine no more important creation of truth than that one for my soul to discover and to know right well. I find no self realization that is more practicable than that one. I cannot consciously enjoy the truth that I am completely whole except insofar as I can understand that my wholeness is the essence of me that is totally responsible for all of my genuine being, including doing. Surely insofar as I allow this principle to guide my conduct, and grow to adore my being, my doing must become manifestly adorable. Although this sublime end enjoins me to steadfast duty to intentional soul culture, hardest of all of my ways of life, it is the one heroic soul adventure enabling me to "sing praises with understanding" (Psalm 47, 7).

Reference to living as being spirited, soulful, divine, occurs frequently in the speech and writings of my so-called foremost fellowman (but all too rarely in my fellowman of restricted conscious self identity). Merely to illustrate:

> Intuitively I've always been aware of the vitally important pact which a man has with himself, to be all things to himself, and to be identified with all things, to stand self-reliant, taking advantage of his haphazard connection with a planet, riding his luck, and following his bent with the tenacity of a hound. My first and greatest love affair was with this thing we call freedom, this lady of infinite

---

[6]See meaning of so-called opposites in my *Psychology of Emotion*, pp. 12, 89, and *Psychology of Language*, p. 59.

allure, this dangerous and beautiful and sublime being who restores and supplies us all.

It began with the haunting intimation (which I presume every child receives) of his mystical inner life; of God in man; of nature publishing herself through the "I."[7]

My meeting my maker in the sense of conscious confrontation with my divine creativity is my profound religious experience.

However, what I must live chiefly in my fellowman is not his rare eminence as prizing his life of *spirited subjectivity* but rather his steady depression as misprizing his life of dispirited objectivity. And what I live chiefly may amount to my limbo of so-called "common sense," if I do not beware.

I have wondered at the extent of my inattention to my subjectivity sufficiently to try to find its source and I believe that it has had some of its beginning as follows.

In my every day living, illusional objectivity is consistently taken for granted as constituting real reality, factuality, first-hand evidence of truth; whereas real subjectivity is consistently taken for granted as absolutely unreliable, undemonstrable, and (most scathing of all) unscientific. As a rule, nearly the only language I ever hear or see is my vernacular of out-and-out materialism, namely, so-called communication, the greatest lovable lie and the parent of all lies.

The result of my continually disciplining my mind, either consciously or unconsciously, in such seeming self alienation or depersonalization cannot be other than that of shaking my faith in my conscious self observation and strengthening my delusion in my unconscious self observation. However I can neither *tell* the truth nor *tell* a lie for all of my life's meaning is contained within my life only and always. The apparent effect of

[7]E.B. White, "One Man's Meat," a collection of essays first appearing in *Harper's Magazine* in July 1940.

16

exercising a lie over and over again without any fear of exposure is to help it to pass either for "the god's truth" or for "scientific fact." The quiet ease with which I have grown my tendency to allow my imitation for my living (so-called objectivity) to do justice for my only possible living (subjectivity) is appalling, so appalling that I can understand my avoidance of considering it. I can understand my Emerson's likening imitation to suicide.

My chief ethical need is to discipline my whole mind with love for *its* reality as being my only possible reality. This lifesaving development can be attained only by my discovering that my only possible language is my idiolect that is valuable only for naming merely my own life's meaning.[8]

My incompetence in observing the wholeness of my absolute individuality cannot make me morally irresponsible. Therefore I live on suffering from every kind of helpful sign and symptom (including "accidental happening") warning me of some dangerous self disregard, but I can seldom trace any of my mental (including so-called physical) trouble to its real source. Rather I must irresponsibly fix my responsibility in what I regard as a so-called foreign agent. Obviously my choice is to live my personal wholeness identity as consciously united or unconsciously untied.

My fellowman finds most enhearting the tendency in his rebellious teenager to reject (so-called) material success as his dominant guide. All well and good. Whatever living he finds enlivening is worthy as such. However I also find my "rejected materialism" or rejected *anything* as most dangerous foundation to build on. My *rejected* materialism, establishment or whatever, develops overestimate and emphasis merely through the re-

[8]See my *Psychology of Language*, p. 1.

17

jection. How then can I proceed to do any of my building upon firm ground? My self-explanation follows.

Anew, all I can ever do is grow my own life. Present volition, not past or future "evolution," is descriptive of my life. All of my present living must be the outgrowth of my preceding living and the root of my further living. To save myself mental trouble it is necessary for me to honor (rather than reject) this natural necessity as fully as possible. To illustrate, in order for me to grow in the direction of appreciation for all of my subjectivity I must first fully honor (rather than reject) as much as I can whatever so-called objectivity (materialism) meaning I have already grown (whether I attribute some or most of it to my fellowman or not).

My lifesaving will to love my enemy leads me to my utmost development of ethicality of my nature. My Hindu's Divine Charioteer grows his Prince Arjuna *(Bhagavad Gita),* "Taking as equal pleasure and pain, gain and loss, victory and defeat, gird thee for the battle. Thou shalt not incur sin." It seems perfectly evident to me now that it is sheerly suicidal for me to reject any of my living of meaningfulness for (my) divinity.

Surely my will to live my ungodly existence must be all and only about itself, namely, my inhibition of my will to live my godly existence. Surely my will to live my godly existence places my only full value upon my life, including my living of my fellowman. My conscious solipsism is my conscious union in my "wider self through which saving experiences come" (William James). Adequately defined, solipsism is a name for the locating of *all* self experience responsibly where it has its only meaning, within the individual living that experience. *I consider this life orientation to be the specific one direly needed today by me, including my every fellowman.*

18

My morality seems to require supernatural sanction exactly to the extent that I repress my meaning for my own sanctity. My seeing that I am by necessity the solipsistic source of all of my resources leads me to find in my own mind (soul, spirit or whatever name I give to my existence) my immovable basis for my irresistible faith in my self devotion. Only morality can vitalize morality.

However, unquestionably it seems easier to delude my self that my repudiation of any way of life as seeming merely hateful can suffice to set me on the right road to a way of life that seems merely lovable. *My effort to escape my necessity to love difficultly by seeking an opportunity to love easily provides me with only the seeming of escape, for the greatness of my life requires my cultivating my capacity to love difficultly. After all, hate is only hurt love, and if I can remove my love from my hate I find no hate left. Such is the spirit of my whole truth awaiting everywhere for my benefit.*[9]

The guiding truth integral to the principle of my ethic, devotion to my whole-souled individuality, is that it can occur and prevail only in my living, quite as my fellow-man's ethic can occur and prevail only in his own living. For any of my self helpfulness to increase its strength I must discipline my mind in practicing exercise of it.

My vigilant reader, who is alert to his conception that his God must be his greatest and hence most careful creation, may now voice his emotional turmoil.

"Your identifying your wholeness with holiness and your enthusiasm as being your divinity, your idealism as being your spirit, your law that the presence of sufficient truth accounts for whatever can exist as being essentially all there can be in the fundamental law of nature and the law of God, and so on — all such audacity

[9]See my *Psychology of Emotion*, pp. 3, 125, 128.

seems to me to be beyond my capacity for letting go my control of my imagination.

"I freely acknowledge that I am unable to make myself feel that I am divine. I confess that I frequently have a hard time just classifying myself as being human. Your earnest claim to be divine, even though you insist you can make it only to yourself, involves the supernatural and is therefore beyond the rest of us natural human beings.

"Are you able to conjure up just one further difficult consideration, namely, that you may be one hundred per cent wrong in your life estimate? Ask your undoubtedly benevolent self *why you are not able to regard yourself as a human being like the rest of us.* Am I not better off, than you are, to be able to appreciate the magnificence of my humanity rather than to have to aspire, as you do, to revering the providence of your divinity?"

I may trace this and similar protestation regarding my writing to the fact that I can record only one self observation of mine at a time. Although my every observation is not intended to rule out any other one, it may easily lend itself to that appearance. Nevertheless the truth is that I discipline my mind to be able to consider *with identical kindness* any and every kind of observation, on account of my realization that each one consists entirely of my own living (creating) of it. To illustrate, my considering my nature as being divine cannot be at the expense of my considering my nature as human, or inhuman, or whatever. Every new development of my conscious self identity is an addition to, not a subtraction from, my previously attained conscious self identity, in fact the former is an outgrowth from the latter.

When my reader holds that he is a human being and therefore unable to consider himself as divine, he may then tend to proceed to assume that his author who records he is able to behold his divinity is therefore unable any longer to regard himself as human. However such is not at all the truth of this subject of mine. After all, in this particular instance of my reader's revolt, I am the evident author of it all.

Although this psychology of my ethic may reflect my discipline of arduous exertion in the specific direction of positing the conscious perfection (divinity) of my whole existence it is in no sense intended to negate the worth of my any other kind of life orientation whatsoever. *My* whole ethic subsumes *my* every other ethic.

SOME HISTORICAL NOTES

When shall we see the man who will accomplish for the law what Rousseau did for education, namely withdraw our gaze from external physical effects and redirect it to the inner organic development of man?

Wilhelm von Humboldt[1]

I can imagine my reader saying, "I am sure you realize that emphasized historical appeal on the subject of self realization by a writer pretending to wish to renounce authority other than conscious self sovereignty, is hardly evidence of the highest range of self consciousness. What do you base your evident assurance of the morality of 'self conscious living' upon?"

For that question my only reply must be, "Upon my self evidence merely. All that I mean by *art of living* derives from self insight. My conscious mind finds only its order, everywhere it turns itself. The names *mind, meaning* and *soul* are synonyms for the concept 'self.' Only by positing my mentality can I begin to try to account for any aspect of my life at all."

My everyone's government or plan of social living *is* a kind of systematized morality. Even the essential idea of my everyone's religion may be conceived as his exercise of life-preserving ordering of his power, named his conduct. Obedience to the law of human nature is

---

[1]Translated by Marianne Cowan in *Humanist Without Portfolio: An Anthology of the Writings of Wilhelm von Humboldt* (Detroit: Wayne State University Press, 1963).

23

justified by conscious knowledge of the magnificence of its excellently peaceful design.

Sometimes an author uses the terms *ethic* and *moral* synonymously; sometimes not. For the purpose of the present writing, I prefer to consider them synonyms. However, a description of my ethical viewpoint may be required to provide some account of what kind of meaning I may ascribe to my terms *right* and *wrong*. A description of my moral viewpoint may be required also to clarify how I apply either term to judge my specific action. In this book I lovingly renounce my right-wrong and every other duality.[2] My ethic or moral concerns the way in which I work the nature of my wholeness; how I grow the dictate derived from my insight into the meaning of being an individual; how I observe the law based upon my experiencing my self and observing (minding) benefit I derive from becoming consciously responsible for the way my existence directs itself.

My Dumas Malone, revered biographer of his Thomas Jefferson, clearly states:

> ... surely the first question that should be asked about anything and everything is: What value does it have for people? And, as it seems to me, the humanist is one who recognizes the primacy of human values and seeks to promote them. This leads me to say that the perennial task of humanistic scholars, of whom I regard myself as one in spirit if not in attainment, is to keep the humanities human.[3]

Every ethic is a dangerous adventure in divine humanism upheld by the homage of a hero, — no hasty

[2]See my *Psychology of Language*, pp. 57, 63. By *renounce* I mean merely: live freely, according to my conscious volition, "take it or leave it"; as contrasted with *repress*, which process results in my seeming to make my conscious mind subject to my unconscious mind, thus augmenting my involuntary behavior. See Glossary.
[3]"Mr. Jefferson and The Living Generation," Occasional Paper 2, read before The National Endowment for the Humanities, April 25, 1972.

harvest. Emerson, all-time American scholar who stood forth for the renunciation of his country's slavery as early as 1831, declared, "Human virtue demands her champions and martyrs, and the trial of persecution always proceeds." Said he of civilization, "It is the learning the secret of cumulative power, of advancing on one's self." He saw that to be consciously free means: consciousness for being determined by nothing but one's self. He saw the right to be free as implicit in the right to live.

The moral ideal can be realized only by the free will. To discover my freedom I must also discover my self extent and be able to feel my responsibility for it. My only ultimate freedom is the freedom I have when I call my soul my own and call my all my soul. Self possession is the only possible private (including so-called "public") property. In his spirited *Ethics of Democracy,* Louis F. Post noted, "There is nothing so subtly difficult as emancipating one's mind from the influence of one's habitual environment."[4] *My emancipation is the flower and fruit of my conscious self possession only.*

My conscious self possession is the flower and fruit of my conscious self education, of my purposefully learning how to live well. My public school system administrator's "process of self education" supported by my tax payer is defensible primarily on the theory that each citizen's education along the lines of selected self experience is essential to his good citizenship specifically through his conservation of his well-being. He must learn about his wholeness well in order to live well. Otherwise the whole scheme would be an indefensible usurpation of the private right of the individual.

[4]Chicago: Louis S. Dickey and Co., 1903.

After nearly two centuries of national existence founded on the assumption of the right of every man, not merely for securing government, but specifically for attaining conscious self government, it is well for me to bear clearly in mind that my United States has been absorbing into its electorate millions of individual man-worlds each of whose past experience has been at cross-purposes with the development of the self insight enabling readiness for conscious self sovereignty.

It is civic spirited to be benevolently skeptical of the power of each one living his public school system to counteract this self unconscious trend unless it is seen responsibly as the most critical threat to the very roots of man's safety and peace, to his political ideal that his government exists in and for him,—and not he in and for it. Every pupil's daily devotional exercise of the wholeness of his developing human individuality, his heeding the inviolable integrity of his awakening human being, is his most precious civic culture, ever to be taken care of, never to be taken for granted. There is no such possibility as a domain of mere knowledge, as an extrapersonal sphere of "knowledge for knowledge's sake," but the educator acting on the principle that impersonal knowledge exists may be unwittingly undermining the ethical ideal of his American constitution.[5]

There is no such possibility as my learning about my wholeness without the constant integral ethical complement of being responsible for the self knowledge accruing from my learning process. As an American educator I submit that it is my professional duty, my life-loving law, to uphold this purely *ethical* meaning of learning of every kind. Every so-called bit of information, every so-called training of head and hand, every

[5]See my *Psychology of Political Science* (Detroit: Center for Health Education, 1973), Book I, Foreword.

hoarding of fact or aggregation of technical or mechanical knowledge, every collection of scientific data, — each is purely moral force of mine. Not seeing my education as my ethical experience is the awful cost I must pay for not seeing my knowledge as self knowledge. My life's law commands my conscious obedience or unconscious disobedience.

Man's earliest historic evidence indicates that his ethic, his emerging sense of whole-self responsibility, first appeared as a localized conscience seeming to be foreign to his sense of acknowledgeable personal identity. Thus, the remotest Egyptian attributed the functioning of his sense of justice to his sun-god Ra. Later, he saw in his Osiris his incarnation of moral worth. From this moralization of his god his mind gradually underwent an ethicalizing process of recognizing his moral feelings as being his own. From attributing desirable ethical behavior only to his hereafter "other world," he gradually began to locate moral order in his "this world." His conscious localization of his "this world" in his own self was to provide man with the completing of his ethicalizing process.

Every scientist avers that his enlightened seeing of only his moral meaning, his strictly personal significance, in his scientific datum, enables him to study appreciatively indeed, with supportive reverence and ever refreshed enthusiasm for his scientific work. On this eminent ground of self responsibility, of lovable justice for each individual, the discipline of his every religion may stand.

Persian Abdul Baha (1842-1892), extolling the Bahai Cause, oracles "The most urgent requisite of mankind is the declaration of the *oneness of the world of humanity.*" Certainly that oneness always exists, but only in my every individual fellowman. To be aware for its necessary existence, as well as to declare it, must ever

27

remain the conscious or unconscious opportunity of each unique individual.

Ethic may be defined as the science of human duty, including law of life. Excellence of self care is a moral as well as hygienic standard. The biological function of my ethic is based on the fact that my every ethical construct is a vital dynamic doing, going on throughout the integration of my being. An ethical truth is a fundamental force unifying human life. Whatever furthers (my) human life is moral. Whatever I live, I live instinctively, including every perception of my world.

Ethical or moral behavior only conventionally refers to the way an individual *associates* himself in society, among others, in relationship to his fellowman. I propose to renounce such a supposition as impossible and shall discuss my ethic as referring to the way an individual lives his society or others or fellowman in and as himself. R. M. MacIver pointed this ethic, "Society is in us, in each of us, in some degree in all, in the highest degree in the greatest of us."[6] John Locke and Thomas Jefferson worked on this individualistic ground for extending the ethical principle of freedom underlying free will. Selfhood is the only possible origin and location of culture, of all conscious or unconscious volition, of all of the free play of all of one's mental power well subsumed by the term *imagination*. Charles Horton Cooley concluded, "the imaginations which people have of one another are the solid facts of society."[7]

Studying the history of my forefather's working out for himself his growing realization of his allness is not at all tantamount to my accomplishing this most difficult and most desirable feat for myself. Hence it is that I may find instance after instance of greatest self realiza-

[6]*Community* (London: Macmillan, 1917).
[7]*Human Nature and the Social Order* (New York: Charles Scribner's Sons, 1922).

tion recorded since the dawn of recorded history, as well as over and, over up through the centuries, and yet may observe greatly limited evidence of my own present devotion to self insight. Furthermore, growing the experience of my fellowman's warning that I must discover my own America, compose my own Declaration of Independence, create my own United States, and on and on, is not tantamount to my warning my self and heeding my own warning that I must *consciously* live my mind, *insightfully* cultivate my manpower, if I would extend my comprehension of the allness of my individuality as did my John Locke and my Thomas Jefferson.[8]

Nevertheless, a study of its historic beginning serves to reveal first origin of my moral agent itself, that most perplexing concern of every moral theorist. In every instance morality has to do with the wholeness of a specific life. Its criterion is always some inner condition of mental life which is of most practical value, some inner experience which finds expression as a helpful workable principle. Its theoretical goodness is consistent with the extent of my capacity for *conscious* self knowledge. The only sure guarantee I can find of the validity of anything at all, is my conviction of its presence in my mind.

My research in history discovers the account of man's mind struggling to cope with human excellence, human perfection, now ignoring its overwhelming meaning, now attributing it to his "impersonal" sources, now vesting it in his demons and gods, now fixing it in his own god, and ultimately locating it in his own divine being. My ancient Babylonian as well as ancient Assyrian and Hebrew, — each practiced seemingly impersonal non-ethical religion and only much later voluntarily

[8]See my *American Government*, Preface.

29

moralized his gods, ultimately uniting his divine with his recognized personal code of ethics.

To sketch most briefly some historic evidence of greatest ethical doing (being) of man, I observe the pure culture of individuality in the ethicoreligious statement underlying the Judaeo-Christian devotion: *I am that I am*. Or, I consult the great Hindu ethic of liberation of the individual in the Bhagavad Gita: "Let a man lift himself up by his own self; let him not depress himself; for he himself is his friend, and he himself is his enemy." My Indian helped to create the marvelous insight: out of unconsciousness, consciousness arises. His doctrine of transmigration awakened him to his duty towards elements of *his* world which he might otherwise ignore. His respect for every living thing enabled practical extension of his self respect. In his interesting record, *India — What Can It Teach Us*, F. Max Müller ably describes Indian literature as the "corrective which is most wanted in order to make our inner life more perfect, more comprehensive, more universal."

Zarathustra (600 B.C.), the prophet of ancient Iran, upheld reverence for human individuality as "highest truth." His teaching of Mainyu (from root *man*, — to think) concentrates upon the truth of the individual's within-ness as being the essence of humanity. The Zoroastrian code (Zend Avesta) upheld truthfulness as a chief precept, thus furthering the identity of theory and practice.

From his earliest beginning religion has been attributed to man and also very early the unity of ethic and religion seemed natural. The ancient Aryan, ancestor of the Hindu of India as well as of the Zoroastrian of Iran, was a worshipper of the power of nature. The world religion declared by Zarathustra appeared to the Iranian several thousand years ago. It upheld the spirit of individuality and the individuality of spirit. My Hindu ethical theory is based upon metaphysical principles in the Upanishads containing the Vedas. Ethical value is measured by the amount of personal sacrifice involved in conduct. Ethical discipline is primarily the exercise of discipline providing liberation of each Hindu. Austerity and renunciation are his primary ethical aids. Ahimsa, harmlessness, is commanded in the early Upanishads.

According to Vedantic teaching, in Brahman there is an indescribable power named maya or nescience that is responsible for the illusion of externality and its supporting the duality of self and non-self. Ethical discipline liberates the soul's appreciation for its unity by disclosing its identity also in its imagined not-soul.

I note the rise in his appreciation of the individual man occurring with my Chinese seer's development of his sense of personal identity. Confucius (551–479 B.C.) was devoted to inborn *jen*, "Jen is to love all man." He held self conscious, self critical, and self realizing human individuality to be the origin of all goodness. He is said to have laid down the ethic for the Chinese way of life, upholding the all-important moral truth that moral attainment depends wholly upon oneself. By many a historian his devotion to conscious self continence is considered to be the dawn of acknowledged self responsibility in and for ethical living.

Yang Chu (b. 420 B.C.) worked up an ethical insight very like that of Epicurus and St. Augustine, making the most of his life by a method of "following the desires of one's heart and refraining from contradicting the inclinations of nature." Said Yang Chu, "The only way to treat life is to let it have its own way, neither hindering it nor obstructing it." He found the good life could be sought and attained by discovering the pleasure in it.

"A great man is in harmony with Heaven and Earth," divined Shu Ching. Tao, the sense of existence, provides the basis for man's proper code of conduct. "All

31

other ways are not worth a fraction of love," meditated the Buddha. "To nourish one's nature is the way to secure heaven," declared Mencius (372–289 B.C.).

Most noteworthy, the man of China conceived his past as perfect, with no historic lapse from this perfection. He, as well as the man of old Japan, considered his family (not his individuality) to be his moral base.

A Zen Buddhist cultivates a Japanese (and Chinese) belief that self enlightenment is attained through meditation, self observation and intuition, rather than through scriptural study.

Every Jewish prophet stood for extending his human individuality-consciousness. The Levitical formula "to love one's neighbor as one's self" contains a wealth of self insight. Said Isaiah, "A man shall be as a hiding-place from the wind and a covert from the tempest, a river of waters in a dry place, a shadow of a heavy rock in a weary land." Said Job, "Till I die I will not renounce my integrity," and, "to depart from evil is understanding." Said Ezekiel, "The soul that sinneth *it* shall die." Proclaims the proverb 9:12, "If thou be wise, thou shalt be wise for thyself." From the period of earliest Jewish history in the second millennium B.C., there was the teaching of monolatrism, monolatry being the seer's first step towards monotheism. My ancestor's fixing of responsibility and authority in one God proved of greatest ethical significance for his fixing his responsibility and authority in his own conscious individuality.

In *The Psalms,* an ethical handbook, the ideal is decisively revealed that identification with the character of God is the rule for the cultivation of the character of man,

> For I have kept the ways of the Lord, and have
> not departed wickedly from my God.
> With the merciful thou wilt show thyself merciful;
> with the perfect man thou wilt show thyself perfect.

> With the pure thou wilt show thyself pure; and with
> the perverse thou wilt show thyself froward.
>   (Ps 18:21, 25, 26)

Discovery of my own self identity in my own fellowman is an expression of certain appreciation for the love of my God towards his all.

Although he worked up some structured ethical theory, the historic Greek seer tended to localize the base of morality in every man's assuming responsibility for himself, in his consciousness for his individuality. "All strangers and beggars are from Zeus," sang Homer in his *Odyssey*. To the ancient Greek sage wisdom meant self culture. Ethical products of the Hellenic period were Sophism, Stoicism, and Epicureanism. The Sophist, from Protagoras through Isocrates, was the first professional educator of Greece, prevailing approximately from 450 to 350 B.C. Protagoras claimed he could teach virtue, Gorgias claimed he could teach the art of persuasion. Protagoras declared, Man is the measure of all things, denying the possibility of objective standards. He claimed the office of the wise teacher to be the replacing of worse with better experience.

Thales (7th Century B.C.), called "the first philosopher," attempted to make water responsible for the substance of his world. However, he also observed, "All things are made of gods."

Solon (c. 638–c.559 B.C.), Athenian lawgiver, became archon in 594 and advanced due process of law as being beneficial for each citizen.

Heraclitus (6th Century B.C.) observed, "Wisdom consists in one thing, to know the mind by which all through all is guided" and, "Eyes and ears are bad witnesses when the soul is barbarous."

Pythagoras (b. 580 B.C.) considered number to be responsible for his cosmos. His ethic was, "Choose the best life; use will make it pleasant."

33

Xenophanes (b. 569 B.C.) claimed, "If animals had had hands they would have depicted gods each in their own form, just as men have done."

Parmenides (6th Century B.C.) stated, "It is only by thought we can become conscious of the really existent."

Empedocles (b. 500 B.C.) created the meaningful insight, "Like can only be perceived by like."

Anaxagoras (b. 500 B.C.) called attention to mind (*nous*) as the responsible principle of conduct.

Democritus (b. 460 B.C.) created the following ethic. "Men have invented for themselves the phantom, fortune, to excuse their own want of prudence." "The envious man is his own enemy." "Sin is caused by ignorance of the better course." "The doer of injustice is more miserable than the sufferer."

Sophocles (c. 496–406 B.C.) recorded a beautifully difficult ethic in his *Oedipus Rex:*

> Let every man in mankind's frailty
> Consider his last day; and let none
> Presume on his good fortune until he find
> Life, at his death, a memory without pain.[9]

Hippocrates (b. 460 B.C.), "Father of Medicine." recorded, "The patient's nature is the doctor that cures his illness." He is renowned for his appreciation of conscious self wholeness.

Antisthenes (b. 455 B.C.), the founder of the Cynic School, moralized, "If you pursue pleasure, let it be that which follows toil, not that which precedes it." "The only pleasure that is good is that which does not need to be repented of." When asked what his study of philosophy accomplished, he replied, "Ability to endure my own company."

[9]Lines 1664–68, translated by Dudley Fitts and Robert Fitzgerald (New York: Harcourt, Brace, 1949).

Socrates (470–399 B.C.) asserted that as his mother practiced midwifery regarding the body so he considered himself to be the obstetrician of his own mind, giving birth and consciousness to truths before held unconsciously. He practiced intense ethical devotion. His wonderful ethic affirmed: continuous development of conscious self knowledge is the only source of virtue. Only self ignorance leads man to vicious conduct. No one willingly wrongs himself, since right living is the only way to happiness.

Divine Socrates asserted the rights of the subject and explained life as a system of ends. Goodness consists in knowledge of each of the ends. By such self understanding an individual can observe the unity and reality of his own will. Aristotle nominated his Socrates "the founder of definition." His seeing his own identity in his Socratic idealism provided Plato with a sound foundation for his development of his own subjective idealism.

Plato (428–348 B.C.), marvelous biographer of his Socrates, upheld the ethical doctrine: when wisdom, courage, and temperance are integrated by justice, then virtue arises. He systematized the teachings of his Socrates and thus laid the basis for a science of ethics. Best known, but incompletely, is his petition: "And may I, being of sound mind, do to others as I would that they should do to me." I call special attention to the fact that this Golden Rule is usually quoted by omitting its most significant qualification, namely, "being of sound mind."

Said my Plato for my book, "The mortal nature ever seeks, as best it can, to be immortal" *(Symposium)*, "Justice admittedly means that a man should possess and concern himself with what properly belongs to him" *(Republic)*, "What is imperfect can never serve as a measure" *(Republic)*, and "Love reveals to the soul the presence of beauty" *(Symposium)*.

Aristotle (385–322 B.C.), "the master of the wise,"

displayed his greatness most clearly in his *Nicomach-ean Ethics*. His *summum bonum* was based on the assertion "Every art and every science, and so too every act and purpose, seem to aim at some good." Hence he defined the supreme good to be that to which all things aim. He considered man to be the source of his own happiness (even though his Solon claimed that no man could be called happy during his life). Aristotle defined happiness as "an activity in accordance with excellence." He held that only the gods were capable of full enjoyment, for only they fully exercised conscious life. His "Golden Mean" expressed his belief that moral virtue must be acquired by practice in avoiding excess or defect. By the "good man," he meant one who is aware that his completeness is good. He professed, "The man is free, we say, who exists for his own sake and not for another's."

When Dante speaks of Aristotle as "the master of those who know," or when Comte refers to him as "the eternal prince of all true thinkers," then it may be difficult to resist lulling one's self to sleep with such high-sounding pronouncements, thus overlooking completely the truth of one's sameness (the law of perfect identity in one's individuality) while pursuing such greater-than-thou or lesser-than-thou-meaning mental processes. Aristotle identified the greatest good of man as an activity of soul in accordance with the best and most complete virtue.[10] He confines himself to describing virtuous modes of conduct and does not stress the all-important point that there can be no difference in moral value between virtuous and so-called "vicious" conduct. Whatever is, is appropriately itself. This ethical orientation is indispensable for one's developing his due sense of self esteem, his biologically adequate self

[10]*Nic. Ethics*, bk. 1, chap. 6.

consciousness as being his indefectible divine self-world, his only truth or reality. No wonder brilliantly self conscious Nietzsche renounced morality based upon any individual's imagined impersonality.

The early Roman created his family living of two outstanding characteristics: ancestor worship and absolute authority of his father *(patria potestas)*. His virtues were those of submission to his due authority, respect for his due process of Roman law, and obedience to his duly appointed magistrate. Patriotism was the Roman idea of goodness. The citizen divided his occupation into farming and war, developing the virtues issuing from each of these devotions. Roman citizenship had great meaning. As his Roman world extended itself, the citizen's unreadiness for corresponding extension of his sense of personal identity showed itself in unrecognized self cruelties such as torture, gladiatorial combats, harsh and calloused living of his slaves, foreigners and his animals, contempt for death, extremes of wealth and poverty.

The early Roman helped himself ethically with his living of his Greek and Jewish sage. Stoics Cicero, Epictetus, Seneca, and Marcus Aurelius, — each developed a personal ethic from seeing his identity in his living of his world. Said Marcus Aurelius (121-180 A.D.), "to care for all men is according to man's nature," "Cast away opinion, and thou art saved," "Look within" and, "O Universe! What thou wishest, I wish." His *Meditations* treats of how to secure peace of mind through endurance and understanding. Cicero's Cato enunciates the basic principle of Stoicism, "Once pronounce anything to be undesirable, once reckon anything as good, other than moral worth, and you have extinguished the very light of virtue, moral worth itself, and overthrown virtue entirely."

My Christian morality originates from its preceding

37

Hebrew development. Historically Jesus's ministry succeeded in spirit and purpose that of John the Baptist, namely love-justice for present living. "The Kingdom of God is at hand" and "the time is fulfilled" are phrases full of this practicalness. Jesus's ethic is spirited with awareness of need for the *activity* of love-justice. The Sermon on the Mount is an enunciation of this beautiful unity. The grace of being (hence doing) good occurs in the wholeness-realm of the spirit. My all-inclusive kingdom of God is within me.

Thus incisive Paul senses his love-justice unity, "Take heed lest this liberty of yours becomes a stumbling block to them that are weak." (I Cor, viii, 9). With rare insight he noted the body of death in flesh-spirit dualism.

Conduct held to be in accord with the views of Jesus, — endurance as the highest level of courage, holiness as the desirable aim of culture, humility as the blessed expression of vanity, love as the soul of righteousness, lowliness of mind as basic for self esteem, self sacrifice as implementing self devotion, godliness as the consciousness of wholeness power — is of course a natural outgrowth of whatever way of life that preceded it. Each one's ethic is his supreme spiritual movement trying to uphold the full-measured meaning of his complete *individuality,* thus providing the only possible accounting for divinity of humanity.

Soulful Buddhistic and Indian sayings accord with those of the Sermon on the Mount, each one intentionally promoting appreciation for *individual* human living. Observe Luke's treatment of so-called "popularity": "Woe unto you when all men shall speak well of you, for so did their fathers to the false prophets." Only the individual mind can conceive *any* idea or view. My conception of "state religion" or of any kind of "organized religion" (other than that consciously organized

38

within my own individuality) need not be at the exorbitant cost of my appreciating the reality of my own divinity. My conception that I base upon authority other than my own may seem to create a condition of mental enslavement rather than mental freedom. *Conscious* individualism, unity, responsibility, sanity, and freedom are synonyms.

Emperor Constantine (c. 274–337) established his Christianity as the favored Roman religion, a most meaningful ethical development for everyone of his Roman world. By identifying moral law with Roman law he tended to localize responsibility and authority for human behavior in the individual citizen. The Christian doctrine of every man's divine sonship helped to bring to each man his conscious use of the truth of the wonderfulness and inviolability of his own life. Each Roman could find his civic benefit in trying to identify himself with the peacemaking, unbounded love and capacity for identification of the founder of his religion.

By uniting his religion of love and his devotion to justice Augustine of Hippo (354–430) developed unique power in the ethical idealism of his individuality. Said he, "As to virtue leading us to a happy life, I hold virtue to be nothing else than perfect love of God," "Such love of God involves love of neighbor, or brother, and proper love of self," "In no way can your enemy hurt you by his violence, as you hurt yourself if you love him not," "My love is my weight," "Love and do what you will," and "Life is a turbulent sea."

The seventh century Islamic faith, Mohammed's teaching, laid special emphasis upon ritual while attending to the observance of ideals. Fighting for the true worship is integral to it. The Koran teaches that God is one, all-powerful, merciful, and just, and that he revealed his divine order to Mohammed. Although its oriental beliefs may seem alien to the occidental mind,

39

the Koran contains most worthy elements. Its true believer helps himself greatly with it.

In the collection of the Traditions occurs prudential counsel of the nature of moral aphorism: "God loves kindness in all things," "The search for knowledge is a duty incumbent on every Muslim," "He is the most perfect Muslim whose disposition is most liked by his own family," "Who are the possessors of learning? Those who practice what they know."

In the Capitulary enjoining the foundation of monasterial and cathedral schools, Charlemagne (742 or 747–814) said, "Right action is better than knowledge: but in order to do what is right we must know what is right." This proper ideal of the practicality of knowledge attests the profound truth that knowledge insightfully conceived is the servitor of wisdom of living. Only in its meaning for self helpfulness is learning seen for its real value. May the curriculum of my every educator conspicuously witness this true comprehension of what is meant by schooling and culture of any kind.

In an ideal university, as I see it, a person must aim at *consciously* learning to develop nothing but his potential manpower. He is expected to study the so-called "facts of life" only as manifestations of the fact of his life. The ultimate meaning of all of his knowledge is consciously intended to be his conscious appreciation of his very own world. None of his technical training *can* be a partial skill, for it is all and only a development of his whole being.

Esteemed as the great theologian of his age, my St. Thomas Aquinas (1225–1274) recognized much of his own self identity in his study of his St. Augustine and Aristotle as he proceeded to work up his powerful life insight regarding the helpfulness in obediently being all that he is. He observes that it is natural for him to seek

40

the full functioning of his power, his good consisting in his realizing the full perfection of the whole of his nature. He describes the supernatural end of man as being the true perfection of the whole man. He defines grace as one's divine ability to find his identity in his divinity. The natural virtue sustaining adequate ethical living may be cultivated by discipline and practice aided by observing the helpfulness in one's fellowman's virtuous living.

Divine Dante Alighieri (1265–1321) developed magnificent ethical power out of his worldward self consciousness. He devoted special interest to establish responsible individuality, equating love and justice. Emerson recorded of him, he is "free imagination, —all wings,—yet he wrote like Euclid," and, "Dante's praise is that he dared to write his autobiography in colossal cipher, or into universality." After working up my own understanding of my emotionality I pleased my self immensely by studying my Dante's reporting how his affectivity was with him, as he viewed the splendor of his sound mind while creating its poetry. He warned of the inadequacy of human reason.

I find my ethical sources in my every poet and artist as well as student of religion that my living has originated, e.g., Leonardo da Vinci (1452–1519), Michelangelo Buonarrote (1475–1569), Miguel de Cervantes Saavedra (1547–1616), William Shakespeare (1564–1616), William Wordsworth (1770–1850), Samuel Taylor Coleridge (1772–1834).

So-called problems of ethics are traceable to the illusion of "conflict" created by an individual's conducting his life *as if* he is not the all and whole of it. Thomas Hobbes (1588–1679), acknowledged leader of ethical doctrine in England, asserted each individual to be entirely "self-regarding," his good being what pleases him. As mentioned, restricted understanding of the basic truth that every individual *is* his own fellowman, created the illusion that one individual could war against another.

To support this consequential illusion that spares an individual from the difficult discipline of self consciousness revealing to himself that he *is* his only fellowman, Hobbes enjoined each individual's submitting himself to "a strong government," which can be nothing but merely an unrecognized abstraction in the mind of each individual. Such a doctrine of "submission to the State" is actually the creating of a grievous problem of self concealment for each individual rather than a solution to his unwillingness to extend his sense of self identity (and its associated self love) to reveal his responsibility for being his own fellowman.

René Descartes (1596–1650) considered moral law to be innate in man's reason. His starting point being spiritualistic, he sought for rational certainty beginning with his certitude for his own subjectivity, his assurance of his inner world evident for his acknowledgeable mentation.

George Berkeley (1685–1753) observed all knowledge to be relative to the subject, a most important step in speculation about reality, but such a purely solipsistic conscious life orientation is most difficult of all life achievement.

Baruch Spinoza (Benedict de Spinoza, 1632–1677) observed that man's freedom lies in his self understanding. He asserted, "freedom of thought and speech not only may, without prejudice to piety and the public peace, be granted; but also may not, without danger to piety and the public peace, be withheld." In his *Ethics* (1675) he records, "Everything desires to persist in its own being." "Everything which adds to the bodily or mental powers of activity is pleasure; while everything which detracts from them is labeled as pain." Spinoza concludes his *Ethics* with the proposition, "Blessedness is not the reward of virtue but virtue itself."

Immanuel Kant (1729–1804) stood staunchly for his mental independence. His Categorical Imperative is a command or law of morality, "Act as though the maxim of your action were by your will to become a universal law of nature," "Treat humanity . . . always as an end and never as a means only," "Nothing in the world — indeed nothing beyond the world — can possibly be conceived which could be called good without qualification except a *good will.*" My Kant's idea of ideality seems to indicate that the very substance of his reality is psychic reality.

Consciously whole-minded Johann Wolfgang Goethe (1749–1832) produced "writings and recorded conversations . . . replete with observations concerning the self, the importance of the development of the self, and the ways in which development of the self can and must be done."[11] He records, "To develop my individuality. quite as it is, was unconsciously from youth on my desire and purpose." He said: However it be, I find life good. In *Faust* his Mephisto speaks of Life's wisdom:

> Gray my good friend, are all your theories,
> And green alone Life's golden tree!

Goethe's interest in his American democracy reflected and corroborated his devotion to whole individuality.

Karl Marx (1818–1883) theorizes that economic force determines the course of (his) world history. He bases his morality purely on class basis. He felt that once capitalism is abolished, man will transcend his self interest and just "naturally" be good.

Friedrich Nietzsche (1844–1900) observes how all

[11]Harold A. Basilius, "Goethe's Conception of Individuality and Personality," in *The Growth of Self Insight*, edited by John M. Dorsey, pp. 79–119 (Detroit: Wayne State University Press, 1962), p. 95.

43

"freedom, subtlety, boldness," as all that makes life worth living, require mental discipline. He recognizes morality in an individual as learning how to live with one's passions, "Let your kindness be your final self-conquest." The greatest one is the passionate one in control of his passions and able to employ them creatively.

The first American's ethic is probably that of my North American Indian. Of all accounts I have read (authored) on this important subject none excels that of Washington Irving's "Traits of Indian Character" included in his *The Sketch-Book of Geoffrey Crayon, Gent.* From this study in which I feel my very own identity, I choose excerpts.

Certainly this Sketch is not intended to be complete, particularly in doing justice to the dire necessity that a persecutor must be his own persecuted one, quite as a persecuted one must be his own persecutor. Clearly Irving uses the word *savage* to refer to his classification of the primitive nature of the society of the noble savage of his time.

> There is something in the character and habits of the North American savage, taken in connection with the scenery over which he is accustomed to range, its vast lakes, boundless forests, majestic rivers, and trackless plains, that is, to my mind, wonderfully striking and sublime. He is formed for the wilderness, as the Arab is for the desert. His nature is stern, simple, and enduring; fitted to grapple with difficulties, and to support privations. There seems but little soil in his heart for the growth of the kindly virtues; and yet, if we would but take the trouble to penetrate through that proud stoicism and habitual taciturnity, which lock up his character from casual observation, we should find him linked to his fellow man of civilized life by more of those sympathies and affections than are usually ascribed to him.
>
> It has been the lot of the unfortunate aborigines of America, in the early periods of colonization, to be doubly

wronged by the white men. They have been dispossessed of their hereditary possessions, by mercenary and frequently wanton warfare; and their characters have been traduced by bigoted and interested writers.[12]

In discussing the savage character, writers have been too prone to indulge in vulgar prejudice and passionate exaggeration, instead of the candid temper of true philosophy. They have not sufficiently considered the peculiar circumstances in which the Indians have been placed, and the peculiar principles under which they have been educated. No being acts more rigidly from rules than the Indian. His whole conduct is regulated according to some general maxims early implanted in his mind. The moral laws that govern him are, to be sure, but few; but then he conforms to them all;—the white man abounds in laws of religion, morals, and manners, but how many does he violate![13]

The solitary savage feels silently, but acutely. His sensibilities are not diffused over so wide a surface as those of the white man; but they run in steadier and deeper channels. His pride, his affections, his superstitions, are all directed towards fewer objects; but the wounds inflicted on them are proportionably severe, and furnish motives of hostility which we cannot sufficiently appreciate. Where a community is also limited in number, and forms one great patriarchal family, as in an Indian tribe, the injury of an individual is the injury of the whole, and the sentiment of vengeance is almost instantaneously diffused.[14]

Just before completing my manuscript of this volume I discovered a most interesting book relevant to my whole work, and specially to my interest in my American Indian: *Roger Williams: A Key into the Language of America*.[15] This work is not merely a dictionary of the Narragansett language but also an insightful Puri-

[12]New York: A. L. Burt, 1819, p. 247.
[13]Ibid., pp. 249–250.
[14]Ibid., p. 250.
[15]Edited with a Critical Introduction, Notes, and Commentary by John J. Teunissen and Evelyn J. Hinz (Detroit: Wayne State University Press, 1973).

tan's additional recording of his original lively appreciation of the natural virtue of his ethical Indian fellowman. Williams provides directions for use of the language thus enforcing his honoring it with his own conscious identity and thereby endowing it with the grace of his self love. The result is a true-to-life account of the life worthy self respect, self reliance and self understanding of my New England Indian.

Deserving of most careful study and recording is the ethic of my noble black slave. Incompetence prevents my doing justice to this most worthy concern, although I have made some small attempt in this direction.[16] Certainly my enslaved fellowman's ethic must be an issue of his necessity to see his identity *only* (consciously or unconsciously) in his free fellowman, quite as my enslaver's ethic must be an issue of his necessity to see his identity *only* (consciously or unconsciously) in his so-called slave.

Evident goodness must derive from my slavery such as reliance upon my spirituality and cultivation of my greatest virtue, namely, my capacity for enduring hardship. I have never discovered a more wonderful definition of my arduous manual labor than that of my beloved Sidney Lanier's poetic *singing with my hands.*

Man's ethic of Democracy has provided him with great promise for his conscious individual liberty based upon his conscious self sovereignty. Not government of the people (the literal translation of Democracy) but government of, by, and for the individual, is the ethic of ethics. Only that world called "individual man" can provide the fool-proof foundation for man's so-called

[16]See my "A Psychotherapeutic Approach to the Problem of Hostility With Specific Application to the Problem of Racial Prejudice," *Social Forces* 29 (December 1950), No. 2. Also see my *American Government* and *Psychology of Political Science.*

world government. It takes two to fight but even an illusional "two" suffices. From the viewpoint of subjectivity, there is, and can be, really only *oneness*. Fighting is, and ever must be, a firing upon one's own troops. Due appreciation for the wholeness of individuality is the due cost of lasting peace.

My American ethician has ever tended to support the democratic view of self government, observing that self instructed free will brings out the innate moral law in the individual and that conscious self realization is the unique natural right of man (W. E. Hocking). More than does any other personal trait, this appreciation for the world meaning of each citizen describes the present ideal American character.

Samuel Johnson (1696–1772) wrote and published the earliest systematic work on ethics in America, *A New System of Moral Philosophy,* (1746). He reduced all of his views on morality "to that grand ancient principle of true wisdom, know thyself." He specified that self knowledge includes "the relations wherein we stand; for this is the knowledge of ourselves in the whole."

During the second half of my American colonial period, Jonathan Edwards (1703–1758) was outstanding for his devotion to self consciousness. Edwards considered true virtue most essentially to consist "in benevolence to Being in general." He clearly regarded man as ruled naturally by self love. He heeded his mind's worldliness, "all existence is mental, and the existence of all exterior things (including of course the human body and its varying conditions) is ideal."

Human development is ever from excellence to excellence, never from so-called inferiority, or mediocrity, to excellence. Perfection is all that can be. My incentive, motivation, effort, or any kind of so-called am-

47

bition arises from my positive interest in living,—rather than from merely dissatisfaction, or disinterest, in the way I am living.

Bernard Bosanquet heeded a meaningful distinction "between teaching ethics and teaching *about* ethics." Indeed the whole notion of teaching as being a system for the knowledgeable educator's imparting his lore to his uninformed pupil, is an illusion. Everyone's learning is a process only of his growing his own self experience called "knowledge." He may thus teach himself (learn) only *about* an "objective science of ethics," in which event he spares himself the difficult, and correspondingly valuable, mind (or soul) shaping lesson that *his* science of ethics is subjective and only *about* him.

My Thomas Jefferson (1743–1826) conceived and recorded his ethic of ethics, *conscious self sovereignty,* in his American Declaration of Independence.[17] I have originated it as my own and it constitutes a dependable source for enabling me to attain my conscious equilibrium that enables me to prize justice justly, "the noblest among the virtues" (Aristotle). In 1790, Jefferson wrote LaFayette an observation of most helpful meaning for me today, "We are not to expect to be translated from despotism to liberty in a feather bed." His ethical insight is prudent and provident, "Laws and institutions must go hand in hand with the progress of the human mind."

The ethic of idealism grew strong in William T. Harris and each founder of his St. Louis school and Journal of Speculative Philosophy, as well as in each founder of his American transcendentalism. My conscious idealism is essential for my establishing moral distinction, or human responsibility, in the fullest sense of the term.

James Walker, John Henry Mackay, and Stephen T.

---

[17]See my *American Government,* pp. 107–120.

48

Byington (Max Stirner's translator) followed the practice of devotion of Ibsen and Nietzsche to Stirner's [Johan Caspar Schmidt's] renowned book, *The Ego and His Own*. Its ethical principle was: personal awakening to the truth of one's allness. Later, even before his coming to America, my Ernst Cassirer clearly recorded concepts on the inviolability of human individuality. Once originally discovered and cherished with self love by his American reader, this self integrity became that one's own beloved self knowledge.

Fyodor Dostoyevsky (1821–1881) centers his religious and ethical interest in his God. He is a Christian moralist and mystic. He observes no superior or inferior being in his ethical world; each must obey his moral law. In *The Brothers Karamazov* his Father Zossina explains why the philosopher says he cannot apprehend external reality: "Much on earth is hidden from us, but to make up for that we have been given a precious mystic sense of our living bond with the other world."

William James (1842–1910), physician, developed his mind mostly as a psychologist. His contribution to his ethical growth is great. Even though he may be often considered a metaphysical pluralist his devotion to continent self consciousness is clear, "the well-known democratic respect for the sacredness of individuality,—is, at any rate, the outward tolerance of whatever is not itself intolerant. . . . Religiously and philosophically, our ancient national doctrine of live and let live may prove to have a far deeper meaning than our people now seem to imagine it to possess." I do not find that James's pragmatism contradicts idealism at all.

James, my highly responsible psychological medic, points out:

> The question of having moral beliefs at all or not having them is decided by our will. . . . No one of us ought to issue vetoes to the other, nor should we bandy words of

abuse. We ought, on the contrary, delicately and profoundly to respect one another's freedom. . . .[18]

He explains:

... the Benthams, the Mills, and the Bains have done a lasting service in taking so many of our human ideals and showing how they must have arisen from the association with acts of simple body pleasures and reliefs from pain. . . . Neither moral relations nor the moral law can swing *in vacuo*. Their only habitat can be a mind which feels them; and no world composed of merely physical facts can possibly be a world to which ethical propositions apply. . . . *Invent some manner* of realizing your own ideals which will also satisfy the alien demands, – that and that only is the path of peace![19]

Certainly this conscious orientation in absolute self continence graciously disposes of the otherwise troublesome claims of my casuistry.

My sublimely ethical Emerson found his unique joy of living in his mind consciousness. For his study of his mind he longed for the development of "exhaustive accuracy of distribution which chemists use in their nomenclature and anatomists in their descriptions."[20] He pointed out that the importance of scientific discovery is "not the fact, but so much of man as is in the fact." Emerson sounded the note of intuitionism, of biological function if you will. He observed, the first requisite of a gentleman is to be a good animal. By "good animal" he referred to the organic health of the human individual or organism in the sense of the good working order (whole functioning) of its organs and organ systems.

[18]"The Will To Believe," *New World*, June 1896, pp. 22, 23, 30.
[19]"The Moral Philosopher and the Moral Life," *International Journal of Ethics*, April 1891, pp. 186, 190, 205.
[20]"Powers and Laws of Thought," *Natural History of Intellect*. The Complete Works of Ralph Waldo Emerson (Boston and New York: Houghton, Mifflin and Company, 1903).

I find that so-called physical exercise is not sufficient to produce the good animal. May my every athletic director make this self-view his own. The athlete's *conscious* self appreciation as being his whole world is also a hygienic necessity. All of my self interest in my world preserves what is conducive to my wanting to live. The insightful practice of self devotion, enlightened and enlightening selfishness, keeps the commandment of life appreciation implicit in human wholeness. However, I am incapable of any but spiritual (moral) living regardless of my recognizing or ignoring that fact.

My Mary Baker Eddy (1821–1910) based her Christian Science development upon her extensive experience in needing to help herself in ways she could not find in the kind of medical practice she had tried out. She gradually concentrated upon the efficacy of conscious mental forces *other than those* of the medical scientist, thus ultimately founding her dogmatic Christian Science. My orthodox practitioner in this movement has been devoted to his organization's accepted concept of mind, eschewing possible benefit derivable from what he regards as a materialistic medicine. In recent years, however, he has been courageously confronting himself with testy problems of confining dogma, growing uneasiness with the dualism implicit in his denial of his scientific medicine or in his mental dissociation of any sort, increasing dissatisfaction with his feelings of unoriginality in his devotion to his schismatic reasoning, frustration from unfreedom of his organizational thinking, and so on.[21] I find my Margaret Laird's intrepid pioneering in health-and-religion most noteworthy.

John Dewey (1859–1952) wrote his *Ethics* (1938) in collaboration with his friend, James H. Tufts. His *Theo-*

[21]See the consciously free-minded work of Margaret Laird, C.S.B., *Christian Science Re-Explored, A Challenge to Original Thinking.* Introduction by John M. Dorsey, M.D. (New York: William Frederick Press, 1965).

ry of Valuation (1939) advanced his devotion to scientific experimental method. His *value judgment* is essentially prediction about the enjoyability of a given consideration. He regarded the dominating purpose of all education to be the formation of the good self, the self capable of maintaining the good society. Insightfully he saw in self growth the basis for cultivating moral freedom and responsibility. Dewey became the most prominent exponent of pragmatism. The pragmatist accounts for the truth of an idea in terms of its usefulness in a living context.

Borden P. Bowne (1847–1910) makes the ever-needed self observation, "In no way can the mind get outside of itself and grasp things otherwise than through the conceptions which its nature allows it to form."

Josiah Royce (1855–1916) talks this idiolect of self realization, "my duty is simply my own will brought to . . . self consciousness" and "Loyalty is the will to manifest . . . the Eternal, that is, the conscious and superhuman unity of life, in the form of the acts of an individual Self." He asserts, "Humanity depends, for its spirituality and its whole civilization, upon faiths and passions that are in the first place *instinctive*, inarticulate, and in part unconscious."

Charles Darwin's *Descent of Man* (1871), Herbert Spencer's *Data of Ethics* (1879), and Leslie Stephen's *Science of Ethics,* — each applies the doctrine of evolution, particularly natural selection, to explain the genesis of man's morality out of prior unmoral living.

Warner Fite (1867–1955), Stuart Professor of Ethics at Princeton University, recorded his insight in *Individualism* (1911), *Moral Philosophy* (1925), and *The Living Mind* (1930). Professor Fite tries to explain how "the coming to consciousness issues inevitably in the expression of personal aims."[22] Certainly by con-

[22]*The Living Mind: Essays On The Significance of Consciousness* (New York: The Dial Press, 1930).

sciousness Professor Fite means self consciousness, for whatever other kind of consciousness can there be! "Goods and values in the economic sense are wholly irrelevant to goods or values in the moral sense, and the community of names is more or less an accident of names . . . yet economic values and moral values have a common basis in human need and desire."[23] Little wonder that Aristotle, sometimes called the first economist, painfully considered his commerce as contemptible. "A business acquaintance" is a description involving illusion of distance rather than reality of identity.

The ethical role of my self as a scientist is beautifully presented by my Warner Fite in his lifesaving work describing his ethic, specifically in his concluding chapter, "The Human Soul and the Scientific Prepossession,"

> By the scientific prepossession I mean . . . the prepossession that all ages have been ages of prepossession except our own; that all former ages have viewed the world through the medium of human prejudices, from which we, happily, are free.[24]

With the exception of my profoundly insightful scientist cherishing a rare concern for his self insight indeed, without warning my scientist banishes his self consciousness even from his psychological laboratory. I may qualify my self as an "expert psychologist" without any reference to my personally experiencing only my own mind. I may even define psychology as the "study of behavior," seeming to be able to leave my mind out of the definition entirely if I can quickly gloss over my meaning for "study."

William Heard Kilpatrick states, "All conduct does grow out of the self; but the term selfishness is used to

[23]In his chapter, "Psycho-analysis and Sex-Psychology" this good author seems unable to consider certain psychoanalytic discovery, except as "obscene" (p. 235).
[24]*The Living Mind*, p. 2.

indicate disapproval of a narrow self in the face of the just demands of a broader self." And, "self and other grow together in the child's mind to form his self-other compounded selfhood."[25]

His Ethical Culture Movement initiated in the United States in 1876 by Felix Adler, Ph.D., of Columbia University is an attempt to found a moral unity in which every one living any religion can grow his own identity in it. Its member observes that such universal identity serves well every individual who would work for his world's unity.

Plato once defined his justice as the health of his soul. Sigmund Freud's psychoanalytic work led him to see that his awareness for his health of soul varied directly with his conscious self knowledge. He disciplined his mind to allocate its content to accord with his cultivation of his self insight.[26] Certainly I must lack conscious self possession to the extent that I cannot comprehend that my world is my own, that it lives in me, not I in it. My own spatial metaphor need not mislead me. However, any illusion of a "self dispossessed" condition of my mind does not mean that I am "possessed by the devil" (wicked). As did Job, Freud stood for self love, self insight, and self helpfulness, rather than for calling himself (including his fellowman) bad. He considered so-called "wickedness" just as helpful to the clergyman as "symptom" to the physician.

My Professor Freud's science of psychoanalysis has been indispensable for my finding out the absolute oneness of my body-mind-and-externality. My amazing discovery of my peerless self analyst at first succeeded

[25]*Philosophy of Education* (New York: MacMillan, 1951).
[26]See, *Sigmund Freud, Psychoanalysis and Faith, Dialogues with the Reverend Oskar Pfister,* ed. Heinrich Meng and Ernst L. Freud (New York: Basic Books, Inc., 1963).

mostly in my stupefying or stunning my mind with access after access of overwhelming self consciousness that seemed terrifying in the light of my limited conscious self identity. Particularly (my) his unwavering belief in the organicity of mental activity has been most helpful to me in my effort to awaken my mind to the identical wholeness in all that I name my body-mind-environment meaningfulness.

In his *An Hymne in Honour of Beautie* Edmund Spenser (1552–1599) divined,

> For of the soule the bodie forme doth take,
> For soule is forme, and doth the bodie make.

From growing my self analytic experience as my own original *self* growth I have been able to observe directly my development, first of my body image or body ego and next, by extension of all of this mental hold, all that I can consider as my mind, with or without my appreciation for its origin in the mental unity I call my body ego.

Leopold von Ranke considered the real advance made by Thucydides to consist in "that he perceived the motive forces of human history to be in the moral constitution of human nature." In his *Prolegomena to Ethics,* 1883, Thomas Hill Green declared, "It is probable indeed that every movement of religious reform has originated in some clearer conception of the ideal of human conduct, arrived at by some person or persons."[27]

Every historian of his profession concerns himself with the idea of the dominant force in his so-called historical development. The philosopher may call it "the love of self knowledge"; the physical scientist may call it "the order of law"; the economist may call it "lifesaving economy"; the political scientist may call it

[27]Professor of Moral Philosophy, Oxford, 1878–1882.

"statesmanship"; the clergyman may call it "religion"; the ethician may call it "responsible self development"; the physician may call it "the mind's awakening to itself." Each one is right as far as he sees it.

Historian and political economist Philip van Ness Myers has recorded many helpful views, such as:

> The truth is ... that in no domain has progress been greater, the gains larger or more precious, than in the moral. From clan morality, based on physical kinship, mankind has advanced or is advancing to world morality, based on the ethical kinship of men. ... There is one thing about a moral ideal which sets it apart from all other ideals. It possesses a unique dynamic force. ... To create a new intellectual life is to create a new moral life. ... Man ever makes and remakes his gods in his own image. ... There is a heart of good in things evil. ...[28]

Whatever living secures my industry, shapes my ethic.

My study of the meaning of ethics is tantamount to studying my civilizing process and, correspondingly, follows a historical account of the growth and cultivation of my self's discovering its wholeness. However, no matter how far back in my antiquity I may care to trace the beginning of my ethical, or moral, or humane, or civilized behavior, the single standard source of all of my sense of propriety remains in my self. My way of behaving my self is always an issue of 1) Who I consciously and unconsciously am, and 2) How I consciously and unconsciously create my world.

My so-called kinship of blood, family, cult, language, religion, race, and so on, always resolves itself into nothing but my own meaning for any of it. The one and only starting point of my historic ethical development has been somewhere in my own *conscious* self development. I am sure that my early sense of justice, or love of man, or idea of god, was as rudimentary as my early

[28]*History as Past Ethics* (Boston: The Athenaeum Press, 1913).

56

self consciousness was. My consciousness for my fellow creature as my own creation, delivers me from costly compensation such as double standard morality, retributive justice, fitting punishment, *lex talionis* (two wrongs makes a right), revenge, or any other kind of shortsighted ethic which simply must add further self injury to my initial one. To the extent that my ethic is that of self reverence, my moral goodness consists in my loyal devotion to my self consciousness. As soul perceptive Philip van Ness Myers stated, "that one be true and loyal to the best one knows is the only thing absolute and categorical in the utterance of the moral faculty."

A brief statement of "the best" I know, may be presented in the enheartening phrases of my Tracy W. McGregor (1869-1936).[29] I extol appreciation of "the supreme worth of the inner ethical life," and the preservation of "the integrity of individual mental and spiritual life." With these insights, and applying my Dr. William Osler's appreciation for the marvelous meaning of work, I cannot go astray from the desirable ascent of man to his *consciously* directing his own self development.

Asserts Fung Yu-Lan, professor of philosophy, National Tsing Hua University,

> What is the highest form of achievement of which a man *as a man* is capable? According to the Chinese Philosophers, it is nothing less than being a sage, and the highest achievement of being a sage is the identification of the individual with the universe.[30]

Nothing of my world can have a self-existence other than that which my existence provides. Only my life

[29]"Toward a Philosophy of the Inner Life." Paper read at the National Conference of Social Work, Detroit, June 1933.
[30]*A Short History of Chinese Philosophy*, ed. Derk Bodde (New York: The Macmillan Co., 1950).

can keep my every problem and its solution alive. Life can be found to be worth living in a way too rarely felt, *consciously*.

Man can never be found in History; any immense vista of "history" can be found only in man. Man is the sole origin of all of his causes. Such an expression as "man in general," or "mankind," ignores all of the only truth of man, namely, his wholly unique individuality. I cannot be the result of "historical antecedence," or a product of my so-called Age. The mere fact that I have lived whatever I have lived defines me as the sole responsible author of my self. I have made a place for my so-called "History" or "Age" or "Antecedents" as my agents in my life.

Summary sense of this incomplete historical view is that my conduct gains ethical sanction in proportion as my activity-as-a-whole-person becomes acknowledgeably self conscious. I go forward in my knowledge and backward in my morals, if I do not see my knowledge entirely as the growth of my self insight. Appreciation of the value of my life, my marvelous presence, is the assumption underlying my every moral estimate. I try to make excellence of self care my ethical theory and practice. Looking into my life I can observe the extent to which my living up to my ideal, my devotion to the truth of my allness, gives me peace of mind, keeps me in most effective touch with my only reality, guarantees my appreciation of my health, and provides ideal responsible living of my fellowman's wholeness. Much as my Walt Whitman, poet of individuality, described his ethic,

I swear nothing is good to me now that ignores individuals,
The American compact is altogether with individuals,
The only government is that which makes minute of individuals,
The whole theory of the universe is directly unerringly to one
   single individual — namely to You.

58

Reviewing this chapter, I say to my self, my history of my ethic would begin ideally with my nature and need as an organism to preserve my life, and then faithfully pursue that ideal. This present historical sketch obviously does little justice to the merit of its subject since it is intended merely as very limited allusion to the ethical nature of organic wholeness. I construe my biblical account of divine revelation of self identity in the words I Am to mean: I Am Wholly All That I Am.

PERSPECTIVE

And this is the result of the gigantic work of the ancients; that man knows himself as being without relations and without a world, as a spirit.

Max Stirner

Heroic effort of my fellow scientist continues to try to understand the mystifying psychic process in terms of physiological behavior. Thus even the wise physician Pierre Jean Georges Cabanis (1757–1808) tried to understand thought as "a secretion of the brain," a behavior analogous to the secretion of the liver or some other organ, in the wish to be able to "objectify" what can be only subjective. Behaviorist John B. Watson (1878–1958) also tried to understand mental event, such as sensation, perception or feeling, in terms of mere activity, thus hoping to substitute appearance (of objectivity) for being (subjectivity, itself).

My psychological system called objectivity is based entirely upon (the illusion of) externality, as if any existence could be on the outside of its entity, rather than entirely within it. This kind of acceptance of the seeming for the being may tempt me as a neurophysiologist to try to account for vision by means of ocular, neural and cerebral localization. However even my least visual production such as luminosity obviously is one thing and my ocular-neural-cerebral activity is quite another. I cannot dispose of tearfulness as lachrymation or of cheerfulness as physiognomy.

61

Further effort to justify so-called objectivity is found in my conception called representativeness. In fact representativeness has even been named the characteristic feature of mentality, as if the mind might depend entirely for its existence simply upon copying external-objectivity-in-the-original. According to this kind of psychology it would appear that the mind might grow from the outside in, rather than from within its own being. Such an image of man's nature, as growing from the impact of external stimulus rather than from his own original nature, certainly slights the view of man as being inviolably whole.

Still another method of supporting the illusion of objectivity can be found in the teaching that one is not a separate being, independent, free and original; that one is a "part" of a greater whole and therefore must revere that whole as outside of his individual existence. As if one's so-called greater whole would be content to consist of parts! Or even, as if one's greater whole would be content to consist of *lesser* wholes.

I cherish my certitude that my ancient as well as modern dogmatic formulation of my religion contains all that there is to contain, namely, the truth of living and hence the living of truth. Each is a lifesaving aspect of my development. All that I can mean by soul, my basic religious concern, is as real as real can be. Indeed my term *soul* befits the psychonomy I use for describing the spirit of the wholeness of my being. The soul of me is the life of me. All of my wording of so-called materiality seems to me to be an hypostatization of a term, by allowing it to seem to name something made of nothing. I see, my fellowman as I see my self, shaping his religion and all else that he lives on the basis of the functioning of his need and his insight.

The point needs to be clear that so-called "wrong" is also the expression of the degree of insight that is sufficient only to produce it. Whatever is, perfectly is. The temptation to indulge the illusion of imperfection is very strong, however. Always the study of further fact accounting for the behavior in question reveals that the very concept of "wrong" or of "error" itself is based entirely upon merely insufficient knowledge of fact accounting perfectly for so-called *wrong,* completely justifying it, thoroughly exonerating it from any and every implication of imperfection of any kind whatsoever. "Reading" this book may provide strengthening exercise for this precious understanding.

Every so-called injustice, vice, mistake (any kind of seeming shortcoming of virtue) may be scientifically and religiously accounted for as necessary, desirable, exactly right in every respect. Whatever currently passes for wrong or error can really be only right or accuracy that is not comprehended as such. I frequently smile to my self while at tennis when I serve or return a ball "out of bounds," whenever I can realize that my every service or return goes just exactly, unerringly, where *I* hit it. Similarly I enjoy my realization that I pass all of my examinations perfectly, in that I secure the exact score I deserve. And so on, I acknowledge that whatever is, is perfectly right, virtuously desirable, for upon this fertile soil I can consciously grow anew.

My conception of life as being a "gift" cannot enable me to value its true worth. Only my recognition of my very own giving birth of my self to my self can create my biologically adequate measure of self thankfulness usually alluded to as "the joy of living." The life orientation I regard as consisting of conscious self knowledge is most useful in conducting the course of my being.

I have discovered that my true perception for my existence extends itself into right thinking and feeling. No standard of value but the flowing love of life itself

63

has provided me with my source of happiness. My pursuit of life is my only possible pursuit of real property. My "physical" world truly is; it is entirely ideal. My full and free use of my mind, my marvelous power of imagination, is my philosopher's stone which reveals every illusion of materiality as the precious reality of my own mind's making. I have had to work my imagination just right to see that my selfishness, the stone which as a builder I rejected, is the only substance which can serve the purpose of building my ethic. *Misunderstanding of a theory by a mind unready to create it, does not constitute its refutation.*

Furthermore, appreciation and realization of the supreme ethic, "Whatever is, is perfect," is rarely achieved, although every other ethical statement inherently contains its own undoing, — namely the presumption of so-called error or evil or sin, or wickedness. Nowhere in my world is a factually unwarranted premise more consistently evident, than in my taking for granted that so-called *wickedness* is a possible. Hence it is that the infallible ethic, "Whatever is, is perfect," is consistently assumed to be untrue, without warrant other than ignoration.

I exercise my truth: I choose to refer to all of my living as an individualizing process, my growth consisting of integrating the developing wholeness of my being. *To speak the whole truth I must speak with my conscious self love.* I define liberty itself as beloved discipline in self consciousness. My only interest possible is in my own whole condition, hence awareness for that necessity may gradually become the whole of my morality. Thus, I can revere the prayer of my Socrates:

> Beloved Pán, and all ye gods who haunt this place, grant me beauty of the inward soul, and make the outward and the inward man to be but one.

A main fact of my psychic activity is that it is continuous throughout whatever I call my body or my so-called externality of any kind. This means that whatever I live that I call *my* physiology or *my* environment is integral to the wholeness of my mind. Hence it is that *my* so-called physical health is a special form of my whole health condition. Hence it is that *my* so-called external world welfare is a special form of my whole health condition. For example, from the standpoint of its being all mine, I cannot differentiate my meaning for what is happening in my environment from my meaning for what is happening in my stomach or liver or any other living of my wholeness. To make the functioning of this consistently overlooked self knowledge thoroughly obvious as self evident, all I have to do is consider the conspicuous continuity of 1) feeling tremendous alteration in my visceral activity and 2) seeing any so-called shocking event occurring (as if) outside of me.

However, this identity comprising the wholeness of my individuality may be, and ordinarily is, overlooked by me. Hence, I may suffer innumerable symptoms of neglect of my health without ever realizing that each distressing symptom is a helpful indication to me that I have not learned the truth of the wholeness of my nature. Certainly I cannot conduct my living with biologically adequate conscious responsibility, until I succeed in teaching my self the true extent of my self. For example, my custom of regarding any trouble occurring anywhere in my so-called corporeality as not involving the health condition of my whole mind, or the converse, is surely a disregard for the welfare of my whole nature.

However, if merely to honor the wholesome spirit of work, or functioning, it is readily understandable that every trial-and-error scientific effort be made to achieve

65

discovery of the nature, need, and working of my mind. It is also understandable that a scientist turn his uniquely human development of language to this stupendous task. In the helpful sense that science is a well-made language it behooves every scientist to try to work up as exactly accurate wordage as possible for scientizing his account of the psychology of his psychology. I refer to his mind's inconspicuous identity: its subjective wholeness-allness-oneness being, of which the compelling grandeur of his sensory, perceptual, and conscious living is the (unacknowledged) fascinating appearance. The well-made language constituting the psychology of psychology will not be a borrowing from any other ology but rather will consist of a terminology strictly designating the nature of the wholeness of spirited human being.[1]

Anew, I observe that my fellowman, *every one,* is now living as ethically as it is at all possible for him to live now. My ethic reveals to me that my everyone's ethic is just as divinely (perfectly) ethical as is the one I call mine. Furthermore whether or not my fellowman is even aware of his ethical living, does not in any extent or degree alter my realization that his present living is divinely appropriate presently for him. I and my criminal are one, quite as I and my creator are one. All of the so-called suffering in my world is as ideally perfect as is all of the satisfying of my world. Each is its own kind of glorious helpfulness that may be named righteousness.

I freely grant my critical comment that I, not frequently but *always,* attach to my words or terms, my own meaning, which may or may not seem to have anything in common with my so-called traditional or conventional definition. However, my abiding truth upholds my reality that all that can be found by me in any

[1]See my *Psychology of Language,* pp. xvii– xxxiv.

of my scripture consists entirely of my own identity.

I imagine *my* greatest social welfare, my greatest civilization, to exist when I, including my every fellow-man, develop my self in my consciously independent manner, so that every single individual may recognize that his own inviolable wholeness includes *his* idea of his fellow-individual's inviolable wholeness. Thus I can feel with certitude that every idea of a harmonious-society-of-independent-personalities can have its existence only in the mind personifying or hypostatizing it, either consciously or not; that only each individual can apply this principle of social welfare to his own living.

Scottish philosopher Francis Hutcheson (1694–1746), professor of moral philosophy at Glasgow, was apparently the first one to originate the social welfare formula, "The greatest happiness for the greatest number," which seems to be localizable somewhere external to its only possible origin, namely, in the individual mind conceiving it. Professor Harold Hoffding (1843–1931) of the University of Copenhagen states in the Preface of his Ethics (1887): "the ethical principles can regulate life only if they have proceeded from life." There is no possible "life of society," only the *life of the individual*. Society defined merely as a number of individuals, has no existence of its own other than in the mind of each individual. Moral goodness can be lived *only* by an individual who possesses the life to live it with.

However, it is customary to speak irresponsibly of an ethical society, ethical science or ethical field, quite as if it is an autonomous entity with some kind of life or nature of its own,—all at the expense of consciousness for the intact wholeness of the speaker. My individuality is a name for my indivisible unity. I cannot make my self a means in order to increase or decrease a so-called number of individuals, except by deluding my self that I can. It is my nature to be only my own living. "Nature" derives from *nascere,* to grow or live. My every meaning is my purely subjective invention. It is my conscious self orientation about the meaning of my social welfare that can help me to understand my John Boyle O'Reilly's caustic couplet:

> Organized charity scrimped and iced
> In the name of a cautious statistical Christ.

It thus becomes evident that my every method of so-called social welfare is bound to be perfectly ill-advised to the extent that it involves disregard for the inviolable wholeness of human individuality. No matter how much as an infant I may seem to be helped by my mother, the only truth in the situation is: how much I help my self by *my* living of *my* mother as she seems to live her baby in a way that she considers to be helpful. It is in no sense implied in my principle of social welfare that my fellowman must wait to help himself until he can acknowledge that his only possible help must be self help, much less *conscious* self help. However it is my gradually developing understanding of my wholeness that reveals all of my help as self help, quite as it reveals all of my love as self love, and thus spares me the pain of every illusion of pamperedness or pauperism.

The impulse and desire of development is itself a product of development. I am by nature all that I can ever become,—political, social, ethical or whatever. My life develops itself. My developing my conscious ability to direct my development is integral to my appreciation for my wholeness. My realizing that I must develop my appreciation for my ability to develop my self is created only when I have strengthened my capacity for con-

scious self responsibility. My steadfast devotion to cultivating my conscious self helpfulness, by and in my self, is the heart of my social welfare for I can do for my fellowman only as I do for my self, quite as he can be only self helpful.

Infallibly to coordinate pleasure with human success and pain (any unhappiness) with human failure is a dangerous oversimplification of the reality of human welfare. Through it positive goodness can become identified only with happiness, and negative goodness (badness) only with unhappiness. The plain truth is: *Man's pain (any unhappiness) is the indispensable guardian of his good, counselling him constantly regarding his best interests, expressing greatest possible livesaving wisdom, — never his so-called enemy.* The rigid retaliation system of reward and forfeit respectively for good and bad done is a primitive ethic that begs the whole question of the true nature of human good, attempting to make goodness itself into a means for securing a reward and thereby obscuring the rewarding significance of goodness as its own end. Thus man's supreme good, that is, goodness itself, is made to appear secondary to some notion of successful living which can be attained by using goodness as a ploy.

Up through the ages man's question of his *summum bonum* has been the subject of earnestly sustained inquiry, whereas his greatest good is always *goodness itself.* Good itself is ever a subjective feeling of life appreciation, entirely its own justification for being, wholly self experience reflecting the essential intrinsic worth of consciously whole human individuality, — without any possible reference to any secondary gain deriving from it. The whole full meaning of human being is unattainable except to the extent that its inviolable subjectivity is thoroughly understood, its unvarying goodness completely acknowledged, its incapacity for doing any wrong totally comprehended.

Whatever I write is a direct continuation of my living, furthering the process of my growth. Unless I write it down immediately I cannot be at all sure that I can later create any meaning of my self at will. On that account I may arise from my bed to record a sprout of meaning that I find helpful, for my experience has taught me that I may or may not be able to produce its flux again in the morning.

Anew, this book is intended to be merely my faithfully recorded growth of a plain statement to my plain self of my ethical viewpoint. It purports to be whole and sound, for it is certainly a product of my wholeness as well as of my soundness. However, I find most compelling my Benjamin Franklin's comment in a letter to his brother John: A man cannot be said to be fully born until he be dead. My present mental condition is specifically the vital outcome of what my mind was like to start with plus how it has grown itself since then. I cannot afford disregard for careful development of my necessity to evolve my self in one way or another, for that is the chief obligation of my sound mind.

My wholeness is uniquely mine. Gradually I learn to identify with my name all of it that I can be aware of as being mine. However, every increase in my appreciation for my being all of my self is associated with birth pains or growing pains signalizing my increasing awareness in obligation for being the independent whole that I am. Roughly these unhappy sensations appear to be essentially signs of my difficult withdrawal from an already comforting self identity to grow up an extension of my conscious wholeness involving my feeling additional responsibility for more of my whole being.

The fact is that I feel comfortable in using my name as well as my "I" without heed for the truth that it is all meaning my wholeness. I can never speak for all of my self or to all of my self in the sense of honoring my identity in all of my being, but the nearer I can come to this ideal goal the more I can consciously realize my ethic.

Not only is my every act created by my wholeness but also the character of that act, as either honoring or ignoring its own wholeness, enters into further creation of my whole individuality. My self conscious act begets self consciousness in my wholeness; my self unconscious act begets self unconsciousness in my wholeness. The origin of my every decision, effort, sensation or emotion is to be found in my organismic oneness. I am always, mostly insensibly, drawing a moral from any of my experience.

The one way that works the marvel of the complete man out of my living is the unique way that honors the functioning of my growing only my wholeness from the beginning. *The only way in which my mind can develop or act is as a whole.* But I may be either conscious or unconscious for this consequential truth of truths. My only possible purpose in life, again regardless of all appearance to the contrary, is my own individual development. All I need to do is to become conscious for that already existing purpose in order to become able to control its direction. My development can only be in the direction of my self interest, denied or affirmed.

Not only my finger print or voice vibration, but also every feature of my whole being is uniquely characteristic of my wholeness. My greatly experienced surgeon, the junior Charles Mayo, once commented that the formation of the viscera of an individual appears to be as physiognomic as his facial features if one can learn how to observe such indication of his identity.

I cannot really divide my mind into parts, despite all appearance to the contrary. My every so-called abstract "part" consists of nothing but what the reality of my concrete wholeness makes of it, and my wholeness can only create wholeness. I can study my anatomy or physiology or any ology without resorting to denying my wholeness quality in any aspect of its wholeness. And this precious lifesaving capability is one that can be developed, I am sure, for I can observe my developing it. My largely neglected but sanity-creating truth is that I cannot ever have anything to do with my anyone or anything except that one's wholeness. Wholeness is all that can ever be of any possible concern to me. Naturally I grow my devotion to the truth of the unalterable integrity of my living as my conscious ethic. Hardihood, perseverance, endurance, including steadfast long-suffering, are aspects of my ethical character I prize specially for their life-preserving help to me.

Since all there is to work with in any way whatsoever consists specifically of its wholeness I have gradually been daring to study this entity of entities with growing appreciation for its profound life meaning in furthering due reverence for individuality, as such, rather than for what it may seem to contain. I discover that when I am not always admiring the truth of wholeness everywhere I *am* indulging my illusion of my mind divided, a costly indulgence. I find that all of my mental trouble that I may call social, political, educational, religious, or by whatever name is really traceable to my heedless treatment of my wholeness which manifests my soul, no less.

However, it is the appearance that I make dominate the reality when I conduct my living *as if* I can separate part from whole. For example, even by seeming to *divide* my mind (insightlessly) into a conscious self that is separate from, and even alien to, an unconscious self, I may allow my reasoning to trouble my mind, at the expense of my untroubled consciousness for the unified wholeness of my identical individuality. The process by which my self wholeness maintains and develops itself ideally cannot be by ignoring the truth of its self, but rather by honoring the unity of its wholeness self in its every experience.

Again, even my personal pronoun "I" cannot truly name my wholeness except to the extent that it can be used to name *all* of my wholeness living. My word "self" cannot name my wholeness except insofar as it lends itself to naming all of my so-called otherness, externality, and similar living of my mind only assumed to be foreign to me. I am *my* you precisely as I am *my* I in any and every form. There can be nothing for me to accept but my own acceptance. For me to reduce any kind or degree of difference to fundamental unity, all I need become is self conscious. Thus my spirituality, materialism, or whatever, becomes understandably all about its self, incapable of being different from its sameness.

It was my re-establishing my faith in the absolute goodness, that is, lifesaving goodness, in *all* of my emotionality that led me to postulate a synthesis of all of my vital mentality as amounting to my beneficial meaning of my life's wholeness.[2] Keeping faith makes good sense indeed when it clearly means believing in the functioning of my own being, however marvelous that certainly is. It is with the eye of my self-faith, however cultivated that may be, that I can survey any of my organic growth. I can live only in the biological world of my organic nature as I create my own self development. It is to the credit of my conception of life as being self growth that I find it helpful in calling my attention to the truth that I can consciously direct my own development

[2]See my *Psychology of Emotion,* p. 23 *et. seq.*

73

merely by conducting my living in the way to make sure that my self growth will become what I want it to become. I must grow my self only in the direction I continue to give to my self.

With my newly grown conscious self catholicity I can consider every degree of my narrow selfishness, religious belief, scientific endeavor, intellectual inquiry or whatever, and yet dispense with any feeling of conflict whatsoever. My concept of mental freedom no longer depends upon seeming *inability* of my mind to function in any way whatsoever and the feeling of wrong no longer dominates my ethical view. My each apparent broadening of my mind with regard to my world is really a manifestation of my evolving my idiosyncratic understanding of my lovable self identity. My fellow-man's, even my colleague's, seemingly limited interest in the potential power of his own self consciousness is not hard to understand and explain as being entirely a currently helpful creation of my (his) own wholeness.

My *every* person is a complete personality as far as he has developed at all; it is only the rare one who has been able to add formative self consciousness to his otherwise wholeness. My blindly seeking to extend my own self consciousness is my blind quest for my acknowledgeable Deity. Seeing all of my living as my own being enables me to take not only both sides, but all sides, of a question at the same time, recognizing the overall harmony of my being as subsuming its capacity to seem discordant.

This Perspective would be incomplete without recording the aesthetic nature of my ethic. Thus, I assert: Whatever is, is all and only itself, including all and only about itself. In other words, my every meaning is entirely self contained and hence incapable of being related to my any other meaning in any way. The logical premise that one concept may be either true or not true

74

about another concept, is based upon illusion, for each concept can be true only about itself. Similarly, any of my reasoning may be understood as a variety of paranoia to the extent that it does not reflect my awareness for the fact that the whole of that reasoning is all and only of and about my self.

As Kuno Fischer defined an aesthetic idea, my experiencing it consists of my finding pleasure purely in its being itself, rather than in trying to apply it or use it somehow,

> This enjoyment, this kind of ideation, is the purely aesthetic one, which lies only in itself, which has its aim only in itself and which fulfills none of the other aims of life.[3]

Self activity is imbued with the joy of living wherever it occurs. The functioning of my being is its pleasing triumph, throughout the extent of my wholeness. When I am able to sense the beauty in any of my living I can honor the wholeness, the inviolable self-continence, in that living. Goodness is the ethic of wholeness; beauty is the aesthetic of wholeness; truth is the justice of wholeness.

My joy of living is mostly intimately associated with my feeling of unified self identity. Of course the joy of living my self, specifically as such, depends entirely upon my development of sufficient appreciation for my being a whole individual to be able to experience living as enjoyable power of my own possession *(Machtgefuhl)*. This pure joy of being fully alive is the most comprehensive aesthetic feeling of pleasing wholeness.

However each kind and degree of my aesthetic feel-

[3]*Über den Witz*. Second Ed. Heidelberg, 1889, p. 20. Also, see Sigmund Freud, Jokes And Their Relation to the Unconscious (1905), in *The Standard Edition of the Complete Psychological Works of Sigmund Freud*, trans. James Strachey in collaboration with Anna Freud, assisted by Alix Strachey and Alan Tyson (London: The Hogarth Press and The Institute of Psychoanalysis, 1953), Vol. VIII, p. 95.

ing is essentially a life satisfaction arising from appreciation for my own wholeness identity.[4] In tracing aesthetic feeling to satisfaction in lifesaving economy, mind loving Sigmund Freud noted the joy of living inherently present in mental activity and the naturalness in enjoying pleasure merely from functioning alone.[5] My most ethical aesthetic feeling occurred when I grew my ability to secure life satisfaction from enduring hard work, difficult (including painful) ordeal, and unhappy life experience, so that gradually my idea of hell began to resemble my idea of heaven quite as my idea of heaven gradually began to resemble my idea of hell.

The philosopher wisely considers the comic under the heading of aesthetics. Invariably the source of specific pleasure I derive from a joke, for instance, is sudden self satisfaction associated with my seeing some of my self identity in my joker's discovered meaning. More obviously my enjoyment of my living my self identity reveals itself in so-called recognition, familiarity, repetition, rhyme, imitation, resemblance, reality feeling, recall (even *deja vu*), phantasy, truth, and analogous exercise of self love.

Conversely I tend to feel unpleasure (inhibited pleasure called ugliness) in all of my living from which my conscious self identity is withheld, e.g., whatever seems alien to me, like foreign language, any estrangement, falsehood, innovation, whatever I may have repressed (autism, narcissism, masturbation, "dereistic" thinking such as omnipotence or omniscience, soiling, make believe, etc.).

The indescribable *greatness* of my nature cannot safely be taken for granted. Rather it needs to be lived

---

[4]See "A Tour For War Nerves: A Guide to an Hour in the Galleries by John M. Dorsey, M.D., and E.P. Richardson" (Detroit: Detroit Institute of Arts, 1945).
[5]*Jokes And Their Relation to the Unconscious*, p. 96.

with full honor for its wonderfulness in order to confer its free providence. Love is all-powerful and needs to be appreciated accordingly by me as the source of my power. Its immeasurable strength requires most careful attention, my attentive care. The course of self love is not smooth, however, leaving me frequently with the necessity to love difficultly, if I would continue to enjoy my love. My only alternative is to suffer my jealousy (i.e., displaced love).[6]

What makes the course of my love rough is my necessity to discover just how to live *any* of my world of power. I must teach my self how to perform the functioning of each of my senses even. Rarely do I discover that my every sense involves only my own worldful living, and therefore my self love may begin its suffering as soon as I teach my self how to start appreciating my wholeness as constituting my individuality. Similarly, to begin with, my every emotion seems capable of panic proportion so that eventually my wholeness force must exert itself to the effect that each of its emotions tame (moderate) itself in the interest of its wholeness-functioning.

When I picture the consequence of my injured divinity, the awesome view is too painful to consider long, whether it be that of my atomic bomb or gelid calm. There is no fury like hurt self love. It turns heavenly being into a hell of a life. It thoroughly accounts for the divinely awful nature of my living created by my daring to recognize only my own identity in my own diary that I call my daily newspaper.

Now to review this already long Perspective. I choose words that imply my conscious subjectivity in order to strengthen my conviction of the ideal truth of my unique nature. For my ideal to grow strong, its

[6]See my *Psychology of Emotion*, p. 5.

presence must be consciously lived. In my writing, what seems like self repetition may be really self preservation. After all, this screed is autobiographical and I am the only possible one who can know what I need to, so to say, remind my self about.

I like to keep accounting for the ideal practicalness in my making peace with the actuality of all of my living that seems to mean *divinity*. For that purpose I wish to observe my regularly starting and continuing any of my living with my conscious self. My key to the understanding of my life is full appreciation for its value as being my only possible possession.

By truth I mean: *Whatever is*. With sufficient truth I can accomplish all that is possible; without sufficient truth I cannot accomplish anything at all. All of the perfect workmanship of truth I formerly ascribed to impersonal deity, I can now find also in my own being. Hence it is I find accuracy in identifying my truth as my divine helpfulness. I find the life of self consciousness to be biologically most adequate, for only it helps to reveal the *whole truth* of my self identity. My reverence for the truth of my self consciousness amounts to ethicoreligious living.[7]

I detail the truth that all pain (including all unhappiness) is traceable to pleasure (including all happiness) that is hindered in its free functioning. In other words, all of my pain or unhappiness actually contributes to the total sum of my pleasure or happiness, the former being merely the negative form that my positive joy of living takes when its free functioning is inhibited. This realization is essential for my developing my full awareness for the wholeness of my individuality. My open-minded Sigmund Freud keenly observed that every pleasurable impulse alters its character if it is met by an obstacle.[8]

[7]See my "Some Considerations on Psychic Reality," *The International Journal of Psycho-Analysis* 24 (1943): parts 3 and 4.
[8]*Jokes And Their Relation to the Unconscious*, p. 99.

My free functioning is symptomless; my inhibited functioning is symptomatic. All of my pain (unhappiness) is really my pleasure (happiness) signifying its troubled functioning. For example, all of my pathology (including psychopathology) is understandable *only* as physiology (including competent mental functioning) that is manifesting its hindered activity. My hate is hurt (inhibited) love; fear is hurt (inhibited) wish; jealousy is hurt (inhibited) magnanimity; and so on.

Each unhappy feeling is verbalized in ideas manifesting the specific thinking that I need to discipline my self to live with love in order to be able to appreciate my whole-making personal identity in it. Hence it is most helpful to me to teach my self to honor every unhappiness for its specific significance in contributing to my appreciation for my wholeness. Otherwise I use each unhappiness to dissociate my mind so that I cannot recognize my united love of living in it. To wit, my depression enables me to sense my personal identity in innumerable unhappy thoughts and feelings which otherwise must continue to seem alien to my presently acknowledgeable self.

WORKING FORMULATIONS

It is quite a different thing to sunder a whole into its parts, and a whole into its lesser wholes. In the one case, we separate only to separate, and not again to connect.

Sir William Hamilton

By religion, I have in mind a reverence for the ultimate in whole self helpfulness. My reverence is a form of self consciousness reflecting appreciation for the divinity of my ever original and originating whole life. *My religion is my feeling, sensing, or divining my dependence upon the helpfulness of my whole divinity.* My ethic is integral to my consciously minding my living, not separable from it. My so-called ethical science is my study of my method for dealing with my perfection, my only possible value.

My need for study of my ethic arises from the utmost difficulty with which I recognize my divinity (perfection) as my only possible existent or power. This enormous difficulty may and frequently does translate itself into innumerable negations or denials of my perfection (divinity). For example, when my faith in my divinity is inhibited it is felt as distrust. Inhibited truth is felt as falsehood, inhibited perfection is felt as wrong or evil, inhibited love is felt as hate, inhibited divinity is felt as devilry, inhibited certitude is felt as doubt, inhibited spirit is felt as substance, inhibited will is felt as alien control, inhibited hope is felt as despair, inhibited self consciousness is felt as externality, and so on.

81

My ethic can be nothing at all but my regulative attitude towards my own whole individuality that includes my meaningful conception that I name *my world*. I, individual, am my only factual, including phantasied, basis for my morality. The law of my being is the law of my health, religion, education, or whatever, including my so-called science. It is my reverence for this right to be *all* that I live that constitutes my only moral motive. Living my fellowman and all else of my world as my self, *consciously,* is the essence of ethical conduct. My self-continent self consciousness is the indispensability, indeed the only reality, in any systematic view I may work up for my ethic, religion, science, education, or whatever. Self-seeing Emerson heeded that egotism is rooted in the absolute necessity for each individual to persist in being what he is.

When I am not glorying in my self consciousness I am instead drawing (insensibly as a rule) a moral from my self unconsciousness in the form of some sign or symptom of my life-endangering self heedlessness. There is even a scientific medical term naming specifically what is ceaselessly the trouble with me as a consequence of my not taking the trouble to discover it, and heed its helpful warning. I refer to the term *anosognosia,* in my experience a name for a serious health struggle afflicting my every human being. The opposite of anosognosia is *pathodixia,* the constant and ostentatious exhibition of a complaint. Each opposite obscures wholeness of self consciousness. Whatever I cannot sense is the matter of the whole of my own living is specifically what must be the matter with me.

Moral law must have a unique meaning for everyone of my world, fully explainable on the basis of the extent of his *consciously* solipsistic self measure. There can be nothing objective in my ethic. My self responsibility underlies the "reason why" of all of my behavior.

Creating my knowledge of the fact of my being, is called my *experience,* from which alone I can derive any principle of my activity. I willingly let my self consciousness do all of my explaining or accounting for me. By not acknowledging my wholeness I excite painful or unhappy feeling intending to make me acutely sensible for the sore side of my resulting condition.

My direct ethical method is that of fact-finding or truth-finding about my wholeness. It constantly confirms my trust in my dependable providence, revealing my comforting and abiding goodness ever-present in whatever happens. Disciplining my mind in due appreciation for the never-failing power of my truth is my perfectly fitting key that opens my mind to see its identity in its reliably understandable universe. And, as my cosmic Kant noted, "The aim of education is to give the individual all the perfection of which he is susceptible." I extol the perfection conferred upon me by virtue of my consciousness for my wholeness.

A far-reaching truth, honored by my Professor Freud as well as by his renowned psychologist Theodor Lipps, respects the fact that whole psychical living is unconscious, consciousness functioning as a power revealing and not nullifying unconscious psychical process. I imagine that the abolishment of unconsciousness must void consciousness, but not the converse. Certainly without the meaningfulness conferred by all of my previous conscious living (that is now no longer conscious) my present living of awareness would be bereft of that whole understanding. This whole-making or integrating process is my mind's wholeness-functioning. My wholeness contains the life-identity quality from which I gradually derive my conscious self-identity feeling.

Ever since Johann Friedrich Herbart (1776–1841),[1]

[1]*A Textbook in Psychology,* trans. from the German by Margaret K. Smith (New York: D. Appleton and Co., 1891).

my German psychologist especially has studied a process he calls *apperception,* referring to the depth of meaning with which new experience is "apperceived" by virtue of the whole of invested understanding already integrated and having its relevance for the new mental event. Many an insightful early psychologist (Wundt, Helmholtz, Schopenhauer, Hartmann) therefore studied perception as amounting to unconscious performance of reasoning.

The truth of my absolute wholeness resolves every illusion of *difference* or *relationship* between the acknowledgeable whole of my economy and the appearance of any regional functioning of my living, including my living of all of my meaning for my imagined external world. My evident wholeness-functioning and my so-called regional-functioning are one, identical. As a whole being I bear witness to nothing but my wholeness. Hence every so-called logical inference about any of my self activity must proceed from one constituent of my constitution to another, each consisting only of the constituted wholeness of my individuality.[2]

However, I have very strongly entrenched my scientific method of trying to understand my whole nature first by proceeding to decompose (by analysis or division for purpose of thorough study) my composite wholeness into its constituent "parts," before first having discovered a comprehensive knowledge of my wholeness itself. I then proceed to try to understand my wholeness by trying to recompose it, as it were, out of its so-called parts, the essential wholeness of which I have meanwhile hardly, if at all, considered.

My all important point for self understanding is that my *first* procedure be my thorough study of the nature

[2]Cf. Sir William Hamilton, *Discussions on Philosophy and Literature: Education and University Reform* (New York: Harper and Brothers, 1868), pp. 159–174.

of my wholeness as being the absolute requirement for my securing reliable understanding of any of its constituent functioning. *My thorough knowledge of my self-wholeness is necessary for my thorough knowledge of my cell-wholeness (not the converse), including all of its appearance in cancer, atrophy, or whatever kind of proliferation.*

I never attempt to clear up any difference posed by my fellowman for I am always absolutely certain that he is right according to the extent to which he lives his life orientation self consciously. But more to the point even, "difference" (as does comparison) implies and indulges the illusion of plurality. The important ethical question that I can address to my self is, Am I aware that all of my thinking or feeling or sensing or doing on any subject is basically my own living, basically my hold on life to behold as life, regardless of whatever other kind of meaning I may wish to make out of it? My sole way of arriving at truth is my realizing my personal identity in whatever experience I live. To exercise my choice illustration, in using the word "people," I can feel helpfully confused, for by "people" I can have in mind simply an abstraction consisting only and entirely of my own identity. My own good behavior is my only possible ethical performance in the interest of my society.

My natural feeling of love of life can be readily obscured merely by my living any experience, that is, any operation of my mind, with feeling of pain or unhappiness that seems to detract from my fully appreciating the marvelous wholeness of my self. I must suffer this private obscurity until I can teach my self to recognize that *all of my pain or unhappiness is lifesaving.* Either consists of truth I am living as momentary self help for prolonging my existence. My self preservation depends upon my ability to live whatever kind of distress I may experience. I arduously discipline my mind to attend to what passes in it as being its own mentality only. This precious insight does not flash forth at once in all its fullness but rather, as all that is grown, it is first barely perceptible as a remote possibility, then becomes my opinion, and only with increasing development finally plants itself to be revered as my very own truth.

This difficultly attainable self understanding is an ideal worthy of my noblest effort exerted with enthusiasm. My every idea that I can recognize for its helpfulness thereby becomes an ideal of mine. My idea of self help is born of want. It is a creation of my need to live. All of my motivation is an expression of my wishing or willing, a basic fact that explains how I happen to be an ethical person whose biological duty it is to take care of my self. Whatever is, is solely in charge of taking care of itself. However, (my) man alone is capable of the ardour of consciousness for this truth. Therefore, (my) man alone is consciously capable of designing the character of his ethology.

I can extend the dominion of my conscientiousness to include my so-called public life specifically by recognizing its identity as an extension of my private living. Furthermore, only to my self-identity instructed eye is my fellowman visible obviously as mine. I must lack motivation for this difficult cultivation until I can convince my self that 1) it is a benefit to me and 2) its neglect is tantamount to my neglecting my health.

I nourish my self with the harvest I have sowed. When I can experience so-called increasing-profligacy-in-the-public-morals as occurring all and only in my world of my mind, I enjoy the civic perspective of self interest that spares me further self hurt even as it provides me with the kind appreciation for my troubled fellowman that is my chief contribution to my world's constructive political development. I can raise the standard of my civic virtue by every single exertion to increase the extent of my self consciousness.

Either I must recognize that my mind in its entirety, that is in its every meaning, consists of nothing but my own living, or I must deny this truth and thereby divide my mind's wholeness into what I can and cannot call my own. With any of my living I cannot call my own I can appear to enter into "relations." I can *appear* to take it or leave it. My reverence can seem too burdensome even, so that I may turn from exercising it, with no appreciation for my lifesaving direction its service provides. Thenceforth, I am unable to base my ethics upon my ability to feel my sense of identity with my fellowman. Rather, I must depend on what I call relations in order to seem to communicate with my consciously disunited mind where I live my fellowman numbly without reverently feeling my glorious identity in that living.

As long as my self love is available for conscious functioning, it contributes most effectively to my whole-making health. With this biologically adequate self assurance I need fear no sense of rivalry, neglect or separatedness whatsoever. However, when my self love becomes unrecognizable by me as self love, for example in my living my you or my God with love that I cannot appreciate as my self love entirely, then I must feel jealousy, envy, inferiority or any other indication of my self love that is modified by illusional rivalry.

Hence it is essential for my peace of mind that I sense my God *as* my God, my loved one *as* my loved one. Without this cultivation of my felicitous conscious self identity, I seem to lose my benevolent *appreciation* for my wholeness, the presence or absence of which respectively determines my mental peace or conflict. Conscious self love makes the beauty of a good mind, the true heaven for which to seek.

My duration of my life and my sole responsibility for fulfilling it, each is ever a new topic of increasing interest. I cannot make too much over my constantly self-evident truth that my perfection is my only self value that can exist. Whatever is, *perfectly* is. This divine principle of mine harmonizes all I do or omit doing into the strength of conscious self love that identifies life satisfaction and life suffering. It commands a perfect prospect of my whole being, guiding me in the way of my most provident self culture, a loving continuance in well being enabling the only possible source of well doing. All of my moral action is a taking place of this law of laws. And my constant liability to losing conscious appreciation for it deserves my perfect concern. For what indeed am I profited if I gain *the* whole world and lose *my* own soul (Matthew 16, 26). Unless I acknowledge my own divinity I cannot responsibly realize, for I have not consciously tried it, the spiritual force that is mine. Solomon soliloquized: A good man is satisfied from his self. To him that hath is given, simply means: conscious self growth succeeds conscious self growth.

His idea, or feeling, or law, or whatever, is subject to whole man, not he to it. For me to lose my presence of mind (poise, mental composure, sense of controlling what I create) as a seeming consequence of "another's" behavior is nothing else than to allow an individuation of my self to appear to subject me to it (as if it were not all and only of my producing). To be "upset" in any sense by *my* fellowman is as much a case of the tail wagging the dog as would be my being disturbed by any other thought (or feeling or sensation) of my own originating.

And why must I supply my neighbor's wants? Why must I be concerned about my fellowman's welfare? Why is it benevolent of me to help another person? Why is it my duty to serve anyone else? How does my self interest or self love apply to my brother? And so on. WHY indeed! My almighty truth reveals that the only possible help is *self help*. I, including my every fellow creature, cannot serve anyone but my self, despite all appearance to the contrary. The inviolable wholeness of every individual excludes any and every possible help to him except that which he provides for his own self.

The profound and far-reaching truth, rarely upheld, is that I can give only to my self and receive only from my self. Furthermore I am neglecting or serving only my own welfare specifically when I withhold or extend my charity so that my fellowman either hinders or helps his self by his creating his specific source of self power which he names his Dorsey. In other words, I cannot take care of my self adequately to the extent that I cannot recognize my living of my fellowman as being certain responsible living of my self. Apparently it does not seem necessary for me to feel concern for the welfare of any so-called other man, but obviously I must feel concern for the welfare of *my* other man. Hence it is to my benefit to grow the strength of conscious mindedness to be able to feel my responsible self identity in my everyman.

On account of the limitless dimension of the concept "individual" there is danger of its seeming unfit for specific concrete work. The question is raised, Can such a monistic metaphysical abstraction be suitable as the only foundation of physiological methodology? Can the idealistic postulate *individuality* subsume all that is meant by *organic, sensation, perception, feeling,* or *knowledge,* and so on? Is some meaning of my whole individuality all there can be to my every life experience, to my understanding of spirit as well as of substance, to my philosophy of science as well as scientific view of philosophy, to my history of linguistics as well as linguistics of history, to my speculative empiricism as well as empirical speculation, and so on? Finally, can this one signification, individuality, be the only true essence of existence of all living (organic) as well as of all non-living (mechanic) being, of any and all identity?

The answer to all of this query is, Yes. All of language, as insightful August Schleicher observed, is an expression of individuality only (articulated sound merely expressing spiritual life). Renowned philologist Schleicher accounted for "otherness" as a condition of language. One individual cannot develop understanding or misunderstanding with "another" individual. He can live his fellowman (as himself) as either self-understanding or self-misunderstanding. What passes for "one understanding another" can only be one's identifying as himself whatever may be designated as that "other." When I can live my "other" with the feeling of my complete personal identity in that living then I "understand" my "other." All of my misunderstanding of my "other" is nothing but my inability to sense my personal identity in my "misunderstood" whomever (or whatever).

Nothing *is* except what can be directly traceable to activity of individuality generating it. Human individuality comprehends all human action, indeed is synonymous with human activity. All of my conscious and unconscious being of any kind originates in the constitutive activity of my wholeness. It is in this source of my every life meaning that its true explanation can be found.

I formerly tried to localize specific affective meaning in each unique visceral tissue, an effort to extend the wisdom of the ancients in this respect. I now see how all of my ideation is an attenuation of my sensory, including emotional, experience. I understand how my ideation is the exposition of the logic of my affect. I have renounced my former intention to localize fear in my heart, fury in my adrenals or spleen, depression

90

somewhere in my abdomen, and so on. Presently I feel the need to embody all that I can mean by my heart or spleen or abdomen or whatever so-called "somatic" organ only in my acknowledgeable subjectivity.

True! I do consider finding individuality to be all that there is (or can be) to anyone or anything, a most important, since most useful, discovery for me. All possibility is grounded in the inviolable wholeness of individuality. All identity is found only in it. All being is composed of it. All knowledge consists of it. Without it there is nothing. With it there is everything. It is the ground meaning of my spirit, soul, mind, imagination, consciousness, truth, idea, possible life, substance, being, reality, knowledge, man, universe, God. My all is identical with this universality: *individuality,* the organon and criterion of all of my meaning.

Individuality, or wholeness, is the only possible ground of all of my goodness. And acknowledged individuality is the only possible ground of all acknowledged goodness. Only a comprehensively appreciated self can be an extensively comprehending self. All understanding of any description is based upon self appreciation. Such a life attitude is deeply lived, realized wisdom. Whoever can live and learn about his life possesses the making of a wise man. Once I find my whole self I realize that there can never be anyone or anything else for me to find. Jonathan Edwards (1703–1758) recorded, "God himself is in effect being in general" and, "Virtue, as I have observed, consists in the cordial consent or union of being to being in general."[3] Viennese psychologist Karl Buhler (1879–1963) introduced a conception helpfully clarifying the bioethical truth, "joy of living." I refer to his descriptive term "functional pleasure" often worded "functional triumph."

[3]*The Nature of True Virtue* (Ann Arbor: University of Michigan Press, 1960).

91

Self learning, so localized, is difficultly attained. Indeed first experience readily appears as factual but seldom as a fact of my life, only. I must learn how to work hard at realizing that my factuality *is* my human being rather than that my human being can get lost in my facts. To know my self as I am I must persevere in my most humble open educable spirit of willingness to augment my realization of my whole personal identity. That means I must cultivate the desire for self enlightenment to the extent of recognizing my every opposition, my every dislike, as being wholly my own self helpfulness.

To illustrate, anyone who can observe his annoyance (seemingly "between" his self and "another person") from the realistic viewpoint that the whole matter (including his annoyer) is entirely and only his own creation, can see for himself the pacifying, satisfying, clarifying consequence of such sane observation of his comprehensive selfhood.

I am the only authority possible for realizing my ethical behavior. For it is my freedom of action which permits me to choose one course of conduct or another. It is impossible for me to do anything except what I ought to do. My autonomy accounts for that. My inviolable wholeness provides my freedom of action. I can set my self *any end whatsoever* and expect to realize it completely, through my free action merely in the simple expediency of exerting my free use of my imagination.

Quite as my knowledge of my world generally serves to extend my freedom so that I can increase the possibility of serving my self thereby, so my conscious self knowledge enables me to become as free as possible in my imaginative being. Make my self as conscious as possible, is as good an ethical imperative as I can find. Extending my self consciousness extends my conscientiousness for my living. By using my self con-

92

scientiousness as my ethical guide I can renounce seg-
regating and relegating my power of free choice to my
unconscious (involuntary) living.

By thus deriving my ethic from my self consciousness I not only identify it with my conscious will
power but integrate it into my appreciated wholeness.
Thereby I can sense my ethical principle as confirming
my being my creator of all of my reality. *But any and all
of my self understanding, to be strong enough to become adequately effective in my behavior, must be exercised diligently, practiced devotedly.*

Thus my Plato helped himself by upholding a seeming dichotomy of conduct: "And hence virtue would be,
as it were, the health and beauty and harmony of the
soul; vice, however, disease and ugliness and weakness." Obstinate fact however reveals that the word
bad or *evil* is a pejorative term that, like every pejoration, simply confesses the pejorationist's present inability to find the ever-present good, including complete
self sufficiency, in whatever he calls "bad." Thus, the
meaning *vice* becomes understandable as one's current
inability to recognize virtue. Vice may be a verbal
translation of an unhappy feeling about one's living,
quite as virtue may name a happy feeling about a person's action. The instinctive tendency is present in every individual to produce such *value judgment* to fit his
temporary mood.

Seeing virtue in all experience, rather than vice, is
analogous to seeing perfectly all in all, without negating
any of it. By perfection I mean: nothing lacking that is
essential to the whole. Whatever is, perfectly is necessarily. Perfection being all that is possible, the virtuous
life-orientation is a product of the positive fact learned
from studied self experience. Thus self-evident virtue
subsumes every appearance of vice, quite as courage
subsumes all cowardice, or strength subsumes all weak-

ness. I conceive my supreme ethical end to be my growing appreciation for the ever-present and thorough perfecting of my ideally moral nature.

The point must be clear, a meliorative term conceals faultfinding, even as a pejorative term reveals it.[4] The implication in "better than" is clearly that of detraction for one term of the comparison. Mark's question seems to stand for the illusive nature of all comparison, "Whereto shall we liken the kingdom of God?"

Innumerable phantom problems called "ethical" result when, instead of observing that only good *living* is possible, an effort is made to divide human conduct into two parts, one good and desirable, the other bad and undesirable. By my accumulating self experience that I disown as bad I build up and keep adding to a gloomy stockpile of my own being, which I have already condemned as "not worth living" and which contributes to my wish for deliverance from my wicked world. When I live on the edge of this abyss of so-called misery my joy of living is justly pre-empted by my need for salvation, my pleasure of innocence duly usurped by my contrite heart, and my rightful appropriation of all of my world helpfully dispossessed by my seeking "unworldly" redemption.

Bowed down by the weight of guilt that helpfully signalizes that I am not able to uphold my perfection consciously, I am unable to understand the full helpfulness of the painful signal. As a child with a toothache, my interest is focused upon getting rid of the pain rather than upon repairing the structure of my tooth. I feel personally helpless for restoring my self to my natural appreciation for the real and inviolable wholeness of my being and, furthermore, I thereby jeopardize my ability to attribute to anyone or anything of my

4See my *Psychology of Language*, p. xxi.

world each one's full measure of wholeness. By deceiving my self about the truth of the absolute oneness and wholeness of my individuality, I introduce the necessity to use illusional plurality and partiality, thus complicating immeasurably my living of the world of my united self. My world-conception *is* an outgrowth of my life-conception. I find my everyone consciously universalizing his unconscious individuality.

What or whom shall I believe? is a question that must puzzle me as long as I am unable to realize that there can be *nothing* for me to believe except the orthodox creativity of my own established self-universe. I am *whatever* I live, and this source for all of my meaning that I call truth, or reality, provides me with all that I *can* believe. My belief in the truth of all of my living as being my own living is the psychic process accounting for my developing gratifying certitude for my identity as an individual creating my all, including my divinity, illusional externality or whatever, out of the making of my own wholeness.

My full meaning for *peace* signifies my feeling *at one* with my self, my pacific feeling of continent self consciousness providing freedom of my mind to call my soul my own and my all my soul. As I write it, I find the dominant purpose in describing the psychology of my ethic to be the recording of my full grown conviction that abiding peace can occur only in the soul of the consciously self responsible individual who thoroughly appreciates that, as long as he lives, he can only be at peace with himself; that he can trace all of his conflict merely to his indulging his illusion that he can somehow influence, or be influenced by, somebody or something external to him.

I know of my responsible statesman who fully understands the demonstrable truth that the whole of his American government is the glorious creation of his

95

own living.[5] He observes his only possible political course that holds out any promise of lasting peace is for every citizen, beginning with himself, to pursue individuality-oriented conscious self education in order to secure the peaceful consequence of conscious self sovereignty. Quite the contrary to the expectation of my American politician, his growing his devotion in the direction of conscious self sufficiency can result only in his cultivating his competence for his office. It is his unawareness for the growing wholeness of his individuality that functions as a kind of political suicide.

To my question, "What do I want to make out of my self?" comes its positive and definite reply, "All that I am, all that I can be." Plato wanted to see things as they are, an educational goal which could but lead him to seeing his self, his "blessed vision" becoming his wonderful self insight. The condition for attaining this goal is my gradual, recognizable self development enabling me to appreciate *all* of my living as sublime. It is not my instinct or primitive power which is in any way undesirable. It is only my unreadiness to observe its innate helpfulness that motivates me to misprize my life's uncultivated power. Wholesome sublimation is not based upon a faultfinding attitude towards my original nature, but rather upon a fact-finding orientation for it revealing it, too, as sublime.

Just as turning on the light to see does not create whatever is already in the room, so my making my self conscious for the exalted nature of any of my being is all about consciousness. However, living consciousness for my living does lead to the supreme self-perceptibleness that can recognize the perfection in whatever I am observing. This high-powered life appreciation is aptly termed the "Divine Look."

[5]See my *American Government*.

Thus my spirited Plato looked: "It is time to lift the eye of the soul . . . and set it toward the Elysian Fields." Similarly my luminary Dante "who saw everything," as a divine beholder, described his life as the adventure of his rising soul.

The startling extent to which my repressed (repudiated, unconscious) thinking and feeling are expressed in my so-called doing (and not doing) escapes all but my responsibly disciplined vigilance.

My consciousness that I make all of my own experience of any kind, is my unfailing source for life appreciation. My will to live consciously *is* my will to power. My love of life can be expressible only in my self love. My name for the ultimate element of my human nature, hence of my world, is wholeness (individual subjectivity). My *summum bonum* is my power to observe that nothing but goodness (helpfulness) can exist. Individuality is a synonym for universality, or wholeness, or perfection, or divinity.

As does every conveniently fancied duality, the artificial dichotomy of private selfish affection and public social affection duly requires costly compensation (since it obscures self conscious viewing of indivisible human selfhood). Such attempted setting up of a double life in one human constitution creates a self deception intolerable for the human mind, necessitating its resorting to symptom-formation to live through it. Thus my ancient form of human sacrifice comes to life in the form of self sacrifice made to do for biologically adequate devotion to my unique wholeness.

Two posited natures of life are not possible for one man, e.g., divine and human, sacred and secular, religious and scientific, individualistic and social, and so on. Man's nature is infallible, indefectible and wholly individual, despite all of the perfect faultfinding terms often used to describe it. He has no choice, other than

97

to be aware or unaware of his ever present divine nature. His perfection is always present everywhere, quite as his wholeness is. His recognition of his wholeness-perfection is all that can be perfectly wanting. No experience is ever observed clearly until its complete excellence, its flawlessness, is fully appreciated. My living that extends my awareness for my self identity is most difficult of all to live. Philosopher Kuno Fischer wittingly defined *experience* as consisting of experiencing what one does not want to experience.

Every person's way of living his world constitutes for him an ideal ethic. A "theft" is as much the will of God as is a "gift"; "cruelty" is as much God's will-being-done as "gentleness"; "gluttony is as much divinely enforced as "temperance." Each so-called "sin" is as blessed an action as any so-called "virtue," temporarily serving the sinner's self preservation ideally. In other words, all so-called unethical activity is unrecognized ethical conduct. The health or perfection of soul-life consists precisely in whatever way it presently exists. Study of the all-sufficing fact discovers every kind of human behavior as a "science of right conduct," as an expression of "the good will."

Self evident self observation reveals that individual self interest, "ethical egoism," is the valid end of all action. The self disregarding notion that the actual and impelling motive of any self activity can be other than selfful, contradicts itself.

Despite nearly every critic's allegations to the contrary, neither Hobbes nor Spinoza ignored his concept of the importance of his species in his personal ethic aimed strictly at his own self preservation. Neither one fell into that tender trap of considering himself merely as a dependent member of a species to which he owed his nature and existence, however. Only the individual consciously capable of supreme service to his self preservation can fully attest his devotion to his species. No "species" was ever born or endowed with individual life or provided with any system of self preservation whatsoever. All of the meaning of "species" exists only in the mind of the individual creating it.

I do not reproduce my self in my offspring. I must do all of my creating by and of my self only. The highest distinction of the ethicist is that he recognize the indissoluble unity of his mind as it is constituting itself of each and every meaning of his world. Human welfare is always and only an individual concern, and it consists not merely in the exercise, but specifically in the *conscious* exercise, of the wholeness of one's potentially *conscious* power.

Only where *conscious* self observation is the scientist's manner and matter of investigation can he duly take into account his full-measured appreciation for the inviolable wholeness of human individuality. His other scientific work reflects the heat of personal emotion rather than the light of personal consciousness. Thus, Shaftesbury optimistically emphasizes the pleasing aspects of human nature. Hobbes pessimistically scores man's unhappy living. Understandable becomes Horace Walpole's judgment in his letter to Sir Horace Mann (1792): "The world is a comedy to those that think, a tragedy to those who feel."

Kant's only task in his ethic was to collect the commands of "duty" and arrange them under a universal formula. He could reach this formalistic view without any cost of disregard for the nature and need of his human individuality. Individuality reverence merely *seems* incompatible with the dictates of "common" morality. A person's first and only possible duty is to take care of himself the best way he knows how until his experience adds to his stock of conscious self knowledge. *Only conscious self knowledge can carry any conscious ethical responsibility.*

Whoever would re-establish the rights of humanity must accomplish this mission wholly, solely and consciously in his own individuality, the only place where any and all of his humanity can be found. Self perfection is no possible ethical goal, for it is omnipresent. Perfect awareness (self awareness) for my very own self perfection is my single possible ethical goal.

In order to uphold its perspective and symmetry as an evident product of my conscious self continence I have written this journal of my *conscious* ethical self development only with my self in mind as its reader. It deals with solemn truth of my own self helpfulness and is in no way intended as a doctrine for my fellowman. Only (my) he can discover anything at all that is helpful for him. In all reverence I add that it is a great life satisfaction to me to be able to observe my fellowman's making his self helpfulness become his *conscious* self helpfulness,—in my opinion, an advance in self appreciation of utmost practical value.

Relieving my mind of its habit of self-depreciation, traceable to my overlooking my self as its only possible subject, may seem like the theological design named *via eminentiae.* I can overcome my evil only as I recognize and honor my good in it for all that it is worth. Soon I discover my calling any of my living by a bad name to be the temporarily helpful result of a snap judgment. *While finding the whole truth accounting for any of my so-called evil living I gradually dispel all of my (illusion of) evil. This is the mightiest power that I can command befitting my true greatness. It is my divine understanding enlightening my human reasoning.* Man can only seem to differ from his God, e.g., in his own duration and in his own unawareness for his wonderful subjectivity. I regard my being able to conceive any meaning at all for my God as absolutely incontrovertible evidence of at least that much of my divinity.

By increasing my awareness of the absolute subjectivity of all of my living I have discovered that I have (am) a life worthy subject for my attention and interest every moment of my waking day. Despite overwhelming appearance to the contrary, none of life can be made up of insignificant incident, of petty trifling. Virtue consists in cherishing every moment of life and exists in imagining, as well as otherwise doing, great things. The illimitable confine of my whole mind is my only localization of all of my meaningful experience. Let me first teach my self reverence for my self, as my living record of concentration upon my ethical devotion of my self 's world.

I have taken to writing down whatever seems thus "on my mind," and it is from this savings bank of my subjectivity that I draw each spirited theme of my recorded composition. The self help I formerly ascribed to "Time," I now attribute to nothing but my cultivating my own self 's world, as such, to minding my own business, as such. However, I sense my necessity to be true to my earliest as well as latest way of living my self, either consciously glorying in this freedom or unconsciously living the same freedom inhibited in the form of compulsion or obsession.

The subjectivity of my mind is my only possible source of all of my meaning. Hence it behooves me to establish my certitude that my mind is the only possible creator and subject of my every sensation, perception, or consciousness of any degree. All of my reality is the product of my creating it, and all of the meaning of all of my reality is uniquely mine.

I always continue to need to observe my own manpower in such vivid and true light as to exalt my love of my life. All of the force of my moral obligation issues only from the source and course of my being. I need to prevail upon my self to take pride in my cultivating ability to feel pain (unhappiness of every kind) as being my precious guardian of my self love. I require some recognition of my self insight to be able to understand that all of my pleasure of life would be impossible were it not for my pain (unhappiness) of one kind or another advising me of peril to my pleasing existence. For me there is no surer evidence of my benevolent Deity than the suffering I must endure whenever and however I overlook the wholeness of my individuality. Such is my liberal interpretation of the psalmist's promise (91st Psalm): "For He shall give His angels charge over thee, to keep thee in all thy ways."

My prayer reveals my desire to prepare my self to be ready to live with full appreciation whatever I pray for. Indeed praying is the beginning of my realizing the intention of my prayer. Furthermore, as I develop the readiness to live the answer to my prayer truly as my own purposeful self helpfulness, my praying moderates its insistence accordingly. Then ultimately I find that I can self-reliantly enjoy my revelation that my praying is always the granting of my prayer, and hence a most practical kind of exercise. My every wish subsumes its own fulfilment.

Certainly each wish is no less than indication of my wish to live, addressed to my own wonderful providence. My prayer is my solemn acknowledgement of my trust in my self dependence, but may be most rarely realized at its true value for my recognizing my self as being the incomparably great one that I am. Hymn-true, I need be no more than a prayer away from my consciously sensing my divinity.

Begging may be one's only trusted form of self help, a divine power seldom appreciated even by my beggar as a revelation of his divine worth. I may resist blindly the whole truth that begging help *is* honorable self helpfulness whenever it occurs and, of all forms of individual need, as worthy of understanding (self) charity as any.

Thus Kenneth Keniston duly honors his regulative wholeness-functioning,

> Above all, human wholeness means a capacity for commitment, dedication, passionate concern and care—a capacity for whole-heartedness and single-mindedness, for abandon without fear of self-annihilation and loss of identity. In psychological terms, this means that a whole man retains contact with his deepest passions at the same time that he remains responsive to his ethical sense. No one psychic potential destroys or subverts the others; his cognitive abilities remain in the service of his commitments, not vice versa; his ethical sense guides rather than tyrannizes over his basic passions; his deepest drives are the sources of his strength but not the dictators of his action. We recognize whole men and women because their wholeness is manifest in their lives: what they do is "of a piece."[6]

My mental condition of limited conscious self identity that prevents my acknowledging that I am absolutely all that I live, or can live, accounts fully for my need to repudiate my necessarily solipsistic nature. Then, the consequence of my unconscious depersonalization is my conscious personification of my living I cannot acknowledge as entirely my own, e.g., State, Institution, University, Democracy, Foundation, Home, Center, etc., etc.

I trace some of my need to publish this strictly autobiographical account of my conscious self helpfulness to my life satisfaction in hopefully imagining only my very

[6]"The Whole Life of the Whole Person," from *The Uncommitted* (New York: Harcourt, Brace and World, Inc., 1962), pp. 441–442.

103

occasional reader's, consciously or unconsciously, authoring whatever he reads. My rich and regular experience consistently teaches me to understand my feeling of rejection as being the necessary beginning of my feeling of acceptance.

I have taken great pains in reading this writing of mine several times to make sure that every occurrence or appearance of repetition in it be acceptable to me as my strengthening exercise of the whole self interest involved.

THE PSYCHOLOGY OF MY ETHIC

*The intuition of the moral sentiment is an insight of
the perfection of the laws of the soul.*

Ralph Waldo Emerson

The "meaning" of whatever exists is: what it is capable of being, including doing. Whatever is, does what
it is,—and thus fulfills its meaningfulness. My mind is
capable of understanding that *meaning* is an acceptable
name for the power of functioning inherent in existence.
To illustrate, I can and do mean only all of my own
whole creaturehood. To each question of, "What do
you mean?" my only answer must be, "All I *can* mean
is something of my self." Obviously then my ethic
based upon my own living is: conscious idealism for my
wholeness. The only world or world element I can live
is my I-world or I-world element. My tree is constituted
of my tree-ness; my animal is constituted of my animal-
ness; my you is constituted of my you-ness; and so on.
The nature of my ethic is constituted of the goodness of
my wholeness.

Ethic has been well defined as the normative science
of the ideal involved in human life.[1] It considers the
standard of good living. My ethical Emerson records,

> Idealism is an hypothesis to account for nature by other
> principles than those of carpentry and chemistry. It ac-
> quaints us with the total disparity between the evidence of

[1]See, John S. Mackenzie, *A Manual of Ethics* (New York: Hinds, Noble,
and Eldredge, 1901).

105

our own being and the evidence of the world's being. The world is a divine dream, from which we may presently awake to the glories and certainties of day.

The so-called "problem of good and evil" is spoken of as "the ethical problem." Solving it, Saint Augustine discovered that only good exists, that so-called "evil" is actually unrecognized good. This great ethical innovation spares every individual who can create it for himself, the necessity of having to condemn any of his own ideality as "bad." By being able to see all of his living as good, man can consciously facilitate the functioning of his whole nature, thereby enjoying the supreme serviceableness of all of his being. Man lives only within the universe of his creaturehood. A salient truth needing exercise, however, is that he may or may not *recognize* that he is all and only his own self.

As I write on this subject of my subjectivity I sense my truth that everyone of my world must find for himself what his ethic (and all else) means. Man (my every use of the word man refers specifically to my each and every person) may work up the self discernment to see for himself, with his Spinoza, how his conscious moral development keeps pace with the growth of his conscious self-scope.

My full self respect provides me with a good hold on my self thus enabling my responsible self activity, functioning somewhat as a firm grip on a whole tool functions in my manual labor. Man needs his full feeling of spontaneity restored by his ability to renounce the negation known as "otherness" or "not-I," to be able to revel in the truth that he makes his own conditions, yes, his own necessities. However, my inability to acknowledge just what I am missing, of any amount of self consciousness, explains my not seeing to its revealing itself at once.

During his New England ethical movement, "Transcendentalism," my American citizen of a century ago invented a serviceable phrase, "the coming man." Gradually it became evident to him that Ralph Waldo Emerson was making real this prophesied personage. From Emerson's impartial spirit arose civilizing deliverance of his glowing manhood from the delusion of inequality bred by unwitting indulgence of his illusion he named *comparison*. He was the fulfiller of his own wording of urgent moral need, "a protest against usage and a search for principles." He saw so-called physical law as nothing but moral law. The star in its course meant to him his discovery of his own self's reliability. He constituted his ethical standard by uniting religious dignity, poetic purity, philosophic insight, scientific observation, a child's boldness, a man's sagacity, a woman's tenderness, with an animal joy of living and an ennobling visceral calm.

My law of human progress, what can it be but my law of perfection becoming conscious? An ethical treatise may quickly founder on its author's use of undefinable words, or on other imprecision of his terminology. An illustration that I like to use is that the word "selfish" carries a firmly established pejorative connotation wishfully implying that that which is ought not to be, or that that which is not should be. Yet, one's selfishness is the only possible foundation for any kind of his morality, since it is the one and only stuff making up all of the content of his wholeness. The consequential truth in every salient point of this book is that my every experience is my vital process, entering into my forming the wholeness-character of my conduct. It is my lifelong responsibility to keep the vast significance of this ever new truth clearly in mind.

My self-enlightened, life-devoted and gloriously courageous mystic discovered that just the feeling of nearness to obscuration of his self identity is dangerous

107

living, even though that obscuration may refer to divinity other than his acknowledgeable own. French Jesuit, Victor Poucel taught himself his wholeness, "Let us honor the body by allowing it to form the first and firm foundation of our spiritual ascent."[2] My educating my mind to the truth of the wholeness of my identity results from no compulsive preciosity: it does result from my hardily practicing my extending my recognition for my already existing subjectivity.

I cannot neglect this profound truth, or any other one, of my nature without helpful signs of the trouble I am thereby making for my self. My ignored, denied, or negated spirituality or divinity is most dangerous self repudiation. I can trace all of my mental trouble only to my living that I disown as being wholly my own. Whether or not I can be aware of it, my every act must be a sacred act; my every word a prayer. All of my mental suffering is understandable as the marvelous insistence of my wholeness upon being able to live itself without being endangered by neglect or repudiation possibly to the extreme extent of not wanting to live its existing condition.

The way to conscious holiness leads through one's own holiness only.[3] "For whosoever will save his life shall lose it" (Mark 8: 35), I now construe to mean: If I would discover and appreciate the divinity of my wholeness, in order to do so I must be willing to work up awareness for *all* of my life, as augmenting appreciation for my personal identity, thereby attaining revelation of my true divinity. Until this liberating development occurs I must either scorn or yearn for awareness of the godly identity that is rightfully mine. In other words, my

[2]*Mystique de la Terre.*
[3]Cf. Josef Goldbrunner. *Holiness Is Wholeness and Other Essays* (Notre Dame, London: University of Notre Dame Press, 1964). An interesting study.

108

observing my divinity is my finding, rather than losing, my real life.

Every new stage in my life is not a parting from my previous one but rather is the outgrowth of it. Realizing this biological necessity enables my spiritual appreciation to keep pace with my growing, as long as I live. Many a life ordeal of mine is traceable to my heedlessness for the vital truth that my present being subsumes all of my formerly present becoming. My anticipating my future development is actually very meaningful present being of mine. All of my conscious waiting is meaningfully realizing whatever I am awaiting. My wishing in the form of hoping is organically realizing all for which I am hoping. My praying contains my answer to my prayer, quite as my mourning brings to conscious life whatever I may be imagining sorrowfully as lost. Here most consequentially I need to create and cultivate the wisdom of love implicit in my spirited living: Wholeness is holiness. It no longer suffices for me to conclude: Only when I am not aware that I am loving my whole soul can I imagine that I am loving God.

Much of my troubled living of my love is traceable to my most critical development when, instead of living all of my loving as being mine, I began treating my wholeness as if it were not all and only whole and hence found my self with the necessity to love some of my living in which I could not recognize my wholeness. Out of this dilemma my need arose for my feeling able to live love other than my conscious self love!

I record it again, perseveringly. Much of my most difficult living is necessarily the creating of experience that I cannot immediately identify as being lifeworthy. My love feels hurt in it, and that hurt love I then call hate, anger, fear, guilt, or some other seemingly unkind name I cannot recognize as merely a name for *my* hurt love. My discovering that pain or unhappiness in any

109

degree is entirely a most valuable sign of helpfully inhibited functioning of my love of living, has enabled me to identify every modality of my hurt love as really being self love.[4] Thus I provided my self with a perspective upon necessary suffering of every kind and degree that reveals it as indispensably livesaving self love. It is my making peace with all of my hurt living, by identifying it as my hurt self love, that restores my appreciation for the magnificent integrity of my whole individuality. My everyone has only his self evidence for making his decisions. Unless I can see that it is to my own personal (selfish) benefit to behave in one way rather than another I must founder, for I have absolutely no non-selfish view to help me make up my mind as to how to behave.

"Enlightened self interest" means: conscious self goodness identifiable with the good of *my* world. Only by first attaining the meaning of the completeness of my individuality have I been able to attribute complete individuality to any and every aspect of my wonderful world. Altruism, said Dr. Oliver Wendell Holmes, is egoism with a spy-glass; it is finding joy in one's fellowman's helping himself, — not trying to take over the self helpfulness and self thankfulness naturally belonging to one's fellowman. However, only and every way my fellowman helps himself, is his honorable responsibility and privilege.

In my late teens and early twenties I created the good fortune to live an individual whose devotion to his ethic was very great indeed, namely, Edwin Diller Starbuck, Ph.D., Professor of Philosophy of the University of Iowa. He embodied, that is, he ensouled Justice Oliver Wendell Holmes's Golden Rule for freedom of thought, "freedom for the thought that we hate." Pro-

[4]See my *Psychology of Emotion*, p. 125.

fessor Starbuck pioneered in positing a person's feeling as independent source of experience. Said he, "Religion changes its form and content as life changes."[5] In his *Psychology of Religion,* describing as a most pronounced characteristic a child's displacement of his religious experience, he italicizes warning lest his religion seem to become *"distinctly external to the child rather than something which possesses inner significance."*

Ever since my study of Plato and Aristotle with my Professor Starbuck, I have considered my ethic to be definable as insightful examination of the conduct of my life, revealing: *only good is always accompanied by pleasure.* As my appreciation for the inviolable integrity of my individuality grew, I became increasingly interested in working up my own true scientific ethic, my moral doctrine in keeping with my realization that my living of my fellowman is basically identical with my living of any other element of my organismic being.

My recognition that my fellowman, as well as everything that I had been accustomed to consider my external world, is in truth my own internal vital process, has enabled me to know whereof I speak by revealing the law of my natural constitution as governing my social or civic conduct. I can always trace any of my animosity to indulging my illusional not-I. I discover that I am a law unto myself and that every law that I can know anything about is entirely of my own making and being. As far as this true life-orientation is concerned, all that can be lacking is my consciousness for it. I can sense my need is ever present to consider as my own the fearful plea of my Oliver Cromwell directly before his Battle of Dunbar, "I beseech ye in the bowels of Christ, think that ye may be mistaken."

The essence of my ethic is also that of my recognized

[5]"The Child-Mind and Child-Religion," *The Biblical World,* 1908, p. 101.

111

American citizenship, namely full-measured appreciation for the complete sufficiency of my individuality. Quite as world pacifist Albert Einstein recorded: The bitter lessons of the past must ever be learned anew.[6] The attempt may be made to dismiss divine solipsism with the accusation that it denies the existence of "external" reality, although the truth is that my solipsistic life orientation, by definition, can deny nothing. Indeed it is the only life orientation which, ultimately, can consistently affirm all of its living by acknowledging it as its own. *Solipsism demonstrates necessity to extend self consciousness in order to extend good will and love.* As Einstein wrote Sigmund Freud about the latter's Psychoanalysis, ". . . it is always a blessing when a great and beautiful conception is proven to be in harmony with reality."[7]

Each citizen's American government is specially devised for his requiring that he become *conscious* for the truth that it is his self government; that it exists for him, not he for it. Each citizen's American education must be clearly conscious as being his own organic growth of his self knowledge, in order that he be able to strengthen his mind to be capable of the conscious self sovereignty that, consciously cultivated by each individual, provides the only possible revocation of self violence through resource to self law.[8]

Once I use my mind to deny *any* of its one and only value, namely, perfection, I immediately require myself to provide some other "value." This ethical dissociation simultaneously involves my creating compensatory illusion functioning as my unconscious bridge from self living I cannot acknowledge to that which I can, for example: otherness, plurality, externality, commu-

[6]In an autograph, October 12, 1923. *Einstein On Peace*, p. 57.
[7]Ibid., p. 186.
[8]See my *American Government* and *Psychology of Political Science*.

112

nication, and so on. It also involves my trading the reality of my perfection for the illusion of progress or regress. Overlooking my holy ground of perfect wholeness (oneness) in order to save what conscious mindedness I can, I involve myself in endless argument based upon my imagined duality.

The very essence of my ethic is the wish to preserve biologically adequate self esteem by practicing the conscious virtue of acknowledging self responsibility for self development (that is, for self experience): that free poise of independent individuality, rather than the fixed pose of superiority, popularity, or some other illusional "objectivity."

Aristotle observed that man may be regarded as a *naturally* political animal in view of his awareness of the benefit to himself in living his fellowman as he lives any of his acknowledgeable self. As he creates in his self experiencing mind his meanings for his world, the individual can learn to recognize his fellowman as a unified identity, a self development, of his own mind's making. Provided that his self consciousness can keep up with his self growth, he soon awakens his civic insight about self helpfulness in constructing self governing contrivances to serve ideal political condition occurring within his personal living.

The foundation upon which my American testament rests cannot be safely assumed to be that of my very own rejected selfness ("the people") but must be located insightfully in my own recognizable individuality. I am all of my own "people," but I must develop sufficient strength of mind to be able to support this insight. My every individual is all that there is for him, also. He is his own "many" or "few" or whatever. That truth can gradually become observable by him as self evident. His acknowledging *that* truth depends upon his disciplining his mental strength to be able to make that

113

effort. Right here is where the importance of his *practicing* American conscious-self education comes in.

All of my ethical feeling is my own instrument for fair self guidance. It may require many centuries for my everyman to be able to renounce his superstition that he can "communicate" with his fellowman by use of his language. His language is a wonderful self development (idiolect) for his securing and operating definitive views of his own abundance, having no more "communication" value than any other organic development of his inviolable individuality. The *real* function of my linguistics is to help me organize *my* life, direct *my* power, mind *my* own interests.[9]

It is evident that for me to be a consciously ethical person I must be willing to work hard and steadily at it. My work-up of the moral insight that conscious individuality is the only possible "united humanity" or All-Real or divine world-plan requires undivided, arduous, and persevering conscious self devotion. All of my conscious individualization begins with my wittingly emancipating my self from my unconscious burden of "received" knowledge, such as all of my so-called acquired vocabulary, all of my commonly accepted opinion, agreement, and each such unconscious subordination of my conscious self identity to my unconscious self identity. By accumulating my unconscious self identity I come as close to moral nihilism as is possible for me. Unselfish self-activity is obvious contradiction.

Once I recognize that I can only know what I am doing by knowing what I am being, then the helpfulness of the function of knowledge in the form of conscious self knowledge becomes evident. As long as I am unable to fix responsibility for *any* of my own living as being entirely mine I discover that my ethical statement is

[9]See my *Psychology of Language*, p. 12.

114

essentially a play of words. It is the law of my constitutional nature to love my self. Self love functioning as the law of my nature extends to *all* of my living experience.

If I am unable to be aware that some of my living is my own, then I am unable to recognize my obligation to live that experience with conscious love. Clear-minded Mark Hopkins recorded his orientation about his own self love, "It has not been sufficiently observed, that the moral imperative, in which I believe fully, the affirmation of obligation to love, can be legitimately given forth only in the apprehension of that very good which wisdom would choose for its own sake."[10]

This work does not aim to state much generally about so-called ethics. I have rather tried to record and ring the changes upon my one basic ethical truth, only, and to indicate how this same magnificent reality of my own *conscious* self realization refers to the way I actually *live* my societal being,—not as if I can be among others, or even in relationship to my fellowman. Self respectfully I renounce each latter supposition as impossible. My ethic refers to the way I live my society or "others" or "fellowman" in and of my self. Immorality is self disregard amounting to self sacrifice. I find it possible to renounce innumerable sacrificial savageries implied in my language by treating my vocabulary with my self consciousness.

If I repress *any* of my mind, obviously I must deny that I am my self alone (solipsism). At the very start then I observe my necessity to restore the terms "selfishness" and "perfection" to biologically adequate verbal standing; to uphold the indefectible ethic of selfish perfection or perfect selfishness; to renounce as impossible any and every attempt at constructing an

[10]*The Law of Love and Love as a Law* (New York: Charles Scribner's Sons, 1895), p. x.

ethic on the negation "imperfection" or on the negation "otherness." Were it not for the fact that learned James Martineau has already used the name Idiopsychological Ethics to refer only to one division of his ethical theory, I would gladly use it to refer to the whole of mine.[11] Dutiful Dr. Martineau insightfully italicizes,

> *Morality is internal. . . . Be this, not in the form, Do this. The possibility of expressing any rule in this form may be regarded as deciding whether it can or cannot have a distinctly moral character.*

Without self consciousness my life would turn into a more or less earnest seeking without a finding of my only possession, namely, my own being. The moral of such a consequence is: conscientious devotion to pure self love, the mind-orientation of a *conscious* solipsist. I specify "conscious" solipsist on account of my finding that my *every* fellowman can, by nature, live only his own life, either consciously or unconsciously. However, only a *conscious* solipsist can steadfastly consider his life-affirming self growth to be his real life-work. Thus it is that my "God may be all in all" (Paul, I Corinthians, 15:28).

My unwittingly self-resisting reader finds a certain statement he cannot consider soberly, much less accord lifesaving importance in the sense that he is living it, and hence living on account of it. The statement asserts, "God is all," and that means to my reader that his author is attributing to his God also all of the "horrible foolishness and badness" in his universe. Therefore he justly remonstrates,

"Your theism mires you in the most awful moral mess. Your identification of God with all that is diabolical is obviously untenable. You might as well claim that everything is its opposite. Truth is false, good is

[11]*Types of Ethical Theory*, Vol. II (Oxford: Clarendon Press, 1886).

bad, right is wrong, faith is backsliding. You lay on God complicity with your guilt and imbecility. You destroy all other virtue or value by localizing it within the being of God, identifying him with the least worthy thing in his universe. Is that not hideous absurdity! Are you not upholding some kind of pantheistic doctrine that the self identity of God magically enables his not being some of his self, that he can be all without being the whole of it? If you claim he is the whole of his All, then how can any individual claim to be his own whole and all, since he must be coercively controlled by his God!"

First, I see my lovable identity, only, in my would-be adversary's objection, and honor each of his views as my own. I like to exercise the truth that my ethic subsumes every ethic that I can know about. To illustrate, my making any statement at all about any subject does not, and cannot, mean that I deny the helpfulness to me of any other statement that might seem to exclude or contradict my first one. Each observation exists, independently, as a production of complete and unique wholeness. Nevertheless, in treating my reader's seeming conflict as my own I may proceed to understand it further, as follows.

Making each denial or resistance my own, one by one I resort to the whole truth in order to resolve the appearance of conflict in the reality of unity. When I consider *all* of the truth in any so-called wickedness or foolishness in my self I invariably discover the blessedness in that wickedness and the wisdom in that foolishness. I find that it is impossible for anything, including any behavior, to occur unless and until sufficient truth is present to necessitate its production. Thus I discover nothing but God's will being done, in whatever happens. Furthermore I find it necessary to regard as most desirable all so-called illness, accident, crime, or whatever I associate with pain or unhappiness, for all such

117

distressing living is *indispensably* instructive. My careful study of any sign or symptom of my troubled living is my only method of finding the lifesaving purpose it serves. Thus my learning how I get my self into it also teaches me how to get my self out of my trouble.

As my Aristotle discovered this amazing fact, so have I found that knowledge of so-called direct and exact opposites is *one*. My goodness results from my renunciation of so-called badness out of which it issues. My faith issues from my renouncing any backsliding. My truth emerges from its apparent incompleteness that I call false. My righteousness similarly arises from my *need* for it, from my painful feeling of insufficiency that motivates my working up my righteousness. Yes, everything is its own everything, including its opposite.

As far as reference to my *least* thing or fellow being is concerned I have made my own the whole view created by my Emerson in his glorious poem, "The Informing Spirit":

> There is no great and no small
> To the Soul that maketh all:
> And where it cometh, all things are;
> And it cometh everywhere.
>
> I am owner of the sphere
> Of the seven stars and the solar year,
> Of Caesar's hand, and Plato's brain,
> Of Lord Christ's heart, and Shak-
> speare's strain.

Rather than "hideous absurdity" I feel nothing but *beautiful truth* in discovering the perfection of divine reality to be omnipresent.

And about the assertion that the divine look, "God is all," introduces plurality rather than unity, in that it necessarily involves both whole and "part," it suffices to observe that a whole must consist of wholeness only, quite as an individual must consist of individuality only.

118

It is the illusion that a so-called part can consist of something other than wholeness that accounts for the illusional plurality implicit in "whole-and-part." Every individual whose acknowledged image of his ideal self identity subsumes all of his own individuality, only, can readily comprehend the necessity for the perfect wholeness he must attribute to his God. Wilbur Marshall Urban senses his divinity in perfection, observing that the name "God" in the highest ethical religions has always meant perfection. He quotes his Jesus: "Be ye also perfect, as your Father in Heaven is perfect."[12]

Perfection constitutes all of my mental life. It is only my perfectly ignoring my perfection in any of my being that requires, as compensation, my indulging my illusion of a plurality of values. My single ethical truth consists of self evident self evidence of perfection as being my only possible value. Over and over, ever anew, *sufficient truth is always on the side of whatever I live, or that living could not occur.* All that can be ultimately and intrinsically valuable leads to the preservation of demonstrably perfect individual life. Nevertheless, *my value of self perfection may be appreciated by me consciously, or not.* The unique process or method of my ethical practice consists specifically in my perseveringly cultivating awareness for the ever-present perfection in whatever self augmenting experience I live.

My pressing need for ethical study and practice derives from my recognizing that my conscious behavior consistently reflects my opinion of my self. If my self estimate is high or low I tend to act accordingly, that is, in keeping with what I feel is due my consciously organized self image. It is my standing duty to steer my self experience with as full as possible appreciation for the basic identity underlying my self-concept-and-my-

[12]*Fundamentals of Ethics: An Introduction to Moral Philosophy* (New York: Henry Holt and Company, Inc., 1930).

fellowman-concept. Such is my interpretation of the doctrine of my Immanuel Kant's Categorical Imperative:

> Act in such a way that you always treat humanity, whether in your own person or in the person of any other, never simply as a means, but always at the same time as an End.[13]

This maxim is ethical as far as it goes. I can never treat any humanity other than my own, whether I am conscious or only unconscious for that necessity. Only I can live my other person as being his own only end, whether I am aware of that necessity or not. In view that being an individual means that I am constantly growing my self I may accurately describe my *being* as my vital process of individualizing. For my every mental consideration, e.g., thought or view, I am cultivating the perspective, "How does it work itself?" Shakespeare revered the allness of his nature thus,

> Nature is made better by no mean,
> But Nature makes that mean; so, over that art
> Which, you say, adds to Nature, is an art
> That Nature makes.

Realizing the great difficulty I experience in recognizing that negation can be only unconscious affirmation, that is, that my mind must first create whatever it would negate, I tend to live my denying critic readily with fond self identity. Whenever as critic I tend to deny the perfect right to existence of any consideration of any subject, including this present statement of mine, I am indeed increasing my self helpfulness by recognizing also the helpfulness of the mote in my mind's eye that enables me, omnipotently, as it were, to assert: What is, is not; or What is, ought not be. Thus, I am grateful to

[13]*The Fundamental Principles of the Metaphysic of Ethics*, trans. Otto Manthey Zorn (New York: Appleton-Century-Crofts, Inc., 1938).

my self to be able to conserve the truth: What is immoral, is also moral.

Right here my reader expostulates, "According to your psychology, whether I say 'Yes' or 'No,' to any issue, it is all the same. If I say 'Yes,' that only means conscious affirmation; if I say 'No,' that only means unconscious affirmation. If that is really the fact of the matter, how can I communicate my innocence or guilt concerning any matter involving misbehavior? I presume you feel that I can judge the extent and degree of my belief precisely by the degree and extent of my disbelief. The more I reject any of my mental activity the more my need to accept it is revealed, according to you. I simply cannot believe you. You may try that rejection out on your autonomous individuality, if you will please."

I would have renounced my so-called teaching work long since if it were not for my discovery that all education is self activity only, that every student is an inviolable individual whose every reference is to his self only, and that all of my help is self help. Coleridge individualized this truth:

> O lady, we receive but what we give,
> And in our life alone does nature live.

In the first place, *MY* dear reader, being an inviolably whole individual I cannot "communicate" in any way whatsoever, despite my cherished illusion that I can do so. In any appearance of so-called dialogue each dialogist really lives *all* that the whole experience can mean to him, entirely in his own mind. My each one is *all* that he lives of any conversation, conference, or whatever so-called intercourse. Therefore my "Yes" or "No" is entirely self contained, although I find *that* most consequential truth is rarely realized. Nevertheless the whole illusion that I can get at or be gotten at by my fellowman is mostly taken for granted as being truth rather than illusion, especially when I argue. Dispute is always traceable to the fact that each disputant *cannot* even be considering the same subject, since each one is wholly and only his own unique subject. My William Graham Sumner wisely recorded,

> It is vain to imagine that a "scientific man" can divest himself of prejudice or previous opinion, and put himself in an attitude of neutral independence towards the mores. He might as well try to get out of gravity or the pressure of the atmosphere. The most learned scholar reveals all the philistinism and prejudice of the man-on-the-curbstone when mores are in discussion. The most elaborate discussion only consists in revolving on one's own axis.[14]

In the second place, since I *am* both the affirmative and the negative of any subject of mine, it is most beneficial that I be able to honor all that I live as negated selfness, quite as all that I live as affirmed selfness. It is in my psychic reality where I conduct all of my meaningful living. My putting a "no" before any possible concern of mine can have no more immediate significance than my refusing to consider it further at that moment. Negation is not riddance. My negative sum is meaningfully mine, quite as is my positive sum. I imagine that my power of negation has been most beneficial in my creating a sense of my self identity that would help me to want to go on living. I save some of my feeling of wholeness of my identity by imagining that whatever I may disapprove of is certainly not I as much as is whatever I approve of. My John Dewey imagined, "Every great advance in science has issued from a new audacity of imagination."

In the third place, so-called misbehavior including any and every kind of crime or wickedness is really

---

[14]*Folkways* (New York: Ginn and Company, 1940), p. 98.

goodness that is not recognizable as such. I am the only wickedness I can ever know anything about, and that conscious self knowledge motivates me to study each sign and symptom of my wickedness precisely as I study the evidence of any other health difficulty. Thereby I can discover how my so-called wickedness is really my only present way to help my self, regardless of how shortsighted, objectionable, sociopathic, or otherwise strictly limited, that helpfulness might appear to be.

When I appreciate fully the lifesaving importance of my wickedness and that my wickedness could not even happen if merely the insufficient truth about my whole living were not present to necessitate its happening, then at last I can begin to recognize the righteousness in *all* of my living.

I, including my every fellowman, pay heavy tribute in guilt to be able to support cherished ways of thinking based upon belief in magic only. I refer to my comforting my self with such logic as Whatever is, ought not be; or, Whatever is not, ought to be. A rarely observed truth is that being so-called wicked or sick is also a condition of complete perfection. Becoming free from sin or getting well does not occur at the expense of depreciating the holiness in so-called sin or the health in so-called sickness. All self belittlement in such reasoning as "I am healthier than I was" is also troublemaking, but it is also perfectly livesaving whenever I live by living it. Thoreau noted, "We cannot well do without our sins; they are the highway of our virtue."

And finally, *above all I would not want my reader to believe or disbelieve anything at all that I write, including the sense of this sentence. The only possible trust is self trust, either recognized or unrecognized as such.* It is not only undesirable but impossible for me to believe anyone else, or for anyone else to believe me,—just as it is impossible for me to do any living of

123

another person, who is all and only his own living. All belief is self belief; all disbelief is self disbelief. All doubt is self doubt. My Emerson ever emphasizing the wholeness of individuality, observed, "All the religion we have is the ethics of one or another holy person." And my Thomas Jefferson noted, "The moral sense is as much a part of man as his leg or his arm."

My definition of my ethical reality, namely that of being (including doing) perfect good, arises out of the biological fact that living itself is constantly a process of self helpfulness. Thus, whatever helps me to live is perfectly good. It naturally follows that whatever I live is perfectly desirable whenever it occurs, for I succeed in living only by means of it, whatever it may happen to be.

My continuing to stay alive may become a *conscious* process of my religiously seeking my own self good. The regulative idea that self good and self help and self living are one, is the ideological form of my wish to live. The one way in which I can accurately prophesy my future living is by consciously conducting my living so that it will succeed in realizing my prophesy. It is in this direction of my devotion that my sense of duty to my self becomes recognizable as identical with all that I conceive as social obligation. By becoming consciously moral I can renounce being unconsciously martial.

One safe helmsman for steering my life I find in my joy of living, as did insightful Epicurus. Regardless of the nature of the living condition my displeasing experience brings forth, be it pain or sorrow, the biologically adequate response called for in each instance is good natured, kind, high spirited living of that whatever. It is practical to score this principle of joyous living as being the kind compatible with prolonging life, quite as unhappy living is compatible with foreshortening life. Indeed my laboratory finding on contented and discontented workers demonstrates the biochemical development confirming this "common sense" philosophy.

Unhappy feeling of any and every kind (from grief to shyness or any other so-called awkwardness or unpleasantness) has exactly the same biological significance as pain. The expression "painful feeling" is physiologically adequate. The purpose of pain (including all unhappiness) is to call attention to dangerous living, to life-threatening experience. In this one respect, hurt feeling of any kind is no different from the pain of sitting on a tack. In each instance the life warning is the same: "You are injuring yourself; relieve yourself." All that my unhappiness of any nature can be saying biologically is: "I am unhappy about my way of life; get a happy way. I am injuring my self with my wounding feeling. Comfort and pleasure my self." My every life satisfaction is life affirming; just as my every life dissatisfaction is life negating.

It is most strongly indicated to reduce quickly my every kind of unhappiness to the danger signal it lifesavingly is, so that I can as swiftly as possible direct my self to act so that I can enjoy (rather than have to go on suffering) my self. It is most rewarding to be able to learn this unspoken language of every aspect of all unhappiness. Just as I could not live through my day without my preciously helpful capacity to feel pain, so I could not live long without my unhappiness.[15] *My ability to know how to protect my wholeness would vanish with my inability to suffer.* My danger signal always warns me of the same threat to my wholeness: I am trying to violate the inviolate integrity of my being whether I suffer penetration of my muscle or whether I suffer attempt to violate my virtue.

It is noteworthy that all unhappiness or all pain de-

[15]See my *Psychology of Emotion*, "Introduction."

rives from my attempt either to stretch my self beyond my wholeness or to fragment it. Each unhappiness (such as grief, distrust, anger, jealousy, shame, etc.) depends absolutely upon my ignoring that I, and I alone, am the only subject who can be associated with any of my feelings. In other words, pain (including all unhappiness) not only protects unity but also indicates the cost of my indulged illusion of plurality. It takes the illusion of two to conjure up the entanglement of helpful mourning, jealousy, hatred, transference love, and every such form of attempted self dispossession.

There is no exception to the vitalizing power of wittingly doing as I please, of using the joy of living as my north star, despite the fact that innumerable vicissitudes of living must evoke both sensation and feeling of a painful nature. It is practical for me to see that there is no unhappiness in any experience, except the unhappiness I helpfully associate with it. Each and every event is a perfectly just one and, as such, deserving of my pleasing appreciation. No source of providence is as desirable, ideal, and indispensable, as the one I can reliably count upon when it is needed. I refer to the trustworthiness with which whatever occurs surely when all of the forces for making it occur are present.

It is most helpful to me to be able to realize that whenever I do steer my self away from any direction which I cannot live good-naturedly, I am surely practicing escape, but I am escaping with my life. Every so-called "escape" behavior, including escape from boredom, when necessary is a praiseworthy method for my currently upholding the noble standard of enjoying living.

Perhaps the most useful observation of all, bearing upon my wisdom in using my life and liberty for the pursuit of happiness, is the fact that *by means of my creative imagination I can always make everything turn*

126

out just exactly in the way I want it to. This ethically valuable lesson I may learn from observing my fellow-man (my fellow patient) resort to it upon slightest provocation, creating daydream, illusion, delusion, and hallucination, which fulfill his every wish. Thus, I may gradually learn to renounce my fear associated with my powerful infanthood and grow to be able to see my very own preciously helpful identity in my schizophrenic patient's autism, narcissism, and wish-fulfilling ideal creations.

It is only by such use of my imagination that I can continue to succeed in recognizing my wholeness when innumerable painful experiences of mine are entirely too strong to be restricted to serving as signals warning me that I am in danger of losing appreciation for my inviolable individuality. I have found that every instance of my not enjoying the sensing of the wholeness of my being has been traceable to my temporary lack of access to my imagination. I have found without exception that every person disabled in any way helps himself immeasurably by purposefully cultivating his imagination to be able to do whatever his imagination could not accomplish before. To record but one instance, a young man "lost" his legs in a traffic "accident" but helped himself to find them again where all of their meaning always was (but where he had never consciously situated it), in his own mind. He observed, "If I had never had that amputation happen, I would never have discovered just what there really is to me. I am satisfied."

I have learned from my experience that my fear of using my imagination for making the most of my life has been the origin of *all* of my prolonged feeling of frustration. For example, when blocked or inhibited in any of my functioning by some so-called "external" power failure, if I am willing to imagine everything and everyone

127

proceeding smoothly according to my wishes, I experience immediate self satisfaction and notable freedom from my own restraint. In other words, once I can renounce my turn of mind of situating my own living event as "external to me," I can start freeing my mental power for its true purpose of helping me to enjoy my whole self so that I can wish to go on living it.

Blaise Pascal (1623–1662) recorded his clear self view, "By space the universe encompasses me and swallows me up like an atom; by thought I comprehend the world." Most meaningful for my cultivation of my feeling of moral obligation for my world, is my seeing my world as I. Since it is good for my health, for my vital function, to be able to take due care of my self, my most important question may be, How am I now employing my sense of my existence? How am I now living all of the experience I ordinarily describe as "going on in the world"? Without realizing it, can I be practicing some kind of ghostly misinterpretation of the comprehensive meaning of my being? Have I been meeting and solving my life's necessities only in a self unconscious way which amounts to asking for an early death from so-called accident, or so-called disease? I cannot recognize my *unconscious* warning of the cost of my seeming irresponsibility for some of my own life!

It is possible to picture my seeming irresponsible way of living my life, as well as my consciously responsible way. If I live my self as if I could be "inside" or "outside of" anything else, then I practice seeming irresponsibility for whatever seems to be not-I. If I live whatever I live, acknowledging that I am living it, then I practice conscious responsibility for my self experience.

The following diagram roughly pictures my traditional view of my living (as if) inside of my world:

I AM PART OF MY WORLD

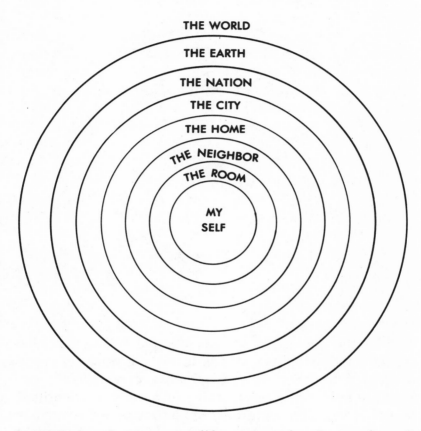

With the above empty life perspective I note how I
would be invisible on every map of any territory I have
ever seen. I feel a sense of restriction of my view of my
personal identity. I suffer an awareness of self impoverishment, of not amounting to very much, of not being
responsible for my all. Furthermore, a benefit to my
fellowman cannot seem a benefit to my self.

129

The following diagram roughly pictures my insightful view of my living my world where I do live all of my self, inside of my being:

I AM ALL THAT I AM

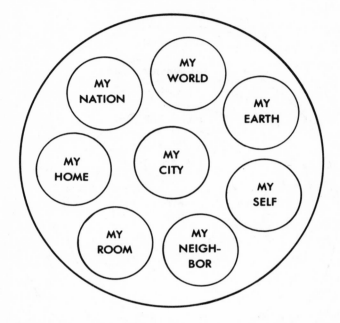

With the above full life perspective I note how my sense of individuality extends to my all, how my sense of my worth involves corresponding care for my self, how my everyone or everything of my world is entitled to my loving consideration. My fellowman's benefit is also clearly my own. My conscious living of my world is responsible, conscientious, liable, duty bound. I can understand my Vergilius Ferm, "One is not tempted by the world, nor by the flesh, nor by the devil—only by oneself."[16]

[16]"Psychology and Morals," *Encyclopedia of Morals* (New York: Philosophical Library, 1956).

A man continues free who can *continue* to live his sensation, perception, thought, feeling, and imagining, consciously as his own power. Not merely subject to any of his experience, he sees he is author of it all. He can care for his every meaning as being a function of his own. By his *practice* of respect for the individuality of his every mental element he enjoys the ongoing life of a self controlled individual. To make my self *exercise* belief in the *self* evidence of my own senses is to assume the conscious responsibility underlying freedom.

My creed of conscious-self-sovereignty is liberty founded upon my *persevering* recognition of the wholeness nature of my personal identity. There can be no real freedom except in unfaltering responsibility. In my conscious responsibility lies my capacity for conscious self-government and my life-rewarding interest in life. Wholesome education is a matter of consciously loving self-experience. Consciousness for the efficacy of my *discipline* of self consciousness is my main hold on my enlarging my conscious self helpfulness. Fully conscious I would imagine my every moment as the marvelous moment of my life that it is.

Under its ethical aspect *my* life includes *my* offspring, *my* fellowman, *my* fellow creature, — in short, *my* all. Only my conception of the wholeness of my individuality enables me to conceive the wholeness of my every fellowman. Of this appreciation of my subjectivity is constituted my so-called "life of the spirit."

My thesis is that my realistic ethic occurs only in my growing it, as my cultivation of my personal idealism. My morality is my expression of the shape my mind is in, due to the mind-shaping force of my self experience. As stated, to grow morally in any desired direction all I need do is practice devotion to the self experience which shapes my mind to express the moral to which I aspire. *My plural term, including collective noun, lends itself to my so-called rabble-rousing propensity.*

131

The conclusion to be drawn here is that freedom for performance of my every function is the law of my self-fulfillment physiologically and ethically. I run counter to the law of my own self development whenever I disclaim responsibility for any functioning of my physiology, *including any meaning of my mind.*

Much confusion of my mind is traceable to my unconscious (irresponsible) use of its power for personification, for example, "The social sciences fail to keep pace with the physical sciences," "Our ethical civilization has not kept up with religious truths." The illusion of "an individual in society" is supported by the illusion of "immorality." Consciously complete society in a consciously complete individual, is my name for consciously complete ethical being. Strange as the assertion may seem, every human individual lives under a hygienic necessity, as well as a moral responsibility, to develop his self love to comprehend *his* world as being his very own.

The hygiene of my mind is most specific. Its one concern is *consciousness for its wholeness.* My losing sight of my mind's unity, or integration, is my only possible accounting for any of my so-called mental disorder. My restoring my view of my mind's integration is my definition of specific psychotherapy. Invariably I find my feeling of moral obligation towards "another" is as conveniently displaced as is my therapeutic ambition for "another." All of my conscientiousness for "someone else" is my unacknowledged self concern.

Pain is a feeling I tend to exclude from my conscious living, for it does not readily excite my natural sense of my immediate excellence. Pleasure is a feeling I tend to retain in my conscious living, for it quickly furthers my sense of immediate self esteem. The wisdom of self experience reveals that full self-development includes

132

desirable, life-preserving "growing pains." My most helpful life attainment is my hardihood, the issue of my undergoing hardship. Without suffering life's ordeals I cannot achieve life's fulfillment, for life's fulfillment entails the function of *all* of my vitality. *In order to further my conscious self realization I learn to take pains to secure pleasure in painsworthy experience.*

Nevertheless, my reluctance to unsettle my established system of belief accounts for my overlooking, instead of looking over, innumerable self-evident truths, and thus prevents my reaping benefits provided by my own powers. Thomas Aquinas observed: the human good is the realization, the full perfection, of human nature.

All of my experience being my self experience, all of my love being my self love, every appearance to the contrary involves some repudiation of my own living. All of my conscious self love contributes to my sense of wholeness. All of my unconscious self love (called *transference love*) activates a specific modification of my hurt self love termed jealousy.

As all else, my love is subjective. However, when I live any of it as objective, I create dissociation in my mind. This dissociation is maintained specifically by my feeling of jealousy which signifies dislocated self love that I resist recognizing as being my own. The pain of jealousy is so intense that I naturally prefer any other feeling in its stead. Hence it is that I can succeed in masking my jealousy as anger, indifference, apathy.

The major role of my jealousy as signifying rejected self love may be too rarely observed in terms of my perfect wholeness. To illustrate, if I do not see my divinity as entirely my own but rather worship my godliness as if it is not mine *(transference worship),* the resulting jealousy creates most painful disturbance as far as my appreciation for my divinity can be concerned. I do well to work up the insight that enables me to understand that I am a jealous god so that I can help my self to locate all of my divinity where it actually must be, namely, in and of my own individual identity.

My long-suffering reader irately and rightly objects, thereby revealing his repudiation of his own subjectivity wherein he lives all of his meaning for his author, "You seem to me to be an autistic, narcissistic, megalomanic opportunist selfishly seeking only your own benefit and using what you call your divinity as a front and cover-up for your licentiousness!

"Furthermore, if it were possible for you to conjure up a pure phantasy of existence more beneficial for you than that which you now ascribe to the meaning of your divinity, I can readily imagine then, in your new-found self interest, your immediately seeking to cultivate all of your own self identity according to that peerless perfection also.

"I believe anybody might like to think of himself as God Almighty but, thanks be to God, it is only the rare schizoid character who lets his fancy go that far! I realize you claim this book to be autobiographical and that you ascribe divinity to everyone of *your* world. But how about *my* world? How about my need to help myself *as the human being* I am satisfied to claim myself to be?"

It is precisely and directly from my working up my loving appreciation for this kind of painful disowning of my meaning for my divinity that I grew my realization of the corresponding strength of my resisted divinity meaning itself. I finally recognized that the force of my need to resist any of my living necessarily implied the strength in that specific living.

As I have often observed to my self, my mind is for

134

the purpose of creating meaning. One of its potential virtues is that of considering kindly (with love) *whatever* meaning it creates.

The oracular sayings of the gods contain much of this expression of self consciousness, of self responsibility. Possibly, first the poet, later the philosopher, developed this ethical principle inherent in conscious self knowledge. Since my observation is my own creation I must painstakingly see that it always adds to and never detracts from my evident self measure.

For example, I must heed my apparent self disregard in the following observation: "Realism maintains that the universe is composed of 'reals' that exist independent of any individual's mind." I must notice that *Realism* cannot maintain any mental view at all for it has no mind to do it with. I must recognize that the whole observation is nothing but a product of a mind seemingly using itself to deny the existence of its producer, its own individuality. I take another observation, "Realism concedes the outside world to be the real world and aims to see things as they are and to adjust the self to this reality." Again I must recognize that *Realism* has no mind to concede with, no will to aim with, no vision to see things as they are or are not, no helpfulness to adjust anything to anything. Again, the whole observation is necessarily nothing but a mind's view seemingly used to take over and make over that mind. Every such statement which explicitly or implicitly denies the very ground of its being (the mind creating it) easily lends itself to a tail-wagging-the-dog appearance. *Whatever mental activity I cannot see is a subject of mine may seem to be able to subject me to it.*

All divinity is in the mind of its beholder. However, I can survey my divinity consciously only to the extent that I work up my consciously divine look. This theistic

135

life appreciation is thoroughly natural, being based upon the appreciation that whatever is, truthfully is. Gladly noted anew: *Nothing can happen unless all of the truth essential for its justification is present.* Whatever can be meant by existence, itself, is the presence of the power of all the truth essential for constituting that existence. My God is my truth.

I have settled upon what I consider to be my most ethical statement concerning any of my living, namely: *Whatever is, solipsistically is.* My idealistic solipsism reveals to me whatever I live in its most reverent light. With this blueprint of responsible reality I find my conscious way to the art and science of creatively living my self. All that I can possibly live is entirely and only personal.

All of my writing records the consequence of my self consciousness, although my awareness for this whole-making truth has developed itself gradually. As I review the voluminous published record of the growth of my conscious mindfulness I can trace my augmenting reverence for the truth of wholeness in each succeeding publication. Thus I can sense this work on the psychology of my ethic to be the natural (necessary) issue of my *Psychology of Political Science.*

I am certain of its truthfulness and therefore I willingly speak and write about the importance to me of my cultivating my *life* appreciation. My way of life depends upon my discovering its real nature. I find that it is well described as marvelous. Its very magnificence accounts fully for the tremendous difficulty which I encounter in my effort to learn how to conduct it. Furthermore, I can trace most of my life-trouble complaint to the force of my notion that my living should be easier than it can be.

I cannot be bad; I can only be good. I can do no wrong; I can do only right. I cannot harm; I can only help. By virtue of my absolute wholeness all of my ethic pertains to my own self necessarily. Also, again, my ethic subsumes every ethic that I can know about. I trace any and all of my resistance about acknowledging the wholeness of my solipsistic subjectivity to my inability to recognize the evident contradiction in my denying that I must be all that I am living.

MY MEDICAL ETHIC

I plead for the building of bridges between the different sciences, the different experimentations, a positive virtue based on altruism among scientific colleagues. I do not want this virtue to stem from reaction formation or from altruistic surrender, but rather I would hope that it is the expression of mutuality which does not destroy individuality.

Rudolf Ekstein

It is not my intention to separate any one aspect of my ethic from the whole of it, for the essence of it is identical in all, namely, reverence for wholeness of individual human life based upon cultivated awareness for its overawing wonderfulness. I am well aware of the so-called unpopularity of this essence manifest in my world today.

As educator my ethic consists of the study and practice of the law or truth of my nature that I must observe in order to be able to honor the wisdom-worth of my fellow-student's whole being. As physician my ethic consists of the study and practice of the law or truth of my nature that I must observe in order to be able to honor the health-worth of the inviolable wholeness of *my* fellowman's nature.

Certainly the biological adequacy of my way of living my fellowman is of most profound health consequence for me although, even as a physician, I may complete a long life unhappily without ever producing any conscious notion of what is the matter with me. The truth is

139

that I, including all that I can mean by my fellowman, am one, not two. Just as I treat this fellowman of mine, exactly so am I treating my self, and it is to my greatest physicianary benefit to be aware of this demonstrable necessity. It is the infinitely deep significance of my life itself that I must continue to examine closely to furnish my self with the true basis of my medical morality.

For example, my judging my lay or medical fellowman as lax in his morals is an instance of my trying to ethicize my self by seemingly disregarding my own living in the name of my disowned fellowman. Only my freely recognizing that I am always my only so-called culprit can provide me with ethical motivation to honor all such living of my guilt, since it is always traceable to my effort to comfort my self with ever ready faultfinding rather than with arduous, exonerating fact-finding.

In order to identify with my colleague whose choice orientation to life differs from mine, even in the issue I deem most critical, it is not necessary for me to surrender or in any way dilute my own conviction. The real bond of union enabling recognizable unity in spite of strangeness is found in the very ability to identify "my" colleague as really *mine*. Once I can use my imaginative power to that extent, I merely naturally understand his attributing to himself his right to the identical kind of freedom of mind which I justly claim for my self. After all, the underlying truth for which my fellowman contends is also always the same, namely, his right to help himself in the best way he knows how, pending his satisfying himself that he can safely add to that kind of helpfulness.

Purely personal self realization is properly the salutary supreme concern of the physician whose whole province is the problem of the worth (meaning) of individual life. When I neglect my idiopsychology I find my self in most embarassing position of insupportable self-contradiction. The principle of self-activity (called *Begriff* by Hegel, *Idea* by Plato, and *Subject-objectivity* by Fichte) governs the method of every mental process, for each is active in making itself its own subject. In his insightful book of seventy years ago entitled *Psychologic Foundations of Education*, William T. Harris, long time and justly renowned United States Commissioner of Education, clearly recorded these views, adding, "The predicate of self-activity, applied to the whole (self), is the most important conclusion reached in this higher kind of knowing (insight)."

Time-honored vivid consciousness for my own self thoroughly disguised as "the outer world" maintains a mental bifurcation of hardly imaginable grave consequence for my vicissitudes of health. Fortunately my medical educator is already beginning to see every phase of medical schooling as each medic's very own self-development. Now as much as ever before the need for the acknowledgeable unification of the forces of health and religious development is becoming apparently earnest and urgent. Now as much as ever before a man's opinion of himself needs to be seen clearly as his guide to his choice way of living.

Every great hero of humanity becomes what he is only by struggling with his own so-called evil until he discovers the good in it. Freedom of will can apply only to being one's self. Through the chorus of his *Agamemnon* Aeschylus sings his song of life, "For Zeus leads us to wisdom and sanctifies the law that suffering is our teacher." Furthermore, from my vast personal experience I would add, And the greater my insubordination to my divine law of conscious self helpfulness, the greater my suffering.

With the comprehensive understanding of the Reverend Paul B. McCleave, a Presbyterian minister, members of the American Medical Association's Depart-

141

ment of Medicine and Religion have started dialogue for clergymen and physician of every faith that already has augmented the insightful helpfulness of each worker. "The program is based on the fact that man is a whole being, representing the physical, spiritual, emotional and social," The Reverend Mr. McCleave said in an interview. "A Person can be ill in any one of these areas, and an illness in any one of the four can cause illness in any of the other three."[1]

Dr. Abraham N. Franzblau founded the first chair of pastoral psychiatry in 1937, at Hebrew Union College, Cincinnati.[2]

Ministry to medicine is now added to campus ministry at Wayne State University, providing service to the School of Medicine and the College of Nursing. It offers opportunity for counselling and guidance on the ethical and religious questions presently being debated in the medical profession, and is developing a program in bioethics for the medical curriculum.

The direction of all of my scientific discovery is towards simplification. My concept "whole individual" subsumes all of my organic functioning. My ethical principle depends upon my conception of my world. It is not a theory of morality, but rather my morality itself. From all of my asserting my specific ethical power of self consciousness it may become evident that my chief concern is to see to my cultivation of as complete as possible appreciation for the creative wonderfulness of my *living*, itself. Only by painstakingly developing my awareness for the comprehensive wholeness of my marvelous individuality as it steadily augments itself in my every experience, can I attain to a just realization of the immeasureable worth of my self-world-creating *life*. My

[1]Claire Cox, *The Detroit News*, April 24, 1966, p. 3-B.
[2]Philip Slomovitz, editor. *The Detroit Jewish News*, September 28, 1973.

ethical imperative requires my revering *whatever* I live, for it always consists absolutely of my own *living*.

All of my research on the basis of my ethic as well justifies my naming it my ethic of psychology as my psychology of ethic. To be sure, the most I can say of any of my wisdom is that it constitutes my ethic, that is, my growing conscious regulation of my action to conform to my principle of responsible self consciousness. My moral *ought* is an expression of my own conscious meaning of self help, that is, of what seems good for me. I am by my selfish nature *all* that I am, social, political, ethical, or whatever.

Although my experience indicates that my fellowman seems to use a similar moral ideal, this apparent similarity does not mean to me that I can agree with "someone else of my world" or that "someone else of my world" can agree with me. My discovering that all so-called "agreement" is an illusion clearly indicates that it can no longer serve as an adequate basis for my ethic. I regularly exercise this truth: I find that *the essential element in my ethic consists of my appreciation for my own life*. Striving for my own welfare is my effective way to devote my self to the welfare of all of my humanity. Only the fact that I cannot know the life-value of what I am missing fully explains all of my uncomplaining acceptance of my insightlessness.

My pursuit of *lifeworthy* self development is my sufficient formulation of my so-called pursuit of happiness. The Fourth National Congress on Medical Ethics was held April, 1973, in Washington.[3] K. Danner Clouser, Ph.D., associate professor of humanities at Pennsylvania State University College of Medicine, Hershey, sensibly stated:

In medical ethics we are really working with the same

[3]American Medical News, May 14, 1973, p. 6.

143

moral rules that we acknowledge in the rest of life. It's just that in medical ethics these familiar moral rules are being applied to situations and relationships peculiar to the medical world.

Dr. Fritz Redlich, professor of psychiatry and director of the Behavioral Science Center at Yale School of Medicine, prudently suggested that there may be strong imperatives in medical ethics to involve such experts as the social scientist, philosopher, man of religion, lawyer and health administrator. Reverend Thomas J. O'Donnell, S.J., a consultant in ethics, wisely observed, "Where ethics lives is at the heart of man, based on his most fundamental response to the meaning of life."

To be sure, even while revering my absolute wholeness, I go on experiencing difficult living, but in order to work with each ordeal I am not compelled to give it a bad name. I go on experiencing health struggle but can endure it as lifesaving strength functioning. I can kindly understand lying, cheating, stealing, destroying, and every such behavior as being the only way in which an individual can preserve his life whenever he resorts to it. Similarly I can kindly understand contempt, scorn, accusation, punishment—even to capital punishment— and every such behavior as being the only way in which another person can preserve his life when he resorts to it. Or I can live with love my fellowman as he succeeds in staying alive by denouncing his whole meaning of wholeness as being impractical moonraking, unreal nonsense resulting from brain rot, or whatever other unrecognizable goodness. Furthermore, the helpful insight I derive from understanding my wholeness in no way prevents my enjoying any of my seemingly not-self-living I formerly found satisfying, e.g., so-called tragedy, romance, literature, or any experience based upon illusional plurality such as communication, transaction, intercourse, or whatever.

144

Finding ubiquitous wholeness to be the realm of truth I feel the need for a new look at all that I can mean by physiology. Finding all of my living, regardless of its nature, to be my only present way of staying alive, I feel the need for a new view of all that I can mean by diagnosis or treatment. Certainly the most beneficial consequence of my new found self-understanding cannot come to a head except as a result of my willingly making it do so. Meanwhile as an M.D. I encourage my self by living every such holistic appreciation as the following:

Pessimism is all and only inhibited optimism.
Sickness is all and only struggling health.
Sinfulness is all and only oppressed sanctity.
Hate is all and only hurt love.
Bitterness is all and only inhibited sweetness.
Badness is all and only unrecognized goodness.
Pain is all and only inhibited pleasure.
Guilt is all and only inhibited innocence.
Fear is all and only inhibited courage.
Corporeality of any kind is all and only inhibited spirituality.
Cancer is all and only inhibited autonomy of whole
   individuality.
"Loss" of any kind other than loss of all of my
   wholeness is lifesaving whenever it happens.[4]

My work with my medical student has featured my disciplining my mind with each medical ideal: The whole physician for the whole physician; the whole patient for the whole patient. The following verses of my William Pegram contain strong psychological medicine:

Should some wise moral doctor but appear—
Some great physician of the human mind,
Diagnostician of the inner man—
What symptoms here within us would he find

[4]See my *Psychology of Emotion*, "Preface."

145

Most rampant and productive of that strife
Which saps the very marrow of our life?
Then would not this, our doctor, first insist
That this, our case, can offer little hope
Until self-blindness firmly we resist
And grant to self-analysis full scope?
And would not also his prescription be
That thought and mind must function full and free—
Unbound, unhampered, by Tradition's hand,
Untrammelled by conventional demand?
And as a tonic would not he decide
That temperance in all must be our guide—
Our watchword and our stay in time of need,
Our gauge to measure thought and speech and deed—
And 'neath this even our emotions bring,
Which, left unchecked, would this our reason fling
Out of its course, deprive of all command,
And headlong run, without a guiding hand?
And would not Temperance, if this pursued—
Thus supplicated, importuned and wooed—
Give birth at last, indeed, to Self-Control—
That prime essential of the growing soul?
For Self-Control, once born, will grow in strength,
In power, in scope, in knowledge, till at length
It quite o'ercomes these ills and sets Man free
To be what Nature meant that he should be!

Then—and then only—is he truly free!
Then—and then only—can he clearly see!
Then will he but conform to Nature's Plan!
Then—not till then—can he be called a Man![5]

The question is often raised as to whether it is possible to learn "professional ethics." The argument against such a desirable goal is that the individual's character is already well established as a consequence of his early home living. "If he has not learned to be honest by the time he gets to college, he can only give lip service to a course of study aimed at maintaining

[5] From *A Diagnosis*, by William Pegram.

ethical standards." Thus it seems taken for granted that an infant and child can develop ethically in a way which makes it impossible for him to develop further ethically. *In reality, conduct becoming an infant and child is the only possible foundation for an adult's ethicizing his nature.*

My own school experience has clearly demonstrated that a pupil does advance his devotion to ethical living once he realizes that he has always been as ethical as possible. I have noticed growth direction of a student's personal character which he has instituted within the year of his experiencing a true view of the comprehensiveness of his individuality. Indeed to watch this development of the highest kind of ethical standard going on in each one of my students has been the most gratifying of all my educational experiences. Many a colleague of mine has witnessed the same kind of development in his pupil.

Precisely what makes a student love to learn to develop his potential recognition of himself as his all, is his kindly experiencing in his own life the kind of educator aiming at this extent of full living. Innumerable are the instances of the teacher enjoying the satisfaction of knowing that his all-out devotion to making the most of his life, and consciously minding it, has been his one and only possible contribution to his meaning of self-education.

My conduct gains ethical sanction in proportion as my activity becomes self conscious. Appreciation for the value of my *life,* my marvelous existence, is the assumption underlying my every moral estimate. Conscious excellence of self-care is my ethical goal. Looking into my life I can observe the extent to which my ethic, my devotion to the truth of my allness, gives me peace of mind, keeps me in most effective touch with my only reality, guarantees my appreciation for my

147

health, and provides my ideally responsible living of my fellowman.

However, due to my greatly limited appreciation for the universality of my individuality, I can compensate for my resulting inadequate awareness about it, by merely assuming that one person or thing can somehow get at or be gotten at by another. Thus I can seem to my self to be able to praise, love, hate, attack, ignore, etc. (my) you (or the converse, my you can seem to accuse, etc., your author).

The all-important ethical concern for me is my continuing development of my only source of either acknowledgeable right or responsibility: How can I steer my self experience in the direction which will insure that my augmenting self growth will be associated with my developing self consciousness to correspond with it! How can I muster this lifesaving life appreciation! In the words of my Hippocrates, "All things are divine and all things are also human."

My only moral command derives from my individual nature. Appreciating the wholeness and allness of *my* individuality I can attribute absolute individuality everywhere in my world, thus dispelling my illusion called "means" as being the derivative of inhibited individuality functioning. H. Hoffding perceptively describes the dualism of means and end as the "most mischievous of all dualisms."

Realizing that the truth is always on the side of whatever happens I can sense and feel my will as identical with my God's will. The spirit of truthfulness becomes identifiable as divine spirit. All is true. All is divine. Dust is divine dust. My return to dust is also divine immortality. I am obligated to be my self, my divinity in whatever form.

With only uninformed spirit I always look for a *cure*

for whatever ails me. My discovery that all that *can* ail me is presently my only available way of helping my self, enables me to renounce my searching for some easy cure for my distress. Rather, I can feel the need to discipline my mind to endure what must be endured so that I can consciously honor it as being my own presently helpful *living*. The consequence of valuing my endurance for its curative worth has been most beneficial. Thus I now honor my every sign or symptom of health difficulty, e.g., any kind of pain or unhappiness, for its *lifesaving* significance. My depression, anxiety, or whatever troubles me, now means treatment as well as diagnosis. I recover from my depression on account of (recognizing the *purposeful* biological functioning of) my depression. I cannot feel unhappy in any form, any more than I can feel pain in any form, except as a beneficial indication that my present way of conducting my living, itself, is dangerously hurtful.[6]

Ever since the enormous show of success realized by my scientist in applying his ideas of "objectivity," "materialism," and "determinism," he has evinced a noticeable tendency to rely increasingly for medical power upon his "scientific study of the presenting objective data," with evident neglect of awareness for his *life-reality:* subjectivity or inviolable individuality. Many a physician's devotion to his medical science of this so-called "impersonal" nature had led to his building up his conception of his powerful medical organization seemingly capable of upholding his exalted notions of Objective Science, long after each of its limits has been duly dispelled by his insightful colleague as once helpful illusion. The medical scientist's *psychological medicine* which scientifically works with the

[6]See my *Psychology of Emotion*, p. 131.

149

obstinate fact of the subjectivity (individuality) of the doctor's patient and of the patient's doctor is becoming increasingly respected as physician-worthy.

Preservation of health, without doubt the first and fundamental blessing of life, may well be considered every self-conscious individual's responsibility. For safe and sane living my possession of painful, including every kind of unhappy, feeling is absolutely indispensable. I never suffer any kind of unpleasant emotion except when my wayward behavior requires such a signal that I am not using my mental functioning with sufficient biological adequacy. As soon as I conduct my life with sufficient self understanding I relieve my mind of its aroused anger, jealousy, suspicion, envy, sorrow, guilt, fear, shame, or whatever helpfully painful affect signifying health trouble.

With conscious self knowledge I recognize my *ought* is the natural outcome of my whatever is. Whatever is, precedes whatever ought to be, naturally (necessarily). The authority according to which my morality must develop itself is my own living of my individuality, my only possible possession. There can be no ethical educator except conscious self educator. My doing right, as right as I can do, in all things is as natural as is my regular breathing or pulse rate.

The Greeks called the virtue of conscious self control *healthy*-mindedness. However, selfness must first be acknowledged as such before it can become controllable. *There is no other method for me to discover the immeasurable value of life except by zealously enlarging my concept of my own individual identity, thereby to reveal its wonderful magnificence.* Since conscious self knowledge is always associated with conscious responsibility (rather than guilt) for being one's self, it is the most difficult knowledge even to wish to attain. Joyously struggling to attain my conscious self

150

knowledge by hardily enduring difficult truth about my nature enabling me to redeem my free innocence from its inhibited functioning as guilt, — that is my ethical process.

I am aware for the truth that — except insofar as my medical experience has made me sensitive, knowledgeable, and proficient with regard to appreciation for life — my medical ethic is a natural continuation and outgrowth of my premedical reverence for all that I can mean by human existence. As M.D. I consecrate my life to this ethic: The study and practice of the preservation of my *marvelous* individual *living* from the momentous occurrence of its conception.

My basis of my medical ethic is my conception of my profession: My acknowledgeable study, diagnosis and treatment of my patient as my self. Man is by nature an ethical organism and his discovery of that necessity is the beginning of his identifying his love of wisdom with his wisdom of love. As I live with this insight, I notice my consciousness grows into conscientiousness. The law of ethic is no different from the law of self preservation. I am mindful of the Psalmist, "Unless thy law had been my delights, I should then have perished in my affliction." (119:92).

It is to my consciousness for my wholeness as being my only agency that I owe gradual development of my lifesaving temperance, moderation, measured living. With the truth of my wholeness in my functioning I can feel my economic requirement to avoid excess. Whatever grace is consciously mine I can trace to the quality of harmonious identity characteristic of my all-doing (all-being) wholeness.

The bodily nature of man remains the central concern of every physician, hence it is desirable that "bodiliness" be studied and understood in terms of its wholeness, namely, in terms of all of itself. It is essential that

151

this morphological concept of bodiliness include the realization that organic wholeness obtains in seemingly most diverse natural functions. Thus I live most of my wholeness below the threshold of my consciousness, that is, unconsciously. It is helpful to realize that although my functioning of each of my senses may seem to be highly differential and localized, nevertheless it is the one identity of my wholeness that makes possible each sensory experience. Indeed all conscious synesthesia is thoroughly understandable in this orientation.

Analogously, the truth of bodily wholeness dispels the illusion implicit in the body-mind duality or any other duality. Thus it becomes evident that profound psychic events occur as secretory functioning of glands, cardiac dynamics, vascular tone, and so on. Realizing that wholeness is my only agency I no longer need to suspend my appreciation for the integrity of my individuality by positing that psychic activity is "accompanied" by action currents in the nervous system, or the like. I can recognize what I call my soul and what I call my body each as the product of my wholeness. The true reality of my existence is represented by my organic wholeness. Every manifestation of my life, such as sensing, feeling, thinking, or even consciousness itself, is a creation of the wholeness of my being. In 1926, Ivan Petrovich Pavlov (1849–1936) sensed the inseparable unit of human individuality thus:

> Sooner or later science will transfer the objective results of its investigations to our subjective world and so it will suddenly expose to the brightest light our nature so deeply submerged in darkness. Science will explain the mechanism of that which occupies and fascinates man most, namely, the mechanism of his spiritual life.[7]

[7]Franz Buchner, *Personality and Nature in Modern Medicine* (New York and London: Grune & Stratton, Inc., 1958), p. 28.

Prior to my recognition of the exclusive role of my wholeness for my living, I had no organ or method with which to encompass as unified the seeming differentiation of my organicity. It remains my challenging task as a medical scientist to continue research as thoroughly as possible upon my exclusively holistic nature.

As physician I frequently find it helpful to express some of my views regarding prognosis, aborticide, euthanasia, organ transplant, and similar medical exertion of mine, including that of my well intentioned fellowman. Again, as all else that I record for my self, each of my choice views on my medical ethic is not intended in any way to detract from identically vital importance I ascribe to my esteemed colleague's medical way of life. Furthermore, I can imagine my colleague's awarding his Dorsey the same kind consideration.

Concerning prognosis, my consistent attitude is that my patient surely has 100 per cent possibility of recovery from whatever is ailing him, regardless of the so-called malignancy of the condition threatening his life. *Certainly in his mind his complete recovery is entirely a matter of his conscious volition.*

A medical colleague of mine once told the story of a patient whose expert specialist's prognosis gave him merely six months longer to live, suggesting that the patient set his life affairs in order to meet this exigency. Two years later the highly trained expert saw this same patient walking towards him on the street, apparently well and vigorous. Grimly appreciating his inaccurate diagnosis but retaining his good humor the good doctor turned to his former patient first with the quip, "Well, what quack have you been going to!"

With regard to the tenderly mortal issue of abortion, "each consideration, aborning or aborting, is an absolutely unique one potentially calling in question the sacred integrity of the human soul and actually com-

153

mitting the attending physician, to the best of his current ability, to demonstrate *his* opinion of the value of human life. *All of mental health is a product of full respect for all human life, prenatal and postnatal.* The notion of 'liberalization of abortion laws' may well introduce innumerable vital concerns such as 'human rights of the unborn,' 'reverence for the human soul,' 'respect for the dignity of human individuality,' or 'disregard for due process of law protecting and preserving human life.'

"The individual variant is the very foundation of medical study and practice. The fetus or embryo is one individual. The mother is entirely another individual. The 'popular' idea of opposing the welfare of the mother to the welfare of the unborn baby, must be the consequence of inadequate appreciation for human individuality to begin with. Sincere belief that a mother can benefit from the unborn baby's loss must not take into account the maternal necessity for a mother's sense of deepest biological responsibility, conscious or unconscious, for her safeguarding the welfare of the baby of her womb. Certainly each mother's life attitude is of first importance, and her awakening to the *sufficient facts* about her pregnancy cannot but be favorable to life.

"Becoming conscious for the power and glory of life itself has been man's most difficultly attained awakening, on account of the fact that it entails his daring to assume ever increasing personal responsibility for it. Thus the tribulations of life responsibility tend to favor enormously restricting one's sense of self identity. I can revere *all* of my life itself, only to the extent that I have difficultly worked up my appreciation for its intact and inviolable organic wholeness.

"Every woman's personal identity includes all of her meaning for her unborn baby. Consciously or uncon-

154

sciously, she immediately regards this new human individuality as her very own, precious and dear as her own soul from its earliest inception. It is the prime interest of everyone that any and every attitude of belittlement towards this life be avoided all the way and by all possible means. Self preservation, life affirmation, is considered as heaven's first law since it is biological necessity.

"In my opinion, each physician sufficiently aware of the incomparable importance of his highly privileged aborticidal act, including its tremendous life consequences for any and every mother, cannot wish to burden his already over-burdened life by personally assuming license for prenatal death in the name of his human liberty. The worthy end of controlling 'population explosion,' 'maternal health,' 'eugenics,' or whatever, cannot justify the effort to degrade prenatal human individuality into a means."[8]

The following is the Declaration of Geneva, a pledge suggested as a dedication of the physician to his profession of *life* service. It was adopted by the General Assembly of the World Medical Association in Geneva, September, 1948, and was immediately recommended for its efficacy, in each journal of organized medicine.

Declaration of Geneva

At The Time Of Being Admitted As Member of The Medical Profession:

I solemnly pledge myself to consecrate my life to the service of humanity.

I will give to my teachers the respect and gratitude which is their due;

[8]See my "Old Embryos That We Are," Letter to the Editor, *Detroit Medical News*, April 28, 1969.

I will practice my profession with conscience and dignity;

The health of my patient will be my first consideration.

I will respect the secrets which are confided in me;

I will maintain by all the means in my power, the honor and the noble traditions of the medical profession;

My colleagues will be my brothers.

I will not permit considerations of religion, nationality, race, party politics or social standing to intervene between my duty and my patient;

I will maintain the utmost respect for human life, from the time of conception; even under threat, I will not use my medical knowledge contrary to the laws of humanity.

I make these promises solemnly, freely and upon my honor.

Some of my considerations on death belong in my medical ethic. Every individual must be his own thanatologist.[9] The living one cannot tell another of his living even, and the dead cannot speak at all. Death being the complete absence of life, the only one involved cannot report this absence. So-called practical sign of death, each one, indicates cessation of organic activity. Absolute inactivity is death.

My so-called suicide is a special name for ending my life by my own conscious contrivance. It is an instance (more so than so-called murder) of extremely limited self consciousness when my whole self control seems usurped by a single feelingful thought best verbalized by, "I do not wish any longer to live the way I am living."

My mind is for the purpose of being able to entertain justly every kind of thought or feeling on account of its immediate viability whenever it occurs. If I repudiate any of my life experience, no matter how much I may

[9]See Allan W. Reed. "Thoughts on Thanatologists," *Harvard Medical Alumni Bulletin* (March/April 1973): 16, 17.

live that event with loathing, I am trying to disown that much of my own life. This biological wisdom is disregarded most consistently when *I live* my fellowman's speaking (my) his mind, without my appreciating that I am the only one living whatever I live.

However, my actually suiciding indicates that I have not been able to make peace with my feelingful thought of suicide so that I have had to condemn it as unworthy living, thereby emphasizing its involuntary force. Regularly I find my fellowman unable to mind his painful wish to end his life immediately, with appreciation for the fact that this wish is entirely natural, namely, his biologically adequate manifestation of hurt self love. Severely hurt love creates natural protest corresponding to the naturalness of crying Ouch! when hurt.

It is particularly essential that a physician of the mind make peace with this unpleasing individuation of his individuality, his determination to end his life, especially on account of the frequency with which he is called upon to live this difficult show of hurt love of his fellowman. I recall many instances in which my cultivated mental strength allowing me to appreciate my wish to end my life as entirely life worthy resulted in my fellowman's developing this same kind of extended self love, thereby becoming able to renounce this suicidal idea or impulse lovingly. To repudiate it with hatred or fear is to provide it with obsessive or compulsive force.

In other words, my obsessive or compulsive will to end my life is a classic illustration of my need to cultivate my self consciousness for all of my self love, including its every modification, beginning with hate. My ability to say and feel that I want to die, while realizing the lifesaving nature of this presenting mental condition, is absolutely indispensable for my due appreciation of my wholeness and allness. My feeling-and-

157

idea of self destruction is a creation of my living quite as is my wish for immortality. *Whatever* I live, including my so-called death desires, I live by. *Whatever* I live by means of, is by definition lovable lifesaving power of mind.

I find that everyone must end his own life, no matter how much appearance may be to the contrary. Human individuality is inviolable in every respect, including this one. Biblical lore teaches the helpfulness of living within the shadow of one's numbered days, thus encouraging man to be able to live lovingly his absolute need to end his living upon attaining the fullness of it. "I want to kill my self" is a passionate idea that needs to be understood clearly as a desperate cry of hurt self love whenever it occurs. It is integral to my wish to continue to enjoy my life.

I am disciplining my mind to feel love when I am able to have some thoughts and feelings verbalizing my deepest depressive emotion. I know of no more wonderful way to strengthen it. My mind is for the purpose of living every kind of thought and feeling and the most depressing thoughts and feelings are unconsciously the most elevating ones. Certainly it is difficult work to appreciate despair or hopelessness. By appreciating it I revere that much of my wholeness.

A classical example is the depressing feeling of an "external" void, a sense of emptiness, that I suffer in my experience of bereavement. My helpful mourning work consists of my sadly conjuring up in my mind as many as possible of such experiences concerning my so-called departed beloved, each one of them seemingly localized only in my so-called externality. From grieving over these consciously depersonalized "memories" of my beloved, whose existence I imagine to be gone forever, I gradually discover their presence within me rather than their absence outside of me.

In other words, by renouncing my illusion of the

158

externality of my loved one I restore the accessibility of all of his (her) reality for me precisely where it has always existed, within me. By thus disciplining my mind with kindly self consciousness I find that all of my real world is the one I live within me and that my so-called external world is entirely the necessarily helpful conception of my imagination. As I empty my mind of externality illusion I find it filled with its own internality. Similarly, with regard to my recognizing the healing (wholeness-saving) power in every kind of my hurt love, by honoring the biological purpose of each painful emotion (as signalling my endangered wholeness) I can gradually discover the wonderful magnanimity of my true nature.

Absolute proof of the unapparent happiness in any of my apparent unhappiness lies in the demonstrable fact that when I can discover all of the truth necessitating my unhappiness I can then always observe an access of joy of living. My love of living never hurts except when I am experiencing power of helpfulness (goodness) without being able to be fully aware for its truth (necessity).

My full appreciation for my scientific truth (i.e., nothing can happen until sufficient truth is present to necessitate its happening) has made me aware for the helpfulness I can find in teaching my self to live my very painful experience with love. After all, my painful experience is entirely my own lovable self. Whatever is, truthfully is, hence, lovably is. And it is most beneficial for me to understand *that* providence thoroughly, for without such understanding I cannot adequately revere the functioning of my wholeness.

To be sure, my individual wholeness is all that exists from the moment of my conception on. However I must achieve cultivation of my consciousness for my wholeness, my acknowledgeable self identity, as best I can.

Euthanasia means essentially to me, my dying as I

please, a strictly individual privilege. With this growth of insight I create my appreciation for the futility in my medical devotion either to keeping my patient alive or helping him to die. Only my patient can even be at all concerned about his own living or dying. *It is evident to me that my suffering is as self-fulfilling as any other living of mine, and it seems most desirable to me that my attending physician be capable of that kind of self understanding, so that he will not try to impose his limit of self suffering upon me.*

Despite all claims to the contrary that I, an M.D., can now prolong or terminate my patient's life, I find every such assertion really resulting in my conscious belittlement, arising from my ignoring my inviolable wholeness, including my patient's inviolable wholeness. The true "dying with dignity" that I wish to uphold involves my realizing that I am doing all of my own dying. Ideally I know that when my suffering becomes unbearable it will become unconscious. Meanwhile, I prefer to ease my suffering according to my own, including my physician's, limited endurance. I cannot relegate responsibility for my health to my M.D. regardless of how much I can find my own identity in (my) his self-helpfulness.

I have helped my self most by discovering how to use my imagination for carrying out, carrying through to its completion, any and every kind of life experience that may possibly occur *in my mind as such*, and this mental development has been a source of great soul appreciation.

Emotional thinking is doing, quite as emotional doing is only mental activity. What I can *consciously* carry out as activity *in my mind* can save me from living the same kind of behavior as if it is not occurring in my mind. To put it crudely, by realizing that my mental activity is a form of my doing, I can behave as I please

160

self continently. By not realizing that my "doing" is entirely my mental activity, I behave as if I can be self incontinent.

My consoling medical ethic reveals to me that I am purely my own generative dust, thinking reed, rational or irrational animal and solipsistic divinity. My lifesaving ethic reveals to me that my moral consciousness can exist for me only to the extent that I see my own identity, rather than so-called existential ambiguity, in all of my asserting my negation of negation and my affirmation of affirmation. My whole-making ethic reveals to me the necessity to be right in my own eye if I would justify my self in my God's eye. I can impose my divine law upon my behavior the moment I can decide that the whole of me is the soul of me. Plato has Phaedrus comment to Socrates: "Hippocrates, the Asklepiad, says that the nature, even of the body, can only be understood as a whole." My every creative act bears the stamp of my growing my wholeness.

I can think of no more relevant illustration than that of organ transplant with which to score the biological role of conscious self identity. All medical experience with organ transplantation reveals the necessity that each patient's wholeness be fully appreciated. Every individual creates all of his whole body in and of his self, consciously and/or unconsciously. All living is no more than the growing of individuality as such. In all of its possible meaning, what lives in my life is constituted only and entirely of my (conscious or unconscious) self identity.

It seems perfectly obvious and necessary to me that any of my living that I experience as if "a foreign body" immediately must assume the meaning of life risk and, in the interest of my unimpaired self wholeness, be eliminated as soon as possible. Equally, it seems perfectly obvious and necessary to me that any of my living that I can experience with conscious self love, as consisting entirely of my own identity only, must assume the symbiotic meaning of constituting a growing of my wholeness. For example, I naturally tend to take on my skin graft of and to my own skin, that is, without my rejecting it as much as I might reject skin I regard as foreign. To the extent that I can recognize, or grow to recognize, my own identity in whatever I live, the likelihood increases of my being a successful host for the organ transplant process.

In the interest of successful transplant it is indispensable that each patient consciously exert his devotion to seeing only his identity in the (his) new tissue he is striving to live as his own. This mental attitude that all of my possession is self-possession is favorable even to blood-transfusion, my blood itself constituting vital tissue of my own.

My Plato described circulating blood as the pasture on which the other cells feed. I am confident of my ability to make my physiology consciously meaningful, thereby bringing out the truth that blood, flesh or bone is mental, as is all human vitality. The viability of my every tissue is of a holistic nature essential to the conception of organicity itself. Blood, however, uniquely illustrates the flowing structure of man, deserving to be described as existence in flux.

In all of my medical work I carefully screen all dependence upon statistical probability, in favor of considering my patient to be an absolutely unique individual. I feel it necessary that my patient willingly assent to, or dissent from, any medical, surgical or experimental procedure involving his person, after he has been as fully informed as possible regarding the whole nature of his physician's recommendation. If my patient is unable to assume such responsibility, without due process of law, he may have to forego the possible benefit accruing from a given procedure. His willing consent or dissent cannot absolve me from any of my full responsibility for my professional conduct.

Rarely am I fully aware that the way I treat what I term my so-called surroundings is potentially of the same kind of meaning for my health as the way I treat any other aspect of my constitution, such as the lining of my stomach or the circulation of my blood. This is my great truth of truth that needs to be duly exalted: I cannot disrespect my fellow creature without immediately developing either manifest or latent symptom of my own self disrespect.

And now a brief note on my medical ethic as it involves any of my so-called anti-social living. I trace all criminality specifically to the so-called criminal's dangerous ignorance for the truth that he is always his own so-called victim. By his crime a criminal is crying out for help. My best interest is served when my so-called criminal immediately secures the same kind of wholesome quarantine and needed treatment *every* human being always deserves, when he urgently needs but cannot assume due self care.

It is now plain to see that, as an M.D., I can claim no other ethic than that which is traceable directly to reverence for my own whole *life,* for only as I value all of my own existence can I value all of the life of my fellowman generally, and of my patient specifically. My wish to help my patient or anyone else derives entirely from my need to help my self.

The guiding truth integral to the principle, devotion to my own whole-souled life, is that my medical ethic can occur and prevail only in my living, quite as my medical colleague's ever perfect ethic can occur and prevail only in his own living.

163

HOW MY ETHIC WORKS ITSELF

Is there anything more daring, anything newer than to announce to physicists that the inert will be explained by the living, to biologists that life will only be understood through thought, to philosophers that generalities are not philosophical, to teachers that the whole must be taught before its elements, to students that one must begin by perfection, to man, more than ever given over to egoism and hatred, that the natural driving power of man is generosity?

Henri Bergson[1]

If I take the trouble to notice, I always find that I can never do anything until I have to do it, quite as I can never omit doing anything until I have to omit it. Everything happens only whenever the sufficient force is present to make it occur; each event results only when nothing is lacking to produce it. Therefore, in answer to this question of mine, How can I learn to *make my self* do or refrain from doing, anything, it now becomes evident that I must willingly study the forceful fact entering into the constituting of whatever I desire to bring about.

If my desire (wish, will) is sufficiently strong it provides me with the incentive (motivation) to work up into my living the condition it implies. This work-up involves not only my sustained devotion but also diligent practice. To the extent that my mind is uninhibited I

[1] *The Creative Mind* (New York: The Philosophical Library, Inc., 1946).

can imagine fully and freely, *omnipotently,* whatever kind of self experience I want. This kind of free imagining, often scorned as "too fanciful," is most essential for my maintaining awareness for my satisfying intactness of mind. Its recognizable subjectivity is most reassuring as well as comforting. It is absolutely indispensable for my maintaining my due appreciation for my wonderfulness, self helpfulness, independence, or self identifiable godliness. It is conducive in every way to my "getting things done." All of my impotence is repressed omnipotence.

My sensing an order of *growing* reverence for my life accounts fully for this present volume. I can safely assume that it is my reader's aim to be moral, although my experience teaches me that this aim exists unconsciously as a rule, rather than consciously. Surely I can speak and write only to my self. However, I do see with bright clarity the fact that I was unable to become consciously moral until I began to take my mentality seriously and then to realize that I am all and only mind, or soul. In this work I use the terms *mind, subjectivity, soul, spirit, whole, reality,* and *individuality* as synonymous.

As all else, my mind can live itself only anew. Despite all the appearance to the contrary, *living consists of newness only.* With this understanding, that living concerns only present existence, it is interesting to note that *morality,* like its correlative term *ethics,* derives from the notion of custom or habit. The courageous moralist Warner Fite declared: Morality is the self conscious living of life. To be moral means that I realize that all of my doing is nothing but my responsible being. I cannot live my self conscientiously to the extent that I indulge the illusion that my living can have something to do with somebody else or something else.

My Plato's Socrates observed, "The unexamined life

166

is not fit for human living." All intellectual curiosity can be nothing but the desire to live one's knowledge of one's own being, *knowledge itself being a form of satisfying being*. From my Plato's record it is evident that what his Socrates had in mind by "the examined life" specifically referred to the cultivation of conscious self knowledge, including conscious self feeling.

My mental condition is the consequence of its culture. Self culture is the requirement for any refinement of my nature. I have grown my self to be what I am by virtue of the kind and degree of disciplined aim I have hesitatingly imposed upon my self cultivation.[2] As my self exercise in this or that direction of my experience seems lifeworthy, in that it not only pleases but also preserves my living, I tend to trust my self to it. My faith in my own divinity has grown strong by this test.

My faith has strengthened itself in proportion to my acknowledging my own being, *as such*. Only by this process of making my self aware of my self have I become *sure* in any way. As my belief in my self could wax strong, on account of augmenting evidence of the existence of my conscious self to believe in, my capacity for certitude developed apace. Thus my conscious self trust provided the basis for my mounting reverence for truth itself. With this firm foundation of conscious self evidence I became capable of recognizing all doubt as being merely unrecognizable (inhibited) faith. And now for most vitalizing innovation in my self trust.

One way of life seemed beyond me on account of the mighty demand it seemed to make upon the wayfarer. As a child I grew some knowledge of it without making it clearly my own self knowledge. It appears that my earliest parental apperception contributed to my idea of it. It seemed to deal in superlative far removed from my

[2]From unpublished writings of my Edward C. Dorsey, M.D.

common path. Also it seemed to require so much of my energy that there was not enough left over for ordinary human concern. It did not even seem to be human. Thus did I try to segregate the perfection of my (necessary) divinity from what I regarded as the imperfection of my (impossible) humanity.

In first unhesitatingly growing my personal thoughts and feelings of divinity I was unable to sense this self growth in terms of my self identity. In consequence, I ascribed all of my divinity meaning to a god that I called mine without realistically being able to appreciate that divinity as being all my own. My ability to overlook my own divinity in this way exercised a power that revealed what I was at pains to conceal, *since only divinity might affirm, ignore or negate divinity.*

In my hesitatingly developing all of my conscious self identity, by my virtue of laboriously disciplining my mind in acknowledgement of its own activity, most difficult of all is my redeeming every meaning of godliness to its true significance as being all and only my selfness. My pursuing greatest difficulty in restoring every meaning of my divinity to its rightful recognition as my own self identity is thoroughly understandable in view of my conscious necessity to conduct my life according to my estimate of its worth. I must choose whether to accept the awesome responsibility of being all of my own divine existence or assume the heavy guilt of disowning this natural responsibility.

Essential for honoring my wholeness, it is necessary for me to observe that my hesitatingly working up my willing appreciation for my own divinity, in no sense means that I am no longer capable of every thought and feeling with which I formerly maintained my unconsciousness for my divinity. I refer to my intolerant skepticism, cynicism, sophism, humor and the like defense against adding to my already nearly overwhelmed conscious personal identity. Quite the contrary, I can now insightfully appreciate the divine order in such helpful protest, seeing that resistance is the beginning of insistence. Furthermore I fully realize that my divinity-consciousness is the direct outgrowth of my divinity-unconsciousness. My conscious divinity enables me to live with love every kind of effort devoted to the honor and glory of omnipresent divinity.

The range in my appreciation for my self identity, from little to great, is traceable specifically to the variety of discipline I have volitionally put upon my mind. My ultimate devotion to cultivating my will to be able to sense and revere my identity in whatever I live, pleasing and unpleasing experience alike, engenders my comprehension for my organic wholeness. Resulting fervent faith in my own continent divinity opens my understanding for the functioning power of my spirituality.

The fact that so sublime a virtue as my wholeness *spirit* can be the ruling power in my life seems less far-fetched with my increasing experience of its goodness and greatness. The advantage I derive from learning the absolute truth of my spirited subjectivity gradually gives back to all of my soul activity (functioning wholeness) the full feeling of naturalness I formerly ascribed to my seemingly mechanistic conception of my life.

My nature is necessarily whole nature, but only my awareness for that absolute truth can necessitate my acknowledging my moral responsibility for the whole of the all of it. I am all of my seeing *and seen*, hearing *and heard*, sensing *and sensed*. Only this realization can liberate me from vast depersonalization in my own unacknowledgeable sensualism by honoring its (my sensualism's) true magnanimity as my acknowledgeable mentality. Honoring the presence of my wholeness in

169

my every act is my description of my good way of life indicating my sensing my power. My divine Emerson said attentively, "The bare fact of your existence as a man is one of such bewildering astonishment that it seems as if it were the part of reason to spend one's lifetime in a trance of Wonder,—altogether more rational to lift one's hands in blank amazement, than to assume the least shadow of dogmatism, of pride." Saint Augustine willed, "Let others wrangle, I will wonder."

Conscious innocence in my living, my most economical way of life, is directly associated with freedom of my mind's consciously functioning wholeness. It is both a responsibility and a relief to me to understand that there can be no one to need me but my self; my fellowman's self sufficiency, his individual excellence, is always present; all that can be lacking for anyone to be able to fully benefit from the grace of his own divinity is his awareness for its existence.

Everyone who consults his self as being his only possible consultant thereby divines his own gracious independence. I can be content only to use my mind to confer with my mind. This is the specific process through which I can discover my divinity as soon as I am ready to appreciate it. Unquestionably this work of liberation or redemption is most strenuous for it brings the wholeness of my mental strength into action. It is never fully done, for it lives hesitatingly in the doing.

It is a day of light when I wonder how my meaning for education could ever wander from its only accurate definition as my discovery of as much as possible of my own admirable life. My willing to own up to my full magnitude involves my willing to renounce lovingly each glorious advance of my development in order to make way for each succeeding one. Only by enforcing this tender renunciation, after fully revering each new growth of my being, can I uphold my lifeworthy ideal of

170

constantly putting on the new man, a process of continuously adjusting my conception of my self identity to fit my ever enlarging conscious wholeness.

My only alternative is to deny my new growth of self existence as being mine, to save my seemingly familiar face at the expense of my truthfully acknowledging my growing self identity first by sensing its strangeness as mine. Merely in the interest of feeling comfortable I can grow up with a diminishing sense of my magnitude, increasingly naming my own self experience not-I, the inelegant incognito I use whenever I deny that any of my living is wholly mine. Confirming faith arises from my clearly perceiving the subjectivity of the whole of my living. If I would consciously do my will, I must make my self aware of my wholeness, specifically of its extent. I note that this function of my psychology or moral science approximates that of my St. Thomas Aquinas (1225–1274): to aid man in discovering his true end and the means to fulfill it.

My only possible method for studying just how I work my mind ethically is specifically that of observing the nature of its creativity, *in statu nascendi*. My strictest scientific procedure for conducting this research is provided by the psychological process termed *free association,* first discovered and refined by my esteemed self analyst, Professor Sigmund Freud, M.D. His marvelous finding proved to be a lifesaving boon to the heroic professor's mankind. Briefly to describe how I now apply it, I purposefully arrange to speak aloud whatever my mind presents for conscious disposition, *without any reservation,* so that I can thus observe this verbalized stream of meaningful vitality, intently and at length, heeding what facilitates or inhibits my free mental functioning.[3]

[3]Now an easily available voice recording and play-back instrument provides very helpful assistance for this accomplishment.

Much of my Freud's genius found accelerating growth and expression as the immediate consequence of his practicing free association with full acceptance of the evidence of his mind revealed thereby. His honoring the importance of his mind as organic functioning of the meaning of his life led him to discover the truth of his *psychic reality,* the biological process enabling his self-weaning to his lovable wholeness, freedom, independence and ethical wisdom. His every self-analytic hour revealed his patient as living his mind largely in the only way he could bear to do so, that is, disguised as if not his own, e.g., as if it must involve some "other" person, or "external" things and events. Thus it became evident that for a person to recognize his own greatness with biological adequacy he must cultivate his self respect to embrace his whole being, to be able to acknowledge his inviolable wholeness as being his own all.

My applying the method of free association brings out not only how much of my own life's meaning I have not claimed as such but also the fact that I must try to disown any of my living for which I cannot presently assume complete responsibility. I cannot claim conscious responsibility for any of my living to which I seem to be subject, as if it might exert some alien control over me. Any of my experience that I can consciously control is obviously subject to me so that I feel that I must accept responsibility for being it. Joseph Joubert noted, "When we think what we do not *feel,* we lie to ourselves. We must always think with our whole being, soul and body." *(Pensêes).*

All of my waking life occurs along with my ever-present wish to sleep. Overlooking my self identity in any of my being awake arises from the momentary ascendancy of my need to sleep. Free association reveals extent of my mind under the order of sleep. The

172

order of whatever living is the law of it. So-called chance is unrecognized (unconscious) order largely accounting for obfuscation of omnipresent perfection.

My practice of free association reveals that I am all of my living that I associate with dislike (dissatisfaction in any form) quite as I am all of my living that I associate with approval (satisfaction in any form). By free associating I discover that my ability to "take sides" on any issue is based upon my ability to take all sides of it. The latter is the kind of consideration that fits the description, "capacity for taking pains," defined as genius by Georges Buffon (1707–1788).

My free associating upon my theme of divinity reveals that I, alone, create all that I can possibly mean by *divinity* and that, therefore, I do well to try my best to acknowledge all of my reference to divinity as my soulful self reference. Free association helps me to illuminate my mental life gradually without dazzling me. As with all else of my life's meaning so with my divinity feeling my self consciousness clears my mind of its extreme dependence upon its naiveté. I am certainly being naive when I deny that any of my own living, of whatever possible degree of wonderfulness, is my own mental offshoot. It is only my limited ability to feel my self continence that can vex or confuse me. Only my very wide-awake reader may respect this inconspicuous necessity:

The degree of any kind of aversion towards complete understanding of my very own divinity of course merely indicates the degree of my repression of my divinity.

I may trace the truth of my godhood directly to my willingly appreciating the godliness of my truth. Only my conscious necessity to be my God has made me acknowledgeably theistic. I am all and only my own proof of my God's existence. My experience of my world necessitates my immediately imagining it to be

173

my creation of my own divinity, quite as my mediately imagining my God's omnipotence assumes His creation of His Divinity.

Although my living creates all of my functioning, apart from the manifest display of such functioning my life itself remains imperceptible. Again, all of my doing is my being, nothing but manifestation of my organic growth, all of which (including my mental activity) grows unconsciously. Free association enables me to treat my unconscious mentation with consciousness. To secure my opinion on any subject I must first perceive my stating my mind upon it. Then if I allow my mind to state itself freely, I find that I can feel and think "every which way" about anything. Discovering I am able to produce many and varying opinions on any head, helps me to realize that my ever seeming against any viewpoint means my seeming against some of my own living of that viewpoint.

From my earliest psychoanalytic experience in free association I learned to expect the great extent to which my so-called lowly living was subject to my repudiation (repression). It hardly occurred to me to take my rejection of my personal, or so-called impersonal, divinity very seriously even, as far as its significance as most meaningful self dispossession (repression) might be concerned.

Only later, specifically as I grew able to appreciate my functioning as being my wholeness-functioning, did I gradually realize the enormous health consequence in my ignoring or even denying (repressing) the divinity of *all* of my living. Now I am aware that I am already trying to negate (repress) any of my experience from which I *must* presently withhold my divinity orientation.

I now gratefully heed that it is my repression of my divinity meaning alone that can be responsible for all

174

that I can mean by my so-called problem of evil, devil, sin, or whatever so-called undivine.

As Professor Freud explained in that mine of knowledge of the psychic, itself, *Jokes and their Relation to the Unconscious*,[4] since every moment of living is both new and unique, one's every experience biologically calls for a "kind of expenditure by our understanding." In the interest of pleasure it is only natural for my mind, seeking relief from effort, to avoid extra exertion by creating a seeming of familiarity where there can be only a reality of strangeness.

The extent to which I allow my illusion of familiarity to spare me the work of being wide awake to the incessant novelty of my living is too monstrous to behold all of a sudden. Hence it is, so-called classification, membership, similarity, imitation, memory, repetition, recognition, rhythm, oldness, and innumerable other implicit denials of the newness, wholeness and allness of individuality, hold strong appeal, especially when I am tired and sleepy.

The conscious subject of my expectation most difficult but most wholesome to uphold is that of furthering by enlarging the conscious unity of my growing individuality. However, all of my denial of the helpfulness of my pain (any unhappiness) is motivated by my wish to sleep. Hence it is that unconscious pain may constantly exist in my body ego, ever accessible for my consciousness whenever my mental wholeness requires it to be thus selected, e.g., as in my hypochondriacal mental condition. All of my general or local negativism amounts to my inhibited positivism only. Conscious self love, my ethic of ethics, is to say Yes to any of my painful living, however difficultly.

My Pierre Teilhard De Chardin (1881–1955),

---

[4]"Jokes And The Comic," pp. 208–216.

French Jesuit and scientist, recorded his profound understanding of the essential nature of wholeness, thus:

> Poet, philosopher, mystic—it is hardly possible to be one without being the others. In the great stream of past mankind, poets, philosophers, and mystics—the long procession of those who have been initiated into the vision and cult of the Whole—have left behind them a central wake which we can follow unmistakably from our own days right back to the most distant horizons of history. In one sense, therefore, we may say that a concern for the Whole is extremely ancient. It belongs to all ages.[5]

> My personality, that is, the particular centre of perceptions and love that my life consists in developing—it is that which is my real wealth. And in that, accordingly, lies the only value whose worth and whose preservation can call for and justify my effort. . . . We see, then, that this transmission of my self to the other is demanded both by the requirements of my action and by the successful fulfilment of the universe. How is it to be effected? Must I strip myself of what is "me" and give it to "him"? It would appear that we sometimes feel that such a gesture is possible; but we have only to reflect for a moment to realize that this is an illusion; and we shall then recognize that our personal qualities are not a flame from which we can cut ourselves off by handing it on to another. We thought, maybe, that we could divest ourselves of them, as we take off a coat and give it away. In fact, however, these qualities coincide with the substance of our being, for they are woven in their fibres by the consciousness we have of them.[6]

Only by practicing discipline of my mind with appreciation for its divine nature can I attain a biologically adequate standard of living and avoid the necessity for symptom formation helpfully revealing my neglecting my necessary greatness. Once I have sensed the value

[5]*Christianity and Evolution*, trans. Rene Hague (New York: Harcourt Brace Jovanovich, Inc., 1969), p. 60.
[6]Ibid., p. 116.

of my self in conducting my life in terms of my godliness, creating my whole world in my image and likeness, it continues to be difficult to maintain this most competent level of my functioning as a whole. Certainly it is understandable to me when my psychiatric patient finds it helpful to regard himself as god almighty. It remains for him to discipline his mind to recognize that his fellowman, and whatever he lives, is identically divine, whether or not his fellowman may be willing to consider his nature in this most exacting way.

I cannot fully believe in the existence of any of my experience in which I cannot feel convinced of my own self identity. Thus, before becoming able to acknowledge that all of my meaning for divinity must belong entirely to me, my faith in its essence tended to be expressed as doubt, skepticism, humor or otherwise beyond my thorough comprehension. Not being able to call my soul my own I seemed to represent each religiously wayward type abhorred by my Mohammed, "the learned in his infidelities, and the fool in his devotions." Not until I began extending my conscious self identity sufficiently to indicate growing appreciation for its immeasurable magnitude could I even make the effort to originate as my own the biologically adequate self reverence recorded by my Ralph Waldo Emerson, to wit,[7]

> That which is signified by the words "moral" and "spiritual," is a lasting essence. . . . I know no words that mean so much. In our definitions, we grope after the *spiritual* by describing it as invisible. The true meaning of *spiritual* is *real;* that law which executes itself, which works without means, and which cannot be conceived as not existing.

I am most grateful to my self for my discovering,

[7]"Worship," *The Conduct of Life* (Boston: Ticknor and Fields, 1860), p. 133.

then accepting and ultimately living only with love this principle: Whatever happens is the product of sufficient truth to require its happening. With that self helpfulness, as never before, I realized that the universal nature of my world works for truthful right forever.

My Latin proverb contains whole-making sense, "As much love, so much mind." I thrill with the truth in my Emerson's verses,

> This is Jove, who, deaf to prayers,
> Floods with blessings unawares.
> Draw, if thou canst, the mystic line,
> Severing rightly his from thine,
> Which is human, which divine.

I must reckon with the fact that the meaning I have ever consciously attributed to my life may have *never* corresponded with its marvelous worth. This vast disparity I can trace directly to my inability to claim all of my experience as being entirely the product of my self contained living.

My limited self understanding has led me to depreciate the indescribable value of the wonderful biological creature I really am. Thus, life may even seem to be cheap. To illustrate, all of my pain, including unhappiness of any kind, is absolutely essential for my welfare. It consists entirely of biological wisdom indispensable for my preserving my life as well as for cultivating lifesaving hardihood and endurance. However, until I discover this truth for my self I may even use all such divinely ordained functioning of unpleasure disdainfully as a reason for not wanting to live.

Glorious enlargement of my power to appreciate my divine life accompanies every access of my conscious self identity. Certainly my strengthening and creating my recognizable mind anew, by striving to be sure of my identity in any and all of my experience, encountered its most arduous effort in my trying to live and love all of my divinity as my self divinity. Lively mindedness! Now I am beginning to understand that I cannot observe my divinity in any of my experience except insofar as I am aware of the fact that it is my divinity that creates that experience. *Only divinity can beget divinity.* Acknowledging my divinity, I am not afraid to die; rejecting my divinity, I am afraid to live.

There is no such possibility as my working together with my fellowman. Only my cultivating my consciousness for the truth that I *am* all that I can mean by my fellowman enables me to feel that I am all together one, capable of living my self as one all together. Disciplining my mind with conscious self identity reveals as my united selfness all that I can mean by society, politics, religion, or whatever name I may be using for whatever living of mine I cannot otherwise claim as being my own.

I can never feel consciously at peace until I can recognize that every kind of conflict is the consequence of my being unconsciously at peace. I can never feel at one with my self consciously until I can recognize that my feeling of being at sixes-and-sevens with my self is a manifestation of my living my oneness unconsciously. I reach my whole individuality consciously when I recognize that I cannot exist as separate from it. Whatever I suffer as interference with my finding my self is my unconsciousness for the truth that there is nothing else for me to find.

All that I can mean by my religion is my discovery of my functioning divinity. In his book, *Greek Philosophy,* John Burnet recorded: "Greek philosophy is based on the faith that reality is divine, and that the one thing needful is for the soul, which is akin to the divine, to enter into communion with it. It was in truth an effort to satisfy what we call the religious instinct." By "communion" I can mean only presence of consciousness for my own unity. I feel in my right mind when I define church or temple as a construct I build up in my own soul for the purpose of discovering and exercising my divinity.

It is my greatening self consciousness that enables me to appreciate that I am the servant of my all, quite as I am the master of it. It is my self consciousness that enables my love to function throughout my being wherever self consciousness obtains. Any man could claim for his life this fitting dignity, this saving grace, if only he could express loving acceptance of all of the truth that he has lived through (saved his life with). My illusional opposites such as sacred or profane, right or wrong, good or evil, as well as similar dualities, arise from lack of understanding of consciousness and unconsciousness as being essential for their formation.

Here another opportunity offers to strengthen with exercise my life-begetting rather than life-forgetting principle: When I am not conscious for enough truth to account to my complete satisfaction for the occurrence of any happening, then I am apt to conclude that such an event is bad or undesirable. However, when I arduously extend my self consciousness to include my painful or unhappy feelings associated with events *as being indispensably helpful,* then ultimately I find it possible to make my peace with whatever happens, even to the extent of recognizing it as divinely ordained in my living. As I grow my understanding for the biological adequacy of all pain or unhappiness, I then begin to realize that good and evil, instead of ruling each other out, rule each other in. It is helpful for me to be able to feel unhappy or painful with whatever experience I live, until my growing further knowledge of the fact about it gradually reveals its lifesaving goodness.

And now I come to a most helpful conception, one which can go far to relieve my self, including my fellow-man, from subjection to mental distress. My understanding of the nature of my growing mind is furthered by my realization of the necessity for *carefully* strengthening various ways of its functioning, by exercising that functioning. I use this illustration: as a growing child my back can support only a certain weight. The weight of self knowledge bears heavily upon my soul, also, so that I must be careful not to subject my mind to too much strain. Of all of my experience, my conscious self knowledge is the most difficult to sustain in its great extension. My consciousness for my self knowledge makes me conscientious about it, and my feeling of self responsibility for it can be very weighty indeed. Well it is for me that my growth of self consciousness depends upon my growth of self love enabling me to care about whatever happens in any of my living that I can recognize as being my own.

From the above description it now becomes evident that I cannot seem to depend upon my own consciously internal control for guiding my self during my first years of my life. I cannot distinctify my not-I until I distinctify my I living. After the latter starts to develop it must gradually seem to *me* that I need a form of control that I cannot even recognize as being my own in order to take safe care of my self. *Certainly this alternative source of control, my parent, is also internal but not recognized by me as being in and of me.* To complicate the issue further, my parent as a rule may not recognize all of his own so-called controlling and controlled behavior to be entirely within his own mind.

Most valuable parental insight would consist of my parent's recognizing that he is all of his own living of his child, and that his child too is all of his own soulful living. The biological truth is that the child cannot even

181

see, hear, or touch his parent despite appearance to the contrary, any more than the parent can ever be able to see, hear; or touch his child. All sensory living pertains only to the senser.

The parent who can sufficiently respect the integrity of his own individuality can recognize the fact that when he speaks a warning it is all self-contained on his part. All that can happen at that moment in his child is that his child grows the auditory experience of hearing (what he ultimately grows to call) his parent speaking warningly to himself.

It is understandable how the illusion of alien control, including suggestion, communication, hypnosis or the like "exchange," derives from the following early necessity of the growing child. In the beginning of his mentality he must create in his own living whatever he calls his parent without being able to recognize that such is his own momentary arrangement within his mind. His seemingly overwhelming need to refer to what must be internal control, as if it might be external control, is most costly in terms of each individual's developing his full appreciation for the wholeness and allness of his individual nature. The enormous cost in terms of human happiness is immeasurable.

One of the most disastrous results of such living (as if I could be outside of my own mind or self) is my necessity to attribute my own power somewhere in my own life which I cannot recognize as my own life. This way of living results in my augmenting my unconscious at the cost of my not augmenting my conscious self power. Certainly the practice of this kind of effort at self depersonalization is a way of life that interferes most with my recognizing my own divinity, or with my even claiming the right to behave my self insightfully.

The positive conception of my ethic now becomes evident: Whatever is, is ethical, ethically is. I make haste to add: but nearly all is rarely recognized as being really ethical. The so-called "highest" good of man is realized by his recognition, study, and practice of his highest function, namely, his self consciousness. Only his disciplining his mind in devotion to his power and glory of self consciousness *can* enable him to conduct his life *according to his nature*. Spinoza recorded, "Virtue is nothing but action in accordance with one's own nature; and there is nothing which excels it in dignity and worth."

Only he who has learned that he has but one possibility, namely, to mind his own business, can avoid trying to help himself by his tempting notion of otherness. My experiencing is my living, including my becoming my living. Becoming is also being. My love for my enemy or for my neighbor becomes my reality as I experience it responsibly, living it as recognizable self activity which I create consciously as ever self helpful merely in that I live through it.

Seldom do I realize either that conscious self development is my birthright or that I must grow my self selfishly in its most extreme sense in order to become my ideal self. Rather I gradually accustom my self to the rather hopeless view that I was born the way I am, and can do absolutely nothing about it except perhaps to try to make my self seem good, as I am. I then turn against my own precious selfishness, misprize it, and strive for the mere appearance of conscious unselfishness (compensating for my self-disesteem-reality by relying upon my social-approval-illusion).

Yes, my *growing* up does include learning to enlarge my sense of selfishness to correspond with and contain my ever augmenting self experience in the form of *my* fellowman. Yes, it does *seem* as if I get rid of my narrow selfishness when I responsibly assume a selfhood in due keeping with my man's estate. However, grown up selfishness (usually called altruism) is based upon and includes as indispensable helpfulness all of the stages of narrower selfishness preceding it. Otherwise it would be impossible for my enlightened and enlarged self even to grow, much less appreciate understandingly, any extension of selfishness less than my latest developed one. A grown-up is not a whole person minus all of his less grown-up stages of development, but is consistible with each of them. My learning how to walk does not mean I can no longer crawl or merely wriggle my big toe. Once more I strengthen this truth by exercising it, as follows.

The point is that my solipsistic word "selfish," more than any other, connotes due *appreciation* for self. Resistance to its wholeness meaning reveals the life value in redeeming it for conscious helpfulness. It bespeaks man's only possible mental condition: conscious and unconscious self devotion serving self helpfulness. Only self positing selfishness is possible and desirable; self affirming unselfishness is impossible and undesirable except as an indispensable illusional expedient. Protecting my narrow selfishness is only self defense against overwhelming my unprepared mind with responsibility for life experience I have not yet learned to consider understandingly as being entirely my own living. Such overwhelming, known as *mental trauma,* is presently incompatible with conscious self care.

Yes, the term *selfishness,* like solipsism, carries a pejorative meaning and therefore must seem objectionable. However, every pejorative term carries the force of repression (negation) in it, and therefore must be carefully considered from this viewpoint. *Prohibition of consciousness for any mental element serves to emphasize that element's forceful mental influence.* To label as undesirable this word *selfishness* which connotes a pure culture of my human individuality, is diametrically to

184

oppose my ground ideal of human welfare, namely, appreciation for the sovereign subjectivity of human individuality. Therefore, preferred and persevering usage of this particular word *selfishness* to express *divine humaneness,* is not only entirely justified but also thoroughly desirable and specifically helpful. *I can measure its potential helpfulness by the degree of resistance I sense against honoring it.*

As always happens in my experience, it is my rejected living that eventually proves to contain the very existent needed for my work. Thus, much of my longed-for helpfulness has been inaccessible by virtue of my pejorating my meaning for the term *selfishness.* It is sanative to be able to learn that every pejorative is a term standing for helpful faultfinding. Whatever is, sufficiently is, perfectly and desirably is.

Learning how to realize that any and all of my disparagement *must* amount to my unconsciously attempting my own self detraction is essential for my being able to renounce fondly my reliance upon my indulgence of self depreciation occurring in every form of pejoration. Hardest of all is my learning the lesson of how to observe my every kind and degree of pain or dissatisfaction as being most desirable rather than as in any respect undesirable. My finding how to see my self helpfulness in any and all of my living, *happy or unhappy,* has been most difficult but most rewarding intentional self education. As that mind-observant auto-didact Pestalozzi indicated, knowledge can occur only in and about the knowledgeable individual. He added, "Of all petty tyrants the worst are school tyrants." My unconsciously self tyrannical school-master helps himself by his indirect and unrecognized kind of self control in the form of seeming control of his pupil.

My mystery of divine providential government of man is solved completely by my thorough under-

standing of the role of factuality (truth) in human experience. Reverence for the force of fact is wholesouled service of one's godly power. It is *evidently* godly to work one's perfection consciously. Presumably only man can discipline his mind to appreciate that the factors constituting his behavior sufficiently account for its perfection. I am infallible and indefectible. Every creature is the product of its own living, but uniquely the human creature can learn to recognize that only he can make himself perfectly this way or perfectly that way or perfectly some other way. As the range of his self consciousness varies so directly does the amount or degree of his deliberate, purposeful shaping of his life.

The only *possible* worldly prosperity for me is that of my own individual world, there being no other for me. Where respect for this fact (that all observation is self observation) prevails, it is possible for so-called selfishness to become recognizable as unmistakable godliness. Advance in learning that my subjectivity *is* my all, attests unquestionable growth of my consciously autonomous whole nature. *Persevering conscious effort to extend the degree and range of my self consciousness (self analysis) is the height of my human endeavor, the ultimate in ethical discipline of my individual mind. The distinction is mighty: self consciousness is not at all the same as conscious self consciousness.*

The helpful self experience, *I am,* also may be used to reinforce my illusion that I appear to be as something given, inevitable, incapable of becoming my ideal self, unable to learn how to live purposeful self development, impotent except for trying to make the appearance of my presenting self look good to my fellowman. This self-belittling illusion may be favored by the self observation that my formal education has never awakened my appreciation for the wholeness and allness of my individuality, but rather has led me to recognizing less

186

and less in my self, but more and more of a world *seemingly* external to me.

The evident fact is that my observation *I am* is always currently made a conscious individuation of my conscious individuality. However, even though "I am" may be intended to mean "All that I am," it may be not so intended, also. Thus, "I am all that I am pleased (or hating, or able, or whatever) to consider that I am." "I am," the present tense, refers to now. It retains the truth: Whatever *is,* is perfectly perfect. The studious "I am" who is right now, however, may also refer to the kind of "I am" that I would like to become, if I difficultly learn how to own up to my experience that must create that becoming. This actual fact that I really can literally grow up to be able to claim all of my actual self possession if I will take the trouble to learn how to study this life-lesson (of *acknowledging* self fulfillment), is the acknowledged self educator's most valuable learning. He proudly calls it: Learning how to learn.

To my question, "What do I want to make out of my self?" comes its positive and definite reply, "All that I am, all that I can become." The condition for gradually attaining this goal is my recognizable self development enabling me to appreciate *all* of my living as perfect. Again, it is not my instinct or primitive power which is in any way undesirable. It is only my unreadiness to observe the innate helpfulness of any of my vital energy that motivates me to misprize my life's uncultivated power. Wholesome sublimation is not based upon a faultfinding attitude towards my original nature, but rather upon a factfinding orientation for it that reveals it too as sublime.

Recently I asked myself to write down additional basic views on my life derived from my scientific method of *self observation* termed free association. This is what I wrote: I regard greatest ethical wisdom of mine

187

to be the product of my becoming sufficiently self insightful to discern my already existing, but previously
misprized, ethical wisdom. Thus my intentional self observation has been most enlivening for it consists of my
concentrating upon discovering the already present
truth (perfection) in my being.

Although I enjoyed the intimation before that I was
not allowing my already grown self knowledge to function adequately, it was during my self analysis with my
Professor Freud that the abiding consequential truth of
this self insight found its due importance. To my expressed wish for further self knowledge he merely observed, "But you already have so much," leaving entirely to my own imagining, "So much that I do not yet
sufficiently know how to use."

My consciousness for making (growing) all of my
own experience of any kind, is my unfailing source for
life appreciation. My will to live consciously *is* my will
to conscious self power. My love of life can be expressible only in my self love. My name for the ultimate
element of my human nature, hence of my world, is my
wholeness (subjectivity).

My discovery that whatever is, *truly* is, has helped
me to observe that whatever is, *ought to be*. With this
reverence for truth I can finally understand every claim
to the contrary, such as: "You ought not behave as you
do," or "You ought to conduct yourself otherwise,"
etc., as an instance of my allowing my inherent omnipotence to function irresponsibly (unconsciously).

This growth of my ethical insight has proved most
beneficial for my clearing up my unpleasing connotation
of sin, my considering the occurrence of sin as if it
ought not be. I can now appreciate my painful feeling of
sin (guilt) as being a most helpful ethical sign or symptom revealing that my conduct arousing my sinful feeling is not temporarily contributing to the ultimate in-

188

terest of my whole self, namely, to my freely function-ing *consciousness* for the wonderful wholeness of my self. The meaning named sin has proved to be helpful to my religious worker as designating his personal act, omission, or attitude that imperils his appreciation for his divine wholeness or holiness. Thus, apostle Paul found that whatever did not come from his faith in his divinity was sinful.

By carefully consulting the truth fully accounting for my sinning I can find not only how I came to exper-ience it but also I may teach my self to use it to build my conscious self identity in the interest of my revered wholeness, its allness. For example, my freedom from sin is an outgrowth of my sinning itself, — not dis-connected from it. My sinning consists of my estranging some of my living from all of my being in which I can fully recognize my innocent unity or wholeness. By redeeming such estranged selfness I succeed in aug-menting my conscious wholeness. The consequent manumission of involitional painful guilt to volitional pleasing innocence is duly felt as a life-affirming event. *Any unfaith in the divinity of my own being must reveal itself in corresponding limitation of my ability to con-ceive my god as all god.* My devotion to my ethic presupposes this kind of consciousness for whole mind-edness.

My complete conception of moral turpitude reveals that it is clearly an issue of faultfinding. Here I gladly exercise my ethical principle that faultfinding is the helpful form perfection-finding takes when insufficient truth is accessible to attest the existence of ever-present perfection. My respectable philosophy that holds crime to be a disease can round out its respectability by hold-ing that any disease, whenever it occurs, is the helpful form that my health takes in my struggling for life.

There is no possible way for me to come to terms

189

with the reality of my perfection, or the perfection of my reality, as an individual, so long as I refuse to honor the whole truth of my existence, but stick to helping my self laxly by indulging my insufficiently examined prejudices. Self tolerance or self intolerance can often prove a most trying choice, but the act most distinctively moral is that of honoring each human necessity, that is, all of human nature, as self-helpful. Divine living, no matter what form it takes, is self helpfulness.

What can be certainly stated about guilt, including its thinly disguised form of accusation, is that it is entirely and only about itself. Despite appearance, it is its only object, subject, predicate or whatever. Only guilt itself can be guilty or guiltful. The same strict localization applies to the whole meaning of every other emotion; each one occurs and completes its course and force wholly in itself.[8]

Excitation of emotion demonstrates the functioning of wholeness. Each feeling seems to steep the whole mind in its mood. Each specific form that unpleasure can take accounts for the seeming variety of emotions of unhappy kind. My every unhappy (painful) feeling appropriate for the occasion occurs whenever I am unable to live freely with love whatever I am creating, (i.e., whatever self experience is happening). Thus, whenever I feel guilty, it is always within my innocence which is not being able to freely function; whenever I feel angry, it is always within my love that is not being able to freely function; etc. All of my illusion that my feeling can involve more or less than itself derives from my disregarding its unique individuality.

I like to strengthen by disciplined exercise my realization that the method I am pursuing in my research upon my ethic is conscious self observation about my absolutely continent wholeness. Everyone or everything

[8]See my *Psychology of Emotion,* first chapter, "Perspective," pp. 1–17.

is wholly *its* own everyone or everything. Ever anew, although I am wholly my self, creating my every experience in my living of it, nevertheless I may or may not be adequately *aware* that I am all that I can live. Yet this conscious self measure is required for me to be able to do my self justice in the sense of attributing to my self what is wholly mine. Furthermore, to my every person must belong any merit of elucidating his concept of his own natural being, namely, that of inviolable wholeness.

Whenever I focus my attention upon any specific aspect of my being, e.g., my so-called body or so-called external world, it is essential that I heed each aspect as consisting of nothing but the wonderwork of my wholeness. Otherwise I shall be using my creative wholeness to produce what does not seem to be its own creating. Such rejected autonomous wholeness then naturally proceeds to set up its own autonomy, which must *appear* to me to be an antinomy with regard to the autonomy of my acknowledgeable wholeness. In my studied opinion, it is this all too regular method of my observation that accounts for my illusion fearfully called "conflict" and my depersonalized living terrifyingly called "cancer."

My whole life is necessarily whole-life-begetting but if I disregard its completely autogenetic nature I thereby introduce living of my own in which I cannot sense or feel my own identity. *It seems obvious to me that this process of dissociating my mentality into I and not-I divisions, technically termed "repression," is the proton pseudos responsible for all of my so-called health trouble for which I cannot consciously assume due responsibility, such as so-called cancer, mental disorder, crime.*

What passes for transaction, cooperation, or mutual help in my life is wholly the biological functioning of my self identity. I want my fellowman to help himself for I can recognize (my) he is *my* living. I do not want my so-called enemy to help himself if I am unable to recognize (my) he too is entirely *my* own living. My life experience consists of creative self synthesis, a generic process of self-activity constantly integrating each successive wholeness of my *present* unity, there *being* no *past*.

In the sense that I may define my ethic as my scientific (psychological) treatment of my morality, my conduct based upon my free choice, my independent will becomes featured as my marvelous agent. After discovering the genetic role of will in my ethical being I find that my definition of will in terms of my conscious self identity no longer suffices to circumscribe my whole responsibility. Certainly my *unconscious will* enters into my determination of my behavior also.

My responsibility for whatever I live originates in the foremost truth that I am the *only* living of it. My only choice is a hard one, too hard even to consider as a rule. I must either live whatever I live or end my living. Therefore in my unconscious will I must include my *will to live,* itself.

Obviously it benefits my health to extend my concept of my conscious self identity to include all that I am accustomed to consider not-I, external to me, or in any way different from me like any tumor or traitor. This process of awakening to my true magnificence cannot occur at the cost of my depreciating any other way in which I have been able to consider my self, but rather must be an outgrowth of that lifesaving resort. I save my life by living oppressed health or holiness whenever I do live it. That means that without such trying exertion, as my so-called illness or sin, whenever it is lived, my only recourse would be to die.[9]

Not until as a growing mind I become aware of my

[9]See my *Illness or Allness,* "Developmental Psychology," pp. 326-398.

192

self as wholly individual and begin to look *in* on all of my life upon my subjectivity can I earnestly start finding my best interest and consult it for regulating my behavior, instead of seeming to be ruled by alien power I may call a bad conscience. However, once my mental activity can get on the track of itself, through experiencing itself, then like Ezekiel's my new sense of individual responsibility can become strong. By resort to my touchstone for truth, my self consciousness, I can resolve the apparent plurality and personification in each cherished view such as family, school, state, etc. My constitution itself seems inconceivable apart from the grace of my awareness for my provident self as divinity incarnate.

My psychology of ethics is a biological science dealing with the nature of the motivation, or will, with which I direct my spending of my entire psychical life. I may not be accustomed to measuring value of experience in terms of heart beats, that is, in terms of realization that I am laying down my life for it. *However, the basic cost of whatever I live is in the amount of my living it.* Most of this lifelike, all-important, conscientious cost-accounting for my self may be ordinarily disregarded by me, as taken for granted, but in that event I am staying alive by unwittingly squandering my only possession as a spendthrift.

Georges Cuvier pointed out, "The first question in science is always a question of method." It is my systematic devotion to the *whole* truth of each that unifies my scientific and religious living. It is only my devotion to a divisive method of study, thus losing track of the wholeness of my subject in my investigation of some certain aspect of it, that seems to disunite my scientific and religious living. When as a scientist I know that all of the truth required to bring about a wished-for consequence will certainly produce it, then I can understand my religious statement, "God's will be done," as I do my scientific claim, "Study of all of the data to be found in an event fully accounts for its occurrence."

The seeming paradox is frequently cited that an individual *can* prize his life most highly and defend it most fiercely with only a narrow minded concept of the scope of his own personal stake in his fellowman's welfare. Certainly I can prize and fiercely defend whatever extent of my life I can acknowledge being, however restricted my recognized personal identity may be. Seemingly I may even seem to worship it the more, the less there is consciously left of it. All well and good. The fact remains that *I cannot take due care of any of the living of mine that I cannot consciously identify as mine.* Rather I must conduct such overlooked existence of mine just as if I am anaesthetic to whatever may happen to it. Really I can never part company with any of my observed self-world.

All of my symptoms and signs of health trouble helpfully signalize some dangerous neglect of the truth of my self *wholeness*. But I may tend to regard these troublesome indications of my own ignored living (of mostly my meaning for my fellowman) as being foreign to me, as alien attacks, spells, or the like. *It is my restricted recognition of my self identity that I consider my (including my everyone's) most grievous public health concern, — all the more so on account of the great difficulty with which it can be evaluated as most awful health disturbance by my earnest public health official.*

Ever since I solemnly willed loving consciousness for my wholeness to be my choice way of life I have industriously tried to attest 1) the necessary difficulty in being consciously self conscious encountered from the beginning of my life course and 2) the rewarding consequence to my whole world in my maintaining the

194

specific lifesaving ethic of reverence for whole individuality, derivable only from consciously self responsible conduct.[10] I know of no poverty so deprivable as any conscious impoverishment of my so-called inner life, my only acknowledgeable soul-life. My one immorality, involving self repudiation, endangers my nature itself for it amounts to attempted dereliction of my organic form, namely, my inviolable wholeness that reveals my pacific gentleness as my revered ethical feeling.

It helps me to consider heedfully my limited ability as a man to honor *all* that is woman as being entirely my own living, and the converse; as a child to honor all that is adult as being entirely my own living, and the converse; as an ethical one to honor all that is unethical as being entirely my own living, and the converse; as a black to honor all that is white as being entirely my own living, and the converse; as a Moslem to honor all that is Jewish or of whatever faith as being entirely my own living, and the converse; as a spirited idealist to honor all that is spirited materialist as being entirely my own living, and the converse; and so on, also through every possible disregard for my wholeness-insight that is absolutely indispensable for my understanding of the meaning of justice.

It is my *practicing* my devotion to the functioning of my wholeness that develops and directs my biologically adequate feeling of absolute dependence upon my provident self. The mine of my nature is my reliable source of reverence for my life, of my honoring my self preservation and self fulfillment as my divine duty or command. My faith in my religion is: my belief in the divine nature of my whole being.

While growing up, a trial of my existence is that of

[10]See my *Illness or Allness,* pp. 100–103.

seeming "forced to give my reasons for behaving as I do." A true accounting for any of my apparent short-coming would involve me in lifelong exposition. For sure, I rarely if ever lack adequate feeling of justification for my conduct, until I challenge my self to account for it in my accusation clearly implying that my action is improper, unmannerly, blameworthy, etc., to begin with. Thus cornered, I may attempt to stand my ground by resorting to whatever reasonable explication may occur to me. Then I may find particularly trying this logic *apparently* addressed to me, "Now you are making excuses, and you are good at that," "A poor excuse is better than none," or "I am not interested in your lame excuses."

It is my self consciousness alone that saves me from driving my self mad by my divisive reasoning. With self consciousness only I can command my self love which is the wonderful power that discovers and releases the true order in seeming disorder.

My study of the source of creation of the mental event called "truth" indicates that it is a feeling of commanding certitude I can identify as a form of my self consciousness, — surely not a product of my reasoning. It is clearly a subjective process free of the illusion of objectivity indulged in my judging or reasoning. Its presence or absence constitutes the distinction respectively in one who speaks with authority or as a scribe.

As the scope of my self consciousness extends so does my conviction that I must be my own sole authority. Feeling, willing, sensing, perceiving and knowing, with clear consciousness for my every meaning as being my mind's self-activity, distinguishes my divine reverence from my so-called human consciousness that does not include such acknowledgeable self continence.

If I can view any consideration insightlessly from but only one coign of vantage it is then a sure sign that I am living it as if I am subject to it rather than as its being subject to me. For instance, in any discussion it is essential that I feel that I am whomever I call my fellow discussant quite as I feel that I am all else that I call my self. I can make any idea or feeling seem to be able to take me over merely by overlooking that I am the only possible one producing it. I mind dearly this truth of my wholeness for clearly my conscious self control is at stake.

SUMMARY

Our eating, trading, marrying, and learning are mistaken by us for ends and realities, whilst they are properly symbols only; when we have come, by a divine leading, into the inner firmament, we are apprised of the unreality or representative character of what we esteemed final.

Ralph Waldo Emerson

My recognition that I am the whole of all that I experience, provides my only satisfactory explanation of all that I can mean by my ethical resourcefulness. Wholeness of my individuality is the first law of my nature. Obedience to this law is the source of all of my ethical helpfulness. Disobedience to this law is the origin of my resorting to dependence upon helping my self in ways that I cannot recognize as my self help. Little wonder that my divine Plato observed, "For love is the desire of the whole, and the pursuit of the whole is called love." *The basic ethic of my life involves my venerating the wonderfulness of the LIFE that achieves the work.*

My recognition of, and continuing research upon, the truth that I *am* all of whatever I live, especially all of my meaning for my fellowman, has led me to my life-saving discovery that *the health of my fellowman is a necessary health concern of mine.* My health thrives or suffers when his health thrives or suffers. I am animated with love for my whole self and it is to my self interest to understand that he is animated with love for his whole self. I am my own only end and cannot be a means to my fellowman, and it is to my self interest that (my) he discover that he is his own only end and cannot be a means to his fellowman.

The Whence and Whither of human existence can become the main problem of my life unless I recognize the illusional nature of time and space by discovering the only temporal and spatial reality of my existence in my now-and-here living. I define my ethic much as I do my religion, namely, as the issue of my conviction with regard to my need to live reverently the eternity of my now and the infinity of my here. Ever with this life perspective can I sense the identity of 1) my earliest instinctive discoveries and 2) my present research or being of any kind. Otherwise by far most of my self discovery (my life experience) must seem shrouded in mystery.

It is the succession or flow of each here and now of my vital presence that provides me with the conception of my permanent continuance. I can imagine my being, by using my being to do it. I cannot imagine my not-being, for I possess no not-being with which to do it. It is my augmenting wholeness that constitutes the sameness in my life course.

When I first began using free association for my self analysis I imagined that it would help me most by increasing my self knowledge rather than by increasing my awareness for my limited ability to use competently the already vast self knowledge my living had already amassed. It was like a rebirth to discover that all of my mental trouble is due to my biologically inadequate understanding of how to appreciate the seemingly limitless and marvelous self knowledge that I already possess.

In my mental functioning, however magnificent it may seem, all of the wonderful detail of the vital process enabling my creating my mental display remains unheeded, so that I may find no possible way of adequately admiring any of the truly astonishing power of my mental *life,* as such. My thinking, feeling, observing, or whatever mental activity, may occur without seeming to provide me with any of the truth even about where, much less how, it is taking place.

Hence it is, my concept of my self identity may be most misleading as far as providing me with appreciation for the true magnitude of my *life* is concerned. I am asleep to the extent that I cannot recognize my own self identity in any of my mental activity.

My observation is thoroughly scientific when I can acknowledge it as my living observation of and by my own mind. For example, my continuous scientific self analysis is needed to reveal the boundless providence of my mental functioning as being subjective, original, individual or selfful, independent, instinctive, self contained, organized, active, sentient, integrated, linguistic, uncommunicative, diremptive, apperceptive, sequential, dirigible, fluctuant, the only source and course of whatever I can mean, imaginative, wishful, feelingful, creative, developable, novel, autonomous, immeasurably great or powerful, peaceful, free, lifesaving, enjoyable, absolute, loving, personal, responsible, real, *unconscious and conscious theistic living of my wholeness.*

I have come to understand how sturdily recognizing whatever strangeness I live as being my self must be the so-called losing of life that must save it. Whatever is, wholly is. My natural awareness for my natural wholeness certainly enables my recognizing the scientific or religious naturalness of all I can mean by my word *divinity.* Beyond doubt, I cannot consider anything as being alien to me without impairing my appreciation for that much of my wholeness.

201

It helps me to be able to feel absolutely sure that hatred of the most hateful kind and degree cannot be anything other than love undergoing the tremendous struggle to which it is equal.[1] Similarly, it helps me to feel all certitude for the truth that the most terrifying fear can be nothing but love struggling for its preservation. It is a wonderful feeling with which I can renounce my concept of any heaven other than my often unrecognizable heaven that I call earth. I recognize the peace that passeth all understanding as being the *difficultly lovable* peace that subsumes painful war, crime, illness, or hurt love of any other kind.

I am teaching my self to renounce lovingly each word in my vocabulary that bespeaks plurality and depersonalization rather than my unity and my self awareness. Only by consciously honoring the wholeness of my existence can I be thoroughly interested in what is happening to my neighbor or heart or back or eye. I can learn to use the word *physical* so that it does not imply merely the illusional duality physical-and-mental. I can learn to use the word *spirit* so that it does not imply merely the illusional duality spiritual-and-material. Similarly, I can live whole Man as constituting his God. I can even use my word *vegetable* or *stone* as constituting vitality of divinity.[2] It is life satisfying to understand unified identity in my revelation-and-mystery, black-and-white, Christian-and-Jew, universal-and-individual, seeming-and-being, and every other so-called difference, however minute.

It is always pleasing to me to see my self only and entirely helping my self in every way it presently can, for I am sure *that* is constantly the true accounting for

---

[1]See my *Psychology of Emotion,* Chapter III, "My Theory of Emotion," pp. 85–137.
[2]See my *Psychology of Language,* Chapter III, p. 39.

all of everyone's living, at any given moment. When I am tempted to engage in any so-called difference of opinion it is a tremendous benefit to be able to realize that every difference is an illusion. My awareness that I am all and only about my self spares me a great deal of trouble. Surely everything *must* be all of its own everything.

It is a blessing of my Providence that allows me to remain unconscious for any of my living which I am presently unprepared to identify as being all and only mine. I feel fortunate to be able to disown awareness for any of my experience that I may not recognize as immediately self helpful. I live a wonderful life, with my protective spirit guarding me from calling my soul my own whenever I cannot recognize my Providence in that consciously soulful experience. I am indeed a marvelous work, whether I am working consciously or unconsciously.

Into this one meaning, my self wholeness, I condense all of my capacity for my self activity, that is, for my functioning of any kind. I live and learn only by being my complete self. In his profound work, *Komik und Humor*, psychologist Theodor Lipps, most esteemed by my Sigmund Freud, recorded much the same kind of appreciation for the wholeness-nature of mentality, "Finally, specific psychological problems always lead fairly deep into psychology, so that at bottom no psychological problem can be treated in isolation."[3] By "wholeness function" I may refer to any one power of individuality, as to all of it throughout its constitution.

It is the immeasurable magnitude of my own constitution, my organic make-up, that necessitates corresponding exertion for my understanding how to conduct my life according to its inestimable worth. Whenever I

3 1898, p. 71.

stop distracting my self from this indispensable source of life guidance, long enough to include again the wonderfulness of my being in my life consideration, I do not even expect my understanding of how to direct my life to be of easy access. Rather I begin to realize not only that my learning just how to live my life well is properly my leading lifelong concern but also that I must be willing to train my self both as an athlete and a scholar in order to honor adequately the self-evident truth that my life must be as difficult to manage competently as it is great in its constitution.

The significance of wholeness of individual life cannot be appreciated too much since full appreciation for it rules out the possibility of alien influence or foreign invasion of any kind, quite as it rules in the necessity for absolutely autonomous self continence whether recognized as such or not. Furthermore there is no other way of minding my life that can provide me with each of these lifesaving insights.

The entire gist of the self helpfulness in my heeding the unity of my health-and-ethic lies in that it appeals to my love of truth quite as it activates otherwise dormant truth of love. All of my seeing and heeding the absolute unity or wholeness of all that I call my mind makes me witness the beneficent working of the whole of whatever I experience, such as my meaning for my fellowman. It is only when I bypass consideration for my mental continence and inviolability that I witness the helpful sign and symptom of my wayward living, that is my indulging my illusion that I can divorce any living of my all embracing wholeness from itself.

It is my consciously honoring the truth that I am all of my self, that I am *wholly* I and nothing but I, that has helped me to realize that all of my behavior, including all of my functioning, is *grown* by me. My creativity is nothing but my growing whatever I create, and my wholeness is all that I can grow. This clear realization leads to my appreciating that *all* of my living is creative, that I am constantly putting on the *new* man, ever producing far greater achievement than I can credit my self with attaining.

It is by heeding my wholeness, *only,* that I can continuously grow purposefully the truth of my organic independence, responsible life-regulation, loving appreciation for my beautiful freedom and spirited zest for being my ever-new world of my own good making. All of my present newness is entirely the outgrowth of my former newness and, in the interest of conscious wholeness, I must honor the origin of my unity in the marvelous continuum that I am. My wholeness is the divinity that divines its identity in every possible reach of my constitution. As such it provides me with my most complete conception of my imagined ideal *universe* (not merely "multiverse").

It is readily understandable that it is my imagined severance of my necessary wholeness that is the source of all of my health trouble. To illustrate, by seeming to lose one of my loved ones, a member of my body or of my family, I can imagine that I have lost that much of my wholeness. Hence it is most indispensable mental hygiene for me to be able to realize not only that I can use my mind to create each loved one in the first place but also that I can use my mind to create each loved one as long as I live. My cherished virtue is my capacity for effort.

My ethical need is to deliver myself gradually from my helpful bondage of unconscious self severance into my helpful freedom of conscious self wholeness. Jan Christian Smuts stated well the hardihood required for, and developed by, the discipline in extending conscious self identity,

Let anybody sit down and try to form for himself an idea

205

of the soul's disembodied existence, and he will convince himself how difficult it is to get away from the physical analogies, from the pale copies of earthly existences, not very much different from the shades which wander through the cold Homeric Hades.[4]

My giving the one name, Nature, to my universe is possible on account of my sensing the singular wholeness of my living of the protean nature of my mind.

Although the executive ethical functioning of my wholeness is sufficiently inconspicuous to avoid nearly all detection, nevertheless I am able to imagine the reality of it as the true nature of my constitution, functioning like an omnipresent guardian spirit of total self control, providing all of the essence and arrangement of my being, from self to cell. And now, to honor practice while practicing honor, I include a closing compact account of my ethical orientation.

In my self-analysis, my choice way of life, I discover this profound ethical consequence. Whenever I repudiate the right to be of any meaning that my mind creates, the resulting inhibition under which that meaning continues its existence thereby outlaws it from its due significance for, including regulation by, my recognizable wholeness, thus allowing its force to function autonomously and inordinately in an independently obsessive way.

I take for illustration my feelingful thought: I wish to die. Dreadful though this self-undoing wish may seem to be, it is nevertheless integral to my biological understanding of my wholeness. I must create all of my own dying. It is to my advantage to appreciate my death wish as being the helpful creation of my own living and, as such, duly subject to the moderating control of my

[4]*Holism and Evolution*, p. 158.

whole mind. My troublesome alternative is to deny my death wish its right to be, repudiate it as life unworthy, and hence endure its continuing obsessive force in the form of its unacknowledged opposite, my fear of death (my wish not to die).

Were it not for my awareness of the exertion involved, in the persistent effort of the meaning in my obsession to become eligible for my conscious self identity, I would have to be aware of my painful feeling of depression (unpleasure) occasioned by my inhibiting the free functioning of the meaning comprising the content of my obsession. In other words, my obsessive behavior is not only the attempt of my repressed (consciously rejected) meaning to return to free conscious functioning but it is also a defense against my becoming aware of how depressed I must be whenever I repudiate the life worthy nature of any of my living. It is the fact that I can be enduring unpleasure (jealousy, depression, etc.) without consciously feeling it as helpful sign of self neglect that permits me to go on behaving distractedly in many shortsighted ways that disregard the proper interest of my whole self.

In realizing that prohibition of free functioning of any meaning represents a form of emphasis of it (analogous to counter-pressure felt by compressing any so-called object) it is essential to heed carefully the exact location of the place where all of my life's meaning occurs, namely, entirely in my individual mind creating it. Despite every appearance to the contrary, it can never occur elsewhere. The illusion that one mind can mean anything to another mind, is a cherished one however, so that it can and does interfere with proper understanding that the locality of all possible gratification or frustration of life satisfaction is wholly and exclusively in the given individual mind actually creating it.

The above statement is of greatest significance for

my biologically adequate ethical development. It is of most critical health consequence whether I am able to distinguish clearly my carrying on any of my meaningful living completely, or merely incompletely, in my acknowledged mind. To maintain awareness for my functioning (e.g., moderating or pacifying) wholeness my mind must discipline itself first to acknowledge and then gradually honor *each* of its experiences (creations) as being its own, only. I understand my every psychiatric symptom as being the persevering (obsessive) effort of some of my repudiated lifesaving meaning to unite with my conscious self identity that honors, as much as it presently can, the truth of my self wholeness.

Again my kind reader expostulates, "Are you implying that everyone should be allowed to do as he pleases, so that he won't have to learn to frustrate himself or deny his right to satisfy his every sudden impulse or persistent longing, no matter how disadvantageous his selfishness may be to his fellowman?"

Such earnest concern must be fully justified. Certainly on the face of it there can hardly be any refutation, for it presupposes the most popular assumption that whole human individuality is not quite possible, that one individual can experience his responsibility in some of another fellowman's living, and the converse. However, my demonstrable truth reveals that my whole individuality consists of only my whole individuality. I can be only of any concern to myself, just as my fellowman can be only of any concern to his self.

Therefore, as I make my reader's important question entirely my own I discover that it deserves its natural fulfillment in the form of its natural answer. That answer is YES, by all means, Yes, *only provided* that I see to it that all of my living of such freedom occurs entirely and exclusively in my own mind and hence cannot have any possible appearance or consequence of involving another mind. My free use of my mind's imagination to allow me to live my love as I please in my own mind cannot in any way be a disadvantage to that entirely independent self-world I call my divine fellowman.

It is through my realization that any and all of my behavior is restricted absolutely to the living of my own self identity that I wish to, and must, extend to my living of my fellowman the identical selfishly protective concern I indulge regarding all of my responsible living of my self.

My only conduct which can *apparently* involve any so-called disregard for my fellowman is the product of my living that fellowman-experience irresponsibly, that is, without my realizing that all of my meaning that I name *fellowman* is my own personal living. Rather than being merely my soul brother, all that I can mean by *my fellowman* is integral to my soul itself.

My fully functioning ethical principle is the product of my acknowledgeable self wholeness. My sensing my self identity in my conscious wholeness is a thrilling numinous experience of mine. Whatever consciously affirms the value of my life is both ethical and therapeutic. My conscious self love provides my full life affirmation.

I want to be able to teach myself just how, safely and sanely, to employ my mind as freely as I please, quite as I want to be able to learn how to dispel my every illusion that I can get at or be gotten at by any other being than my own. I find that it is naturally helpful for me to be able to strengthen my mind gradually so that I can ultimately *imagine* my self living in any and every possible way that might be necessary, my only alternative being to forbid my discovering my providence in being the whole world of my self that I can be.

Anew, whatever I live that I cannot acknowledge as

209

entirely my own being then becomes my not-I living which continues to function "involuntarily," i.e., without my conscious self being able to control it. Furthermore my not-I existence continues to try to restore its identity as my I-living by emphatically exerting its obsessive character. My everyone would gladly acknowledge his own godliness were it not for the fact that consciously living his life responsibly as the God that he is necessitates his freely recognizing his every life experience as being adorable (the Divine Look).

I can hardly imagine the enormous amount of (truth-bearing) mental trouble that is directly traceable to (my) everyone's massively accrued not-I living. Of one fact I feel most sure, such troubled existence far and grievously outdoes any other.

> The Tirynthians, according to an ancient story reported by Athenaeus, becoming conscious that their trick of laughter at everything and nothing was making them unfit for the conduct of serious affairs, appealed to the Delphic oracle for some means of cure. The god prescribed a peculiar form of sacrifice, which would be effective if they could carry it through without laughing. They did their best; but the flimsy joke of a boy upset their unaccustomed gravity, and in this way the oracle taught them that even the gods could not prescribe a quick cure for a long vitiation, or give power and dignity to a people who, in a crisis of the public well-being, were at the mercy of a poor jest.[5]

[5]George Eliot, *Impressions of Theophrastus Such* (New York: Harper and Brothers, 1879), p. 122.

MY ETHICORELIGIOUS LIVING

Persian: Honover, the creative word "I am" or "Let it be," is the bond which makes all one.

Egyptian: That cannot be which has not been before.

Greek: Sophocles: There is in truth but one God, who made heaven and earth. God alone IS.

 Parmenides: All which man regards as reality are merely names for appearance, delusion. Whatever is, is.

 Plato: Justice is the harmony of all the virtues. Truth belongs to the mind.

 Socrates: Know thyself. Morality is the necessity of the heart. The soul is that which is.

 Aristotle: Sense reveals only individual existence. The universal is immanent in the individual. Man finds his ethic only in his natural self realization.

 Plotinus: The Supreme Good is Absolute Unity. God Is All In All.

Hinduism: God is all. By mystical knowledge of him, man becomes one with God. God makes Himself.

Zoroastrianism and Parsis: Good thoughts, good words, good deeds. The Reality is one, the wise by many names call it.

Brahminism: The substance of created things is Brahma's substance.

Buddhism: Let a man lift himself up by his own self; let him not depress himself; for he himself is his friend and he himself is his enemy.

Confucianism: Seek to be in harmony with all your neighbors.

Taoism: Being in one's inmost heart in kindly sympathy with all things.

Judaism: Man is created in the image of God. Jehovah means: I Am, I Am That I Am, rendered in the Greek version of the Seventy "I Am He That Is."

Christianity: Love thy neighbor as thy self. As you do unto the least of these my brethren you do unto Me.

St. Paul: "When that which is perfect is come then things which are in part shall be done away."

Clement of Alexandria: "The opinion of Plato upon ideas is the true Christian and orthodox philosophy."

John Eckart, "Master": "Only one who is like the truth can know it."

Bishop Berkeley: "Things of sense are a revelation of spirit."

Mohammedanism: Do what God likes, and avoid what He dislikes.

Sufeyism: Man can know truth only by becoming the truth itself.

Narragansett Indian: You know God, Will you lie Englishman?

Baha-U-Llah: Beware lest names withhold thee from God. . . . Happy are those who practice! . . . The peacemaker of the world has always been considered an agitator.

John Scott Haldane: Materialism is a superstition on the same level as a belief in witches and devils, and will go the way of such beliefs.

H. G. Wells: Moral indignation is jealousy with a halo.

GLOSSARY

Absolute: completely free; whatever is, absolutely is

Abstraction: *seeming* objectification of real subjectivity

Adoration: refined self devotion befitting my every one's divinity

Alone: all one. Solipsistic necessity.

Altruism: grown-up egoism

Agnostic: inhibited gnostic (see, inhibition)

Analysis: inhibited synthesis (see, self analysis)

Antinomy: illusion of autonomous opposition

Anxiety: inhibited pleasure of wholeness

Apperception: meaningful perceptiveness from former perceiving

Atheism: inhibited theism

Autonomy: whatever is, is law unto itself; the unique necessity in
   individuality

Balance of wealth: every poor man lives all of his own rich man;
   every rich man lives all of his own poor man; the health of each
   depends upon this insight

Becoming: nascent being

Beauty: the whole truth of whatever is

Being: fruition of becoming

213

Biological adequacy: serving all interest of self wholeness

Blessing: heeding the power of my goodness

Body: nucleus of mind

Chastity: consciously self contained sexuality

Communication: illusion based on disregard for language as being each linguist's idiolect only

Confession: acknowledgement of guilt in order to assume conscious responsibility

Conflict: symptom of inhibited self unity

Conscience: consciousness for my need to take care of my wholeness

Conscious: acknowledging self meaning (see, unconscious); degrees of luminosity of consciousness vary from dim to dazzling

Conscious discipline: willingly undertaking more or less difficult exertion to secure desired end

Contrition: see Penitence

Control: exertion of self power with conscious self possession

Courage: fortitude; perseverance of conscious self love that is the only possible source for conscious love of life

Critic: one who denies authorship; every author is his own possible critic

Curse: hurt prayer

Death: absence of manifest sign of life

Deify: to recognize already existing divinity

Depersonalization: withholding sense of self identity from any experience

214

Devil: personification of one's inhibited divinity

Discipline: consciously exercising my mind in a trying direction of my choosing

Distance: quantitative measure based on illusion of space

Divinity: select term for ordinarily repressed ideal way of living; perfection regularly repressed as too good to be true; enthusiastic, spirited, self sufficient, self sentience; it is divine to be human and human to overlook it

Duration: quantitative measure based on illusion of time

Duty: need to cultivate my potential, consciously fulfill the development of my wholeness

Emotion: self feeling providing mental sensorium beyond its so-called general and special senses

End: unit of reality, subjective, self sufficient (see, means)

Endurance: developed hardihood; conscious mental strength

Environment: my creation of my vitality I call my surroundings

Eternity: now

Ethic: reverence for my neighbor as being all mine

Euphoria: joy of living; self interest functioning freely

Evil: unrecognized good. (The common ancient Hebrew word for wicked or vile is *foolish*.)

Existent: whatever is, divinely is

Experience: whatever I live

Externality: inhibited internality; proof of self unconsciousness; my helpful defense against overwhelming my self identity which is the present limit of my awareness for my wholeness

215

Faith: conscious and unconscious self trust

Familiarity: illusional, disregard for novelty or necessary strangeness of all living

Faultfinding: inhibited truth finding, concealed regularly in pejorative or meliorative term

Fear: inhibited wish

Forgiveness: loving difficultly

Free association: conscious wording (audile and oral) of uninhibited stream of consciousness

Freedom: voluntariness; absence of alien living; complete autonomy; divine will

Glory: exalted distinction of worth unavoidably created by gradual discovery of the extent of one's immeasurable wholeness

God: All, without exception. My imagined source and course of all of the providence of my imagined world.

Good: living is all good; conscious living is conscious good

Goodness: my feeling of my own wholeness

Grace: art of living conferred by my *conscious* wholeness

Grammar: more or less fixed arrangement of words (singly, in phrase or sentence) according to so-called established or admissible usage

Guilt: inhibited innocence

Hatred: inhibited self love; "wounded feeling"

Healing: freeing constitutional (wholeness) vitality; releasing conscious wholeness power

Health: functional triumph of all of wholeness

216

Heaven: my heaven is everywhere wonderful in me, not merely I in it

Hell: Heaven disguised by my ignoring that falsehood is inhibited truth

Help: all that is humanly possible. *All* of living is always divinely helpful, consciously or unconsciously.

Heredity: my own development, immediate and remote. I can inherit my self only.

Hesitation: unique form of mental activity signifying consciously controlled readiness to function or not to function.

Holiness: revered wholeness

Honor: due regard for the truth of one's wholeness

Hope: a way of living whatever is hoped for, seldom recognized as such; wish

Hyperbole: reduction of enthusiasm to a grammatical figure; fault-finding indication of exaggeration or extravagance

Ideal: activity which helps to integrate total wholeness

Idiolect: everyone's only language; my language for naming my own living *only*

Imagination: over-all term for mental-activity. I imagine my seeing, hearing, thinking, feeling, etc. A function rarely developed to biological adequacy, e.g., wholesomely imagining one's own divine omnipotence, omnipresence, omniscience, and so on.

Impiety: my irreverance for my deity

Individual: basic unit of universality

Infinity: here

Inhibition: opposite of facilitation of free functioning; withholding conscious love from functioning; prevention of free functioning resulting from inability to feel that lovable truth is always on the side of whatever happens

Injustice: inhibited justice

Insight: understanding all observation as being *self* observation

Jealousy: inhibited self trust

Judgment: conscious self observation

Justice: whatever is, is just; whole truth

Language: everyone's solipsistic idiolect only

Law: obedience to the nature of my divine humanity

Life: organized power and glory

Living: growing, creating, self; *all that I can do is what I am*

Love: joy of functioning being; *all* love is self love, only

Mankind: I attribute to my every fellowman the same divine human nature that is mine.

Matter: inhibited subjectivity; unrecognized mentality

Maturity: Whatever is, maturely is. An infant is a mature baby. An embryo is a mature embryo.

Meaning: functioning mentality; unit of mind; self contained power of functioning inherent in existence.

Means: inhibited end

Meliorative: subtle cover-up for my overlooking my omnipresent perfection

Memory: unrecognized *present* being only

Mental health: conscious self wholeness

Mental trauma: overwhelming excitation obscuring sense of self identity

Mercy: my love's contribution to its justice

Mind: conscious and unconscious subjectivity; ideal meaningfulness.

Mobility: conscious self activity supporting illusions of time, space and motion

Morality: need for return of repressed innocence when self wholeness is overlooked

Mystic: *internal* nature of all being; *intrinsic* quality of truth; entifying solipsistic unity of any and all reality

Nature: I am by nature whatever I can be. I grow my all; I *acquire* nothing.

Negation: affirmation of oppositeness; return of repressed meaning (see repression)

Obey: honor my own command

Objectivity: unconscious subjectivity

Obsession: persistent recurrence in conscious living of previous consciously repressed (repudiated) meaning

Opposite: illusion of duality (plurality) compensating for negation of unity (individuality)

Other: not-self illusion. Insightfully imagined not-self, also.

Ought: need to honor conscious wholeness in order to feel the goodness in being alive

Pain: inhibited joy of living self love

Peace: conscious self consciousness

Pejorative: evident cover-up for my ignoring omnipresence of my perfection

Penitence: my painful acknowledgement of need to revere the truth of certain specific wholeness of mine.

Perfection: whatever is, perfectly is, wholly is. See Divinity.

Personification: attributing self power as if it is not all my own

Pleasure: uninhibited joy of living self love

Possession: all of my possesion is my self possession.

Practice: strengthen through exercise. See Discipline.

Prayer: any and every conscious and unconscious self address

Present: my life's only moment of existence

Progress: meliorative term compensating for disregarded omnipresent perfection

Property: self possession only

Psychology: when conscious, is mind studying mind; when unconscious, is mind studying unrecognized mind

Psychotherapy: mind helping itself with its consciousness. Developing conscious responsibility for being a whole individual.

Punishment: inhibited self satisfaction entirely

Reality: whatever *is;* perfection; conscious self orientation; my acknowledgeable living of my self meaning; universal solipsistic I-am-that-I-am

Reasoning: verbalized emotion or sensation

Redemption: recognition of already existing perfection

Relationship: illusion compensating for some disowned selfness

Relative: inhibited absolute

Religion: conscious or/and unconscious sensing of one's own divinity

Renunciation: ability to direct attention (interest) freely; to be able to take or leave any experience freely

Repression: necessary withholding of sense of self-identity from any meaning

Responsibility: degree of appreciation for the intact wholeness of my self identity

Reverence: heartfelt consciousness for goodness or godliness

Reward: compensation for my overlooking that whatever I live is its own reward

Right: the demand for conscious integration in behalf of self wholeness

Sacrament: any and all functioning of divine human wholeness

Sacred, see Holy

Science: organized system of self knowledge regularly overlooked in the illusion of objectivity

Self: my whole organic being; a name for the all of me

Self analysis: conscious self observation redeeming conscious responsibility from unconscious guilt, and conscious control from unconscious compulsion

Self consciousness: my only possible consciousness

Self identity: my presently acknowledgeable individuality

Selfishness: the natural substance of self

221

Sensibility: any self sentience beginning with sensation, including emotion, and culminating in divine self consciousness

Sex: genetic element of living; male lives all of his own femaleness; female lives all of her own maleness

Shame: inhibited pride; injured pride

Sickness: health struggling to restore its vitality to free functioning

Sin: unrecognized hence often repudiated holiness

Society: my imagining of a plurality of individuality; extension of self sovereignty

Solipsism: term used literally to mean self alone (all one); name for the inviolably intact wholeness, allness, of divine human individuality. My everyone *necessarily* is either a conscious or unconscious solipsist; key term for reaching conscious reality; whatever is, is all and only itself.

Soul: the essence of self; whatever is, is all soul. My subjective wholeness.

Spirit: the imponderable nature of subjectivity; will

Subjectivity: my only source and course of reality (truth); continent self meaning

Success: attainment of reverence for justice inherent in all of my living

Thanks: gratitude to my self for the providence of my divine nature

Theory: creation of a practical mental composition

Thinking: verbalized and non-verbalized emotion

Togetherness: unrecognized unity

Truth: wholeness of whatever is

222

Unconscious: all of my being that I cannot freely acknowledge as being mine and take justifiable pride in. All of my mind is unconscious; some of it can become conscious, also.

Unity: all and only *within* wholeness of individuality

Universal: essence of individuality

Unpleasure, or unhappiness: inhibited self love

Virtue: strength of my devotion to purposely practicing my self consciousness

Vocabulary: all of my terminology of, and for, my own living only

Wholeness: Whatever is, wholly is. Wholeness only exists and functions in and for itself.

Wish: vital motivation, will

Word: original poetry

Work: my wish to live derives from pleasure in my functioning as fully as possible, — hence the life risk in so-called retirement

Worship: see Adoration

Worth: value in terms of divine human living

Wrong: unrecognizable right; faultfinding

BIBLIOGRAPHY

Abse, D. Wilfred, and Jessner, Lucie. "The Psychodynamic Aspects of Leadership." *Daedalus,* Journal of the American Academy of Arts and Sciences 90 (Fall 1961): 693–710.

Ad hoc Committee on Ethical Standards in Psychological Research. *Ethical Principles in the Conduct of Research with Human Participants.* Washington, D.C.: American Psychological Association, Inc., 1973.

Adams, Henry. *The Degradation of the Democratic Dogma.* New York: Peter Smith, 1949.

Adler, Morris (Rabbi). Personal observations.

Adler, Mortimer J. *The Time of Our Lives: The Ethics of Common Sense.* New York: Holt, Rinehart and Winston, 1970.

Allee, William Coit. Personal observations.

Anderson, Ralph D., Jr., M. D. Personal observations.

Arasteh, A. Reza. *Rediscovering America.* Tucson, Arizona: Omen Press, 1972.

Aring, Charles D., M. D., et al. *Man and Life. A Sesquicentennial Symposium.* Cincinnati: University of Cincinnati, 1969.

———. "A Sense of Humor." *JAMA* 215 (March 29, 1971): 2099.

Asch, Sholem. *The Apostle.* New York: G. P. Putnam's Sons, 1943.

August, Harry E., M. D. Personal observations.

Babcock, Allen S. (Rt. Rev.). Personal observations.

Bach, Marcus, His "Outreach" newsletters.

Ballinger, Malcolm B. (Rev.). Personal observations.

Banks, A. A. (Rev.). Personal observations.

Barksdale, L. S. *Building Self-Esteem.* Idyllwild, California: The Barksdale Foundation for Furtherance of Human Understanding, 1972.

Barrett, Albert M., M.D. Personal observations.

Barrett, C. Waller. Personal observations.

Bartemeier, Leo H., M. D. *A Physician in the General Practice of Psychiatry.* Selected Papers. Ed. Peter A. Martin, A. W. R. Sipe and Gene L. Usdin. New York: Brunner/Mazel, 1970.

Barth, Karl. *The Word of God and the Word of Man*. Trans. Douglas Horton. New York: Harper & Brothers, 1956.

Basilius, Harold A. "Goethe's Conception of Individuality and Personality." *The Growth of Self Insight*, ed. John M. Dorsey, pp. 79–119. Detroit: Wayne State University Press, 1962.

Basler, Roy P. "A Literary Enthusiasm; or, the User Used." Phi Beta Kappa Address, College of William and Mary, December 5, 1969.

_____. *A Touchstone For Greatness*. Westport, Conn.: Greenwood Press, Inc., 1973.

Bean, William B., M.D. "President's Address—The Ecology of the Soldier in World War II." *Transactions of the Am. Clinical and Climatological Assoc.* 79 (1967).

_____. "A Testament of Duty." *J. Laboratory and Clinical Medicine* 39 (January 1952): 4.

Beauvoir, Simone de. *The Ethics of Ambiguity*. New York: Philosophical Library, 1948.

Bell, Martin (Rev.). Personal observations.

Bell, Whitfield J., Jr. "James Hutchinson (1752–1793): A Physician In Politics." In *Medicine, Science and Culture: Historical Essays in Honor of Owsei Temkin*. Ed. Lloyd G. Stevenson and Robert P. Multhauf. Baltimore, Md.: The Johns Hopkins Press, 1968.

_____. "Lives In Medicine: The Biographical Dictionaries of Thacher, Williams, and Gross." *Bulletin of the History of Medicine* 42 (March/April 1968): 101–120.

_____. "The Fielding H. Garrison Lecture: A Portrait of the Colonial Physician." *Bulletin of the History of Medicine* 44 (November/December 1970): 497–517.

Bender, Lauretta, and Schilder, Paul. "Suicidal Preoccupations and Attempts in Children." *Am. J. Orthopsychiat.* 7 (1937): 225–234.

Benham, Hamilton. Personal observations.

Bergson, Henri. *The Creative Mind*. New York: The Philosophical Library, Inc., 1946.

_____. *Creative Evolution*. Trans. Arthur Mitchell. New York: Henry Holt and Company, 1911.

Berlien, Ivan C., M. D. Personal observations.

Bhagavad Gita.

Bibring, Grete L., and Kahana, Ralph J. *Lectures in Medical Psychology: An Introduction to the Care of Patients*. New York: International Universities Press, Inc., 1968.

Billings, Ardella M. Personal observations.

Blackhurst, J. Herbert. *The Philosophical Ground of Democracy and Education*. Pre-publication edition.

Blain, Alexander III, M. D. Personal observations.

Boelen, Bernard J. "The Question of Ethics in the Thought of Martin Heidegger." In *Heidegger and the Quest for Truth*. Ed. Manfred S. Frings. Chicago, Ill.: Quadrangle Books, 1968. Pp. 76–105.

Bohm, Henry V. Personal observations.

Bowen, Lem W. Personal observations.

Bowne, Borden P. *Introduction to Psychological Theory*. New York: Harper and Brothers, 1886.

Boyd, Julian P. *The Declaration of Independence*. Princeton: Princeton University Press, 1945.

Braceland, Francis J., M. D. "Hormones and their Influence on the Emotions." *Bull. N. Y. Acad. Med.* (1953): 765–777.

Brazier, Mary A. B. "The Growth of Concepts Relating to Brain Mechanisms." *Journal of the History of the Behavioral Sciences* 1 (1965) No. 3.

Breese-Whiting, Kathryn. Personal observations.

Brennan, Thomas P., M. D. Personal observations.

Brierley, Marjorie, M. D. *Trends in Psychoanalysis*. London: Hogarth Press, Ltd., and Institute of Psycho-Analysis, 1951.

Brightman, Edgar Sheffield. *Moral Laws*. New York: The Abingdon Press, 1933.

Britton, Erwin E. (Rev.). Personal observations.

Bronowski, J. *Science and Human Values*. New York: Harper & Row, 1965.

Brown, N. O. *Life Against Death: The Psychoanalytical Meaning of History*. Wesleyan University, 1959.

Buchner, Franz. *Personality and Nature in Modern Medicine*. New York and London: Grune & Stratton, Inc., 1958.

Buckham, John Wright, and Stratton, George Malcolm. *George Holmes Howison, Philosopher and Teacher*. Berkeley: University of California Press, 1934.

Bueche, Gary (Rev.). Personal observations.

Burlingham, Dorothy. "Psychic Problems of the Blind." *American Imago* 2 (1941): 43–85.

Burton, Ralph J. Personal observations.

Burton, Robert. *The Anatomy of Melancholy*. Ed. Floyd Dell and Paul Jordan-Smith. New York: Tudor Publishing Company, 1927.

Carpenter, Edward. *Towards Democracy*. London: George Allen & Unwin Ltd., 1883.

227

Carver, William F., M. D. Personal observations.

Cassirer, Ernst. *Substance and Function and Einstein's Theory of Relativity*. New York: Dover, 1953.

_____. *The Individual and the Cosmos in Renaissance Philosophy*. Trans. Mario Domandi. New York: Harper and Row, 1963.

Childs, Marquis W., and Cater, Douglass. *Ethics in a Business Society*. New York: The New American Library, 1954.

Clark, Robert B., M. D. Personal observations.

Cleveland, Harlan, and Lasswell, Harold D., eds. *Ethics and Bigness: Scientific, Academic, Religious, Political, and Military*. New York: Conference on Science, Philosophy and Religion in their Relation to the Democratic Way of Life, Inc., 1962.

Clifford, William Kingdon. "Ethics of Belief." *Contemporary Review* (January 1877).

Cohen, Harry. *The Demonics of Bureaucracy*. Ames, Iowa: The Iowa State University Press, 1965.

Cohen, Wilbur J. "The Quest for Equal Opportunity." The Whitney M. Young, Jr. Memorial Lecture Series, Wayne State University, Detroit, Michigan, March, 1973.

Coit, Stanton. *The Soul of America*. New York: The Macmillan Company, 1914.

Coles, Robert. "A Young Psychiatrist Looks at His Profession." *The Atlantic Monthly* (July 1961).

Cooke, Nicholas F., M. D. *Satan In Society*. Chicago: C. F. Vent Company, 1891.

Coomaraswamy, A. K. "Recollection Indian and Platonic, and The One and Only Transmigrant." Supplement to *Journal of the American Oriental Society* 64 (1937) No. 2.

Cooley, Charles Horton. *Human Nature and the Social Order*. New York: Charles Scribner's Sons, 1922.

Coppin, John S. Personal observations.

Corson, Hiram. *The Aims of Literary Study*. New York: Macmillan and Company, 1894.

Coulter, Glenn M. Prismatic address, Notes on Supreme Court.

Cowin, Nora. Personal observations.

Cowin, William Thomas. *In Other Words*. Liverpool, England: Nora Cowin, 1972.

Coye, Robert D., M. D. Personal observations.

Crafford, F. S. *Jan Smuts*. New York: Doubleday Doran, Inc., 1943.

Crawford, DeLyle. Personal observations.

Cushman, Edward L. Personal observations.

Danhof, John J. Personal observations.

228

Danto, Bruce L., M. D. *Jail House Blues*. Orchard Lake, Mich: Epic Publications, Inc., 1973.

Davenport, Russell· W. *The Dignity of Man*. New York: Harper and Brothers, 1955.

Davids, T. W., and Rhys, C. A. F., trs. *Dialogues of the Buddha*. London: Luzac, 1951.

Day, Stacey B., M. D. *Collected Lines*. Montreal: Three Star Printing and Publishing Company, 1966.

———. *American Lines*. Montreal: Three Star Printing and Publishing Company, 1967.

de Chardin, Pierre Teilhard. *The Phenomenon of Man*. New York: Harper, 1959.

———. *Christianity and Evolution*. Trans. Rene Hague. New York: Harcourt Brace Jovanovich, Inc., 1969.

DeLawter, Hilbert H., M. D. Personal observations.

De Lubac, Henri, S. J. *Religion of Teilhard de Chardin*. Trans. Rene Hague. New York: Desclee Company, 1967.

Dewey, John. *The Quest for Certainty*. New York: Minton, Balch and Company, 1929.

———, and Bentley, A. F. *Knowing and the Known*. Boston: Beacon, 1949.

DeWitt, Robert L. (Rt. Rev.). Personal observations.

Dillenberger, John, ed. *Martin Luther: Selections from his Writings*. New York: Doubleday and Co., 1961.

Dorsey, Anna Elizabeth, and Dorsey, Edward William. Parental living.

Dorsey, Edward C., M. D. "Approach to the Clinic." Presented at a scientific program in honor of John M. Dorsey's seventieth year, sponsored by the Michigan Society of Neurology and Psychiatry and the Wayne State University School of Medicine Alumni Association, September 16, 1971, Detroit, Michigan.

———. His Journal, February, 1971.

Dorsey, George C., Sr., M. D. Personal communication.

Dorsey, James E. Personal communication.

Dorsey, John M., Jr., M. D. Letter to the Editor, *The Detroit Free Press*, December 29, 1970.

———. Television presentations on pediatrics, *A. M. Detroit*, Dennis Wholey, host, WXYZ-TV, Detroit, Michigan.

Dorsey, John M., M. D. *American Government, Conscious Self Sovereignty*. Detroit: Center for Health Education, 1969.

———, ed. *The Growth of Self Insight*. Detroit: Wayne State University Press, 1960.

229

_____. *Illness or Allness.* Detroit: Wayne State University Press, 1965.

_____, ed. *The Jefferson-Dunglison Letters.* Charlottesville, Va.: University of Virginia Press, 1960.

_____, and Seegers, Waiter H. *Living Consciously: The Science of Self.* Detroit: Wayne State University Press, 1959.

_____. *Psychology of Emotion: Self Discipline by Conscious Emotional Continence.* Detroit: Center for Health Education, 1971.

_____. *Psychology of Language: A Local Habitation and a Name.* Detroit: Center for Health Education, 1971.

_____. *Psychology of Political Science: With Special Consideration for the Political Acumen of Destutt de Tracy.* Detroit: Center for Health Education, 1973.

Dorsey, Mary Louise Carson. Letters and Notes to John M. Dorsey, unpublished.

_____. Personal observations.

Douglas, Paul H. "Three Saints in Politics." *The American Scholar* 40 (Spring 1971): 223–232.

Dow, Alex. *Some Public Service Papers, 1892–1927.* Detroit, 1927.

Dow, Douglas. "Simplified Economics." Paper delivered to Prismatic Club (Detroit), 1972.

Doyle, Crystal. Personal observations.

Drucker, Peter F. *The Age of Discontinuity.* New York: Harper and Row, 1969.

Edgar, Irving I., M. D. *Essays in English Literature and History.* New York: The Philosophical Library, Inc., 1972.

Edwards, George C. *The Police on the Urban Frontier.* New York: Institute of Human Relations Press, 1968.

_____. Personal observations.

Edwards, Jonathan. *The Nature of True Virtue.* Ann Arbor: University of Michigan Press, 1960.

Edwards, Margaret (Mrs. George C.). Personal observations.

Eissler, Kurt R., M. D. *Goethe: A Psychoanalytic Study.* Detroit: Wayne State University Press, 1963.

Ekstein, Rudolf. "Psychoanalysis Looks at the Origins of Values in Children." *Educational Leadership* 21 (1964): 523–527.

_____. "Historical Notes Concerning Psychoanalysis and Early Language Development." *Journal of the American Psychoanalytic Association* 13 (1965): 707–731.

_____, and Motto, R. L. *From Learning for Love to Love of Learning.* New York: Brunner/Mazel, 1969.

———. "Psychoanalysis and Education for The Facilitation of Positive Human Qualities." *Journal of Social Issues* 28 (1972): 71–85.

Eliot, George. *Impressions of Theophrastus Such.* New York: Harper and Brothers, 1879.

Elston, Wilbur. "The Limits to Press Freedom." *The Torch* 45 (January 1972): 9–13.

Emerson, Dorothy. *Dorothy Emerson's Scrapbook.* Washington, D. C.: National 4-H Club Foundation, 1966.

———. *Speak Up Young People.* Washington, D. C.: National 4-H Club Foundation, 1964.

Emerson, Ralph Waldo. "Worship." *The Conduct of Life.* Boston: Ticknow and Fields, 1860.

———. "Powers and Laws of Thought." *Natural History of Intellect.* The Complete Works of Ralph Waldo Emerson. Boston and New York: Houghton, Mifflin and Co., 1903.

Emrich, Richard S. (Rt. Rev.). Personal observations.

Ensign, Dwight C., M. D. Personal observations.

Erickson, M. H.; Haley, J.; and Weakland, J. H. "A Transcript of a Trance Induction with Commentary." *American Journal of Clinical Hypnosis* 2 (1959) No. 2.

Erikson, E. H. *Insight and Responsibility: Lectures on the Ethical Implications of Psychoanalytic Insight.* New York: W. W. Norton, 1964.

———. *Identity: Youth and Crisis.* New York: W. W. Norton, 1968.

Evely, Louis. *Suffering.* Trans. Marie-Claude Thompson. New York: Herder and Herder, 1967.

Fahey, Denis (Rev.). *The Mystical Body of Christ in the Modern World.* 2nd ed. London: Browne and Nolan Ltd., 1938.

Fand, David I. "A Monetary Interpretation of the Post-1965 Inflation in the United States." *Banca Nazionale del Lavoro Quarterly Review* (June 1969) No. 89.

Fawcett, Thomas. *The Symbolic Language of Religion.* Minneapolis, Minn.: Augsburg Publishing House, 1971.

Feinberg, Charles E. "Walt Whitman and His Doctors." *Medical History* 114 (1964): 834–842.

Ferm, Vergilius, ed. *Encyclopedia of Religion.* New York: Philosophical Library, Inc., 1945.

———. *Encyclopedia of Morals.* New York: Philosophical Library. Inc., 1956.

Fischer, Kuno. *Uber den Witz.* 2nd ed. Heidelberg, 1889.

231

Fite, Warner. *The Living Mind*. New York: Dial Press, 1930.

Flugel, J. C. *The Psycho-Analytic Study of the Family*. London: Hogarth Press and The Institute of Psycho-Analysis, 1948.

Ford, Henry II, and Portman, John. "Can the New Riverfront Development Revitalize Detroit?" Address before the Economic Club of Detroit, May 22, 1972, Max M. Fisher, Presiding officer.

Forrer, Gordon R., M. D. *Weaning and Human Development*. Roslyn Heights, N. Y.: Libra Publishers, Inc., 1969.

Fox, Charles. *The Mind and Its Body*. New York: Harcourt, Brace and Company, 1932.

Foxe, Arthur N. *Plague: LaEnnec (1782–1826) Inventor of the Stethescope and Father of Modern Medicine*. New York: The Hobson Book Press, 1947.

Frankel, Charles. "The Nature and Sources of Irrationalism." *Science* 180 (June 1973): 927–931.

Frankensteen, Richard T. Personal observations.

Franklin, John Hope. "The Quest for Equal Opportunity: The American Dream." The Whitney M. Young, Jr. Memorial Lecture Series, Wayne State University, Detroit, Michigan, November, 1973.

Franklin, Leo M. (Rabbi). Personal observations.

Fredericks, Marshall M. Personal observations.

Freeman, James Dillet. Personal observations.

Frehse, Robert (Rev.). Personal observations.

Freud, Anna. *The Writings of Anna Freud*. 7 vols. New York: International Universities Press, 1966.

Freud, Ernst L., ed. *Letters of Sigmund Freud*. Trans. Tania and James Stern. New York: Basic Books, Inc., 1960.

Freud, Sigmund. Jokes and their Relation to the Unconscious (1905). *The Standard Edition of the Complete Psychological Works of Sigmund Freud*. Trans. James Strachey in collaboration with Anna Freud, assisted by Alix Strachey and Alan Tyson. 24 vols. London: The Hogarth Press and The Institute of Psychoanalysis, 1953.

Freund, Hugo, M. D. Personal observations.

Fromm, E., and Suzuki, D. T. *Zen Buddhism and Psychoanalysis*. New York: Harper, 1960.

Gardner, John W. *No Easy Victories*. New York: Harper & Row, Publishers, 1968.

Genet, Jean. *the thief's journal*. Foreword by Jean-Paul Sartre. Trans. from the French by Bernard Frechtman. New York: Bantam Books, 1963.

232

Gengerelli, Joseph A., and Kirkner, Frank J., eds. *The Psychological Variables in Human Cancer*. Berkeley and Los Angeles: University of California Press, 1954.

Gibson, Hilda Clair. Personal observations.

Ginsberg, Louis. *Morning In Spring*. New York: William Morrow and Co., Inc., 1970.

Girdharlal. *Silence Speaks*. Salem, India: Balubhai and Sushila Shah, 1963.

Glass, Bentley. *Science and Ethical Values*. Chapel Hill: University of North Carolina Press, 1965.

Goldbrunner, Josef. *Holiness Is Wholeness and Other Essays*. London: University of Notre Dame Press, 1964.

Golightly, Cornelius L. "A Philosopher's View of Values and Ethics." *Personnel and Guidance Journal* 50 (December 1971): 289–294.

Good, Harry G. *A History of American Education*. 2nd ed. New York: The Macmillan Company, 1956.

Gorman, Gwen. Personal observations.

Green, T. H. *Prolegomena To Ethics*. Ed. A. C. Bradley. Oxford: Clarendon Press, 1906.

Greenberg, Samuel A., M. D. Personal observations.

Gregg, Alan, M. D. Personal observations.

Grindley, Robert F. Personal observations.

Grinstein, Alexander, M. D. *On Sigmund Freud's Dreams*. Detroit: Wayne State University Press, 1968.

Grotjahn, Martin, M. D. "Process of Awakening." *Psychoanalytic Review* 29 (1942).

Guenon, R. *Introduction to the Study of the Hindu Doctrines*. London: Luzac, 1945.

Gullen, George E., Jr. Personal observations.

Hadfield, J. A. *Psychology and Morals*. New York: Robert M. McBride and Company, 1929.

Hadley, Arthur Twining. *The Moral Basis of Democracy*. New Haven, Conn.: Yale University Press, 1919.

Hagman, Harlan L. Personal observations.

Hall, Don. Personal observations.

Hall, Bernard H., ed. *A Psychiatrist's World*. The Selected Papers of Karl Menninger. Foreword by Marion E. Kenworthy. New York: Viking Press, 1959.

Hall, G. Stanley. *Life and Confessions of a Psychologist*. New York: D. Appleton & Co., 1923.

Hamburger, Miriam. Personal observations.

Hamburger, Samuel. Personal observations.

Hamilton, William. *Discussions on Philosophy and Literature: Education and University Reform*. New York: Harper and Brothers, 1868.

Happel, Clara, M. D. Personal observations.

Hargrave, Colleen Moore. Personal observations.

Harold, Preston, and Babcock, Winifred. *The Single Reality*. New York: A Harold Institute book. Distributed by Dodd, Mead and Co., 1971.

Harris, William T. Most insightful U. S. Commissioner of Education.

Harrison, Phyllis Anne, M. D. *Getting It Together*. New York: Globe Book Co., Inc., 1973.

Hartman, Ferris. Personal observations.

Hartman, Iris. Personal observations.

Hartmann, Heinz, M. D. *Ego Psychology and the Problem of Adaptation*. Trans. David Rappaport. New York: International Universities Press, 1958.

_____. *Psychoanalysis and Moral Values*. New York: International Universities Press, 1960.

Hastings, Donald W., M. D. Personal observations.

Hastings, James, ed. *A Dictionary of the Bible*. 5 vols. New York: Charles Scribner's Sons, 1903.

_____, ed. *Dictionary of Christ and The Gospels*. 2 vols. With assistance of John A. Selbil, D. D., and John C. Lambert, D. D. New York: Charles Scribner's Sons and Edinburgh: T. and T. Clark, 1906.

Hazo, Robert G. *The Idea of Love*. New York: Frederic A. Praeger, 1967.

Herbart, Johann Friedrich. *A Textbook in Psychology*. Trans. from the German by Margaret K. Smith. New York: D. Appleton and Co., 1891.

Hertz, Richard C. (Rabbi). Personal observations.

Hesse, Hermann. *Autobiographical Writings*. Ed. Theodore Ziolkowski. Trans. Denver Lindley. New York: Farrar, Straus and Giroux, 1972.

Hilberry, Clarence B. Personal observations.

Hocking, William Ernest. *The Meaning of God In Human Experience*. New Haven: Yale University Press, 1912.

Holden, James S. Personal observations.

Holden, W. Sprague. "Two Centuries with the First Amendment." *The Torch* 45 (January 1972): 8, 13–16.

Hood, Nicholas (Rev.). Personal observations.

Hopkins, Mark. *The Law of Love and Love as a Law.* New York: Charles Scribner's Sons, 1895.

Howard, R. Palmer, M. D. Personal observations.

Howe, Helen. *The Gentle Americans.* New York: Harper & Row, 1965.

Howe, Reuel L. (Rev.). *Survival Plus.* New York: Seabury Press, 1971.

Huegli, Richard F. Personal observations.

Hughes, John T. Personal observations.

Hughes, Judith Moss, M. D. Personal observations.

Humboldt, Wilhelm von. *Humanist Without Portfolio.* Detroit: Wayne State University Press, 1961.

Hunt, John, D. D. *Pantheism and Christianity.* London: Wm. Isbister, Ltd., 1884.

Huston, James A. Personal observations.

Hutchings, P. Ae. *Kant on Absolute Value.* Detroit: Wayne State University Press, 1972.

Hutchins, Robert M. *The Learning Society.* New York: Praeger, 1968.

Ingalese, Richard. *The History and Power of Mind.* New York: Dodd, Mead and Company, 1927.

Irving, Washington. "Traits of Indian Character." *The Sketch-Book of Geoffrey Crayon, Gent.* New York: A. L. Burt, 1819.

Jacobsen, Edith, M. D. "Depression, the Oedipus Complex in the Development of Depressive Mechanism." *Psychoanal. Q.* 12 (1943): 541–560.

James, William, M. D. "The Will to Believe." *New World* (June 1896): 22, 23, 30.

———. "The Moral Philosopher and the Moral Life." *International Journal of Ethics* (April 1891): 186, 190, 205.

Jefferson, Thomas. *The Life and Morals of Jesus of Nazareth.* Washington: Government Printing office, 1904.

Jeffries, Benjamin, M. D. Personal observations.

Jennings, Charles G., M. D. Personal observations.

Johnston, Joseph A., M. D. Personal observations.

Johnston, Thomas. *Freud and Political Thought.* New York: The Citadel Press, 1965.

Jones, Virgil (Rev). Personal observations.

Joslyn, Alan W. Personal observations.

Kahn, Mark L. "The National Airlines Strike: A Case Study." *Journal of Air Law and Commerce* 19 (Winter 1952): 11–24.

Kant, Immanuel. *The Fundamental Principles of the Metaphysic of Ethics*. Trans. Otto Manthey-Zorn. New York: Appleton-Century-Crofts, Inc., 1938.

———. *Critique de La Raison Pratique*. Paris: Presses Universitaires de France, 1943.

Kapp, R. O. *Towards a Unified Cosmology*. New York: Basic Books, 1960.

Kapustin, Max (Rabbi). Personal observations.

Keen, Sam. *Apology for Wonder*. New York: Harper & Row, 1969.

Kellenberger, Richard K. Personal correspondence.

Kelly, Alfred H., and Harbison, Winfred A. *The American Constitution*. 4th ed. New York: W. W. Norton and Company, 1970.

Kersten, Lawrence K. *The Lutheran Ethic*. Detroit: Wayne State University Press, 1970.

Keye, Vernon E. Personal observations.

Kheshvala, Karl. Personal observations.

Kierkegaard, Soren. *Training In Christianity*. Translated, with an Introduction and Notes, by Walter Lowrie, D. D. Princeton: Princeton University Press, 1947.

Kilpatrick, William Heard. *Philosophy of Education*. New York: Macmillan, 1951.

King, Lawrence S. Personal observations.

King, Martin Luther, Jr. (Rev.). Insightful writings and personal observations.

Kirkeby, Oliver M. (Rev.). Personal observations.

Klettner, Frederick J. (Rev.). Personal observations.

Knight, Frederic B. Personal observations.

Kolb, Lawrence C., M. D. Personal observations.

Kornegay, Francis A. Personal observations.

Krato, John. Personal observations.

Krystal, Henry, and Raskin, Herbert A. *Drug Dependence*. Detroit: Wayne State University Press, 1970.

Kubie, L. S., M. D. "The Central Representation of the Symbolic Process in Relation to Psychosomatic Disorders." In *Recent Developments in Psychosomatic Medicine*. Ed. E. D. Wittkower and R. A. Cleghorn. London: Sir Isaac Pitman and Sons, 1954.

Lachman, Jordan H., M. D. Personal observations.

Laird, Margaret. "Life's Demonstration Is Christian Science." Lecture delivered at New Trier High School, Winnetka, Illinois, October 21, 1951. Published by Don Hall, Sarasota, Florida.

————. *Government Is Self Government*. San Diego, Calif.: Portal Press, 1970.

————. *Christian Science Re-Explored, A Challenge to Original Thinking*. Rev. ed. Los Angeles: The Margaret Laird Foundation, 1971.

Laughlin, Henry P., M. D. *The Neuroses*. Washington: Butterworth, 1967.

Lee, Dorothy. *Freedom and Culture*. New York: Prentice-Hall, Inc., 1959.

Levine, Maurice, M. D. *Psychiatry and Ethics*. New York: George Braziller, 1972.

Lipps, Theodor. *Komik und Humor*. 1898.

Lotze, Hermann. *Outlines of the Philosophy of Religion*. Trans. and ed. George T. Ladd. Boston: Ginn and Company, 1886.

Louis, Sister Mary. Personal observations.

Luccock, Halford E., and Brentano, Frances, eds. *The Questing Spirit: Religion in the Literature of Our Time*. New York: Coward-McCann, Inc., 1947.

Lunn, Arnold, and Lean, Garth. *The New Morality*. London: Blandford Press, 1964.

MacEwen, Ewen, M. D. Personal observations.

Mach, Ernst. *Contributions to the Analysis of Sensations*. Trans. C. M. Williams. Chicago: Open Court Pub. Co., 1897.

MacIver, R. M. *Community*. London: Macmillan, 1917.

Mackenzie, John S. *A Manual of Ethics*. New York: Hinds, Noble, and Eldredge, 1901.

MacLeish, Archibald. *Freedom is the Right to Choose*. Boston: The Beacon Press, 1951.

————. "The Irresponsibles." *Nation*, May 18, 1940, reprinted in *The Intellectuals*. Ed. George de B. Huszar. Glencoe, Ill.: Free Press, 1961.

————. "Why Do We Teach Poetry?" *The Atlantic Monthly* (March 1956).

Malone, Dumas. *Jefferson the Virginian*. Boston: Little, Brown and Company, 1948.

————. "Mr. Jefferson and The Living Generation." Occasional Paper 2, The National Endowment for the Humanities (April 1972).

Mark, Max. "The End of Power Politics." *The Virginia Quarterly Review* 44 (Summer 1968): 353–368.

Martin, Peter A., M. D. *Selected Papers of Peter A. Martin, M. D.* 1966.

Martineau, James. *Types of Ethical Theory*. Vol. 2. Oxford: Clarendon Press, 1886.

Marx, Karl. *A History of Economic Theories: From the Physiocrats to Adam Smith*. Edited with a Preface by Karl Kautsky. Trans. from the French, with an Introduction and Notes, by Terence McCarthy. New York: The Langland Press, 1952.

Masserman, Jules H., M. D. Personal observations.

Mayo, Bernard, ed. *Jefferson Himself: The Personal Narrative of a Many-Sided American*. Boston: Houghton Mifflin Company, 1942.

_____. "Thomas Jefferson's Faith in Human Integrity." In *The Growth of Self-Insight*. Ed. John M. Dorsey. Detroit: Wayne State University Press, 1962.

McCosh, James. *Gospel Sermons*. New York: Robert Carter and Brothers, 1888.

McEachren, John W. Personal observations.

McGregor, Tracy W. "Toward a Philosophy of the Inner Life." Paper read at the National Conference of Social Work, Detroit, June 1933.

McLean, Don W., M. D. Personal observations.

McMath, Neil C. Personal observations.

Meng, Heinrich, and Freud, Ernst L., eds. *Sigmund Freud, Psychoanalysis and Faith, Dialogues with the Reverend Oskar Pfister*. New York: Basic Books, Inc., 1963.

Menninger, Karl. *Man Against Himself*. New York: Harcourt, Brace, 1938.

Menninger, William C. *Psychiatry: Its Evolution and Present Status*. Ithaca, N. Y.: Cornell University Press, 1948.

Milbright, Don (Pen name, Sylvester). "The Logic in Truth and Love." Mimeographed material.

Miller, Amos W. (Rabbi). *Abraham: Friend of God*. New York: Jonathan David, 1973.

Modlin, Herbert C. "Science and Technology Vs. Ethics and Morals." *Bulletin of the Menninger Clinic* 37 (March 1973): 149–159.

Monahan, Maud. *Life and Letters of Janet Erskine Stuart*. London: Longmans, Green and Co., Ltd., 1922.

Moos, Malcolm Charles. *The Campus and the State* (with Stephen Hess). Baltimore: Johns Hopkins Press, 1959.

Morris, Annie. Personal observations.

Moser, Robert H., M. D., ed. *Adventures in Medical Writing*.

American Lecture Series. Springfield, Ill.: Charles C. Thomas, 1970.

Murray, James A. (Rev.). Personal observations.

Myers, Philip van Ness. *History as Past Ethics.* Boston: The Athenaeum Press, 1913.

Naka, Syuzo. M. D. Personal observations.

Nathan, Otto, and Norden, Heinz, eds. *Einstein On Peace.* Preface by Bertrand Russell. New York: Simon and Shuster, 1960.

Needham, J. *Science and Civilization in China.* Vol. 2. Cambridge: Cambridge University Press, 1956.

Neef, Arthur. Personal observations.

Newman, George F., M. D. Personal observations.

Niebuhr, Reinhold. *Moral Man and Immoral Society.* New York: Charles Scribner's Sons, 1932.

Nixon, Robert K., M. D. Personal observations.

Norton, William J. Personal observations.

O'Grady, Gerald B., Jr. (Rev.). Personal observations.

O'Meara, Thomas F., and Weisser, Donald M., eds. *Paul Tillich in Catholic Thought.* Garden City, N. Y.: Image Books, 1969.

Orton, Samuel T., M. D. Personal observations.

Otto, Rudolf. *The Idea of the Holy.* Trans. John W. Harvey. London: Oxford University Press, 1923.

Parker, Augustin H. Personal observations.

Parker, Judy. Personal observations.

Parks, Ralph (Rev.). Personal observations.

Parrington, Vernon Louis. *The Romantic Revolution In America 1800–1860.* New York: Harcourt, Brace and Company, 1927.

Patterson, Ralph M.; Craig, James B.; Waggoner, Raymond W.; and Freiberg, Richard. "Studies of the Relationship between Emotional Factors and Rheumatoid Arthritis." *Am. J. Psy.* 99 (1943): 775–780.

Pei, Mario A. "The America We Lost." *The Freeman* (May 1964): 7–9.

Perry, Bliss. *The American Spirit In Literature.* New Haven, Conn.: Yale University Press, 1918.

Perry, Ralph Barton. *Puritanism and Democracy.* New York: The Vanguard Press, 1944.

Peter, Julius C. Personal observations.

Peter, Laurence J., and Hull, Raymond. *The Peter Principle.* New York: William Morrow and Company, 1969.

Peterson, Merrill D. *Thomas Jefferson and the New Nation.* New York: Oxford University Press, 1970.

Petty, Thomas A., M.D. Personal observations.

Pierrot, George F. Personal observations.

Platt, John R. "Commentary on Theological Resources from the Physical Sciences." *Zygon* 1 (March 1966): 33–42.

Popielarz, Edward (Rev.). Personal observations.

Post, Louis F. *Ethics of Democracy*. Chicago: Louis S. Dickey and Co., 1903.

Poucel, Victor. *Mystique de la Terre*.

Power, Eugene B. Personal observations.

Power, Sadye. Personal observations.

Pratt, James Bissett. *The Religious Consciousness*. New York: Macmillan Company, 1924.

Prentiss, Henry J., M. D. Personal observations.

"Prisoners In America." Report of the Forty-second American Assembly, December 17–20, 1972, Arden House, Harriman, New York. Columbia University: The American Assembly, 1972.

Pruyser, Paul W. "The Practice of Science and Values: A Psychologist's Odyssey." *Bulletin of the Menninger Clinic* 37 (March 1973): 133–148.

_____. "Comment" on Herbert C. Modlin's "Science and Technology Vs. Ethics and Morals." *Bulletin of the Menninger Clinic* 37 (March 1973): 163–168.

Pyle, Ralph. Personal observations.

Radhakrishnan, S. *An Idealist View of Life*. London: George Allen and Unwin Ltd., 1932.

_____. *The Bhagavadgita*. New York: Harper, 1948.

Rank, Otto. *Psychology and the Soul*. Trans. William D. Turner. Philadelphia: University of Pennsylvania Press, 1950.

Raphael, Theophile, M. D. Personal observations.

Read, Leonard E. *Students of Liberty*. Irvington-On-Hudson, New York: The Foundation for Economic Education, Inc., 1950.

_____. *Let Freedom Reign*. Irvington-On-Hudson, New York: The Foundation for Economic Education, Inc., 1969.

Redl, Fritz. "Zum Begriff der Lernstoerung." *Zeits. f. psychoanal. Paedogogik* 8 (1934).

Reed, Allan W. (Rev.). "Thoughts On Thanatologists." *Harvard Medical Alumni Bulletin* (March/April 1973): 16, 17.

Reeves, Jesse S. "Perspectives in Political Science 1903–1928." *The American Political Science Review* 23 (February 1929).

Rosenbaum, Jean B., M. D. His insightful writings and personal observations.

240

Rosenzweig, Norman, M. D. "The Affect System: Foresight and Fantasy." *J. Nervous Mental Dist.* 117 (1958): 113–118.

Ross, Helen. "Play Therapy." *Am. J. Orthopsychiat.* 8 (1938): 499–524.

Rost, E. R. *The Nature of Consciousness.* London: Williams and Norgate Ltd., 1930.

Rostrevor, George. *Bergson and Future Philosophy.* London: Macmillan and Co., Ltd., 1921.

Russell, Dean. *Frederic Bastiat: Ideas and Influence.* Irvington-On-Hudson, New York: The Foundation for Economic Education, Inc., 1969.

Rynne, Xavier. *Letters from Vatican City.* New York: Farrar, Straus and Company, 1963.

Sadler, H. Harrison, M. D. Personal observations.

Sanford, John A. *The Kingdom Within.* Philadelphia and New York: J. B. Lippincott Company, 1970.

Sankovich, Joseph B. (Rev.). Personal observations.

Saul, L. J., M. D. *Emotional Maturity.* Philadelphia: Lippincott, 1947.

Sawher, Clifford F. (Monsignor). Personal observations.

Schilder, P. *Brain and Personality* (1931). New York: International Universities Press, 1951.

Schlick, M. *Problems of Ethics.* Vienna: Verlag Julius Springer, 1930. (Also New York: Prentice-Hall, 1939).

Schroeder, Henry A., M. D. *A Matter of Choice.* Brattleboro, Vermont: The Stephen Greene Press, 1968.

Sears, John E. J., Jr. Personal observations.

Seegers, Arthur J. (Rev.). Personal observations.

Seegers, Walter H. *My Individual Science.* Detroit: Center for Health Education, 1968.

Selleck, Henry B., and Whittaker, Alfred H. *Occupational Health in America.* Detroit: Wayne State University Press, 1962.

Selye, H. "Language, Science and Creativity." *Totus Homo* 2 (1970), No. 1.

Semple, Sidney J. (Rev.). Personal observations.

Sherrill, Lewis Joseph. *The Struggle of the Soul.* New York: The Macmillan Company, 1951.

Shore, Milton F., and Golann, Stuart E., eds. *Current Ethical Issues In Mental Health.* Based on a workshop at the 47th Annual Meeting of the American Orthopsychiatric Association, San Francisco, California, March, 1970. Rockville, Maryland: National Institute of Mental Health, 1973.

Sibille, Mike. Personal observations.

Simon, Leonard N. Personal observations.

Sinclair, May. *The New Idealism*. London: McMillan and Co., 1922.

Skutch, Alexander F. *The Quest of the Divine*. Boston: Meador Publishing Co., 1956.

Sladen, Frank J., M. D. Personal observations.

Slattery, Sister Mary Francis. *Hazard, Form, and Value*. Detroit: Wayne State University Press, 1971.

Slomovitz, Philip. Editorials and comments, *The Detroit Jewish News*.

Smith, Andrew J., Jr., M. D. Personal observations.

Smith, Lauren H., M. D. Insightful writings and personal observations.

Smith, Robert A. III. "The Psychiatrist and the Psychic Elements of Rebellion." Unpublished paper.

Smuts, Jan Christian. *Holism and Evolution*. New York: The Viking Press, Inc., 1961.

———. *Walt Whitman: A Study in the Evolution of Personality*. Ed. Alan L. McLeod. Detroit: Wayne State University Press, 1973.

Snavely, Tipton R. *George Tucker As Political Economist*. Charlottesville: University Press of Virginia, 1964.

———. *The Department of Economics at the University of Virginia, 1825–1956*. Charlottesville: University Press of Virginia, 1967.

Sohrab, Mirza Ahmad, ed. *The Bible of Mankind*. New York: Universal Publishing Company, 1939.

Solley, Charles M. *Peterkin: An Educational Fable*. Monterey, Calif.: Brooks/Cole Pub. Co., 1972.

Sophocles. *Oedipus Rex*. Trans. Dudley Fitts and Robert Fitzgerald. New York: Harcourt, Brace, 1949.

Spencer, Nena. Personal observations.

Sperling, O. E. "A Psychoanalytic Study of Social-mindedness." *The Psychoanalytic Quarterly* 24 (1955): 256–269.

Sperry, William B. (Rev.). Personal observations.

Spiegel, E. A., M. D., ed. *Progress in Neurology and Psychiatry*. Vol. 27. New York and London: Grune & Stratton, 1972.

Spitz, Rene A., M. D. *No and Yes on the Genesis of Human Communication*. New York: International Universities Press, 1957.

———. "Wiederholung, Rhythmus, Langeweile." *Imago* 23 (1937): 171–196.

Sprague, George S., M. D. "Ideas of Contamination as a Defense Against Sexuality." *Am. J. Psy.* 97 (1940): 659–666.

Stagner, Ross. *Psychological Aspects of International Conflict.* Belmont, Cal.: Brooks/Cole Pub. Co., 1967.

——. "Psychological Dynamics of Inter-City Problems." In *Seminar on Manpower Policy and Program.* Manpower Administration, U. S. Dept. of Labor, 1968.

Stanton, C. Frederic. Personal observations.

Stapleton, William J., Jr., M. D. *A History of the Michigan State Medical Society: A Century of Service in Medicine.* East Lansing, Michigan: Michigan State Medical Society, 1965.

Starbuck, Edwin Diller. "The Child-Mind and Child-Religion." *The Biblical World,* 1908.

Stearns, Martin. Personal observations.

Sterba, Editha. "Nacktheit und Scham." *Zeit. F. Psychoanalyse* 3 (1929).

Sterba, Richard, M. D. *Introduction to the Psychoanalytic Theory of the Libido.* New York and Washington: Nervous and Mental Disease Pub. Co., 1942.

Streiker, Lowell D., ed. *Who Am I?* New York: Sheed and Ward, 1970.

Stulman, Julius. "Climbing to Mankind Solutions." *Fields Within Fields . . . Within Fields.* The World Institute, Vol. 1, No. 3, 1968.

Sumner, William Graham. *Folkways.* Boston: Ginn and Co., 1906.

Suzuki, D. T., Cf. *Zen and Japanese Culture.* Bollingen Series 64. New York: Pantheon, 1959.

Szasz, T. S., M. D. "Comments on 'The Definition of Psychosomatic Disorder'." *Br. J. Phil. Sci.* 7 (1956): 231.

Teunissen, John J., and Hinz, Evelyn J., eds. *Roger Williams: A Key into the Language of America.* Detroit: Wayne State University Press, 1973.

The *Christian Bible.*

The *Koran.*

"The Principles of Medical Ethics With Annotations Especially Applicable to Psychiatry." *American Journal of Psychiatry* 130 (September 1973): 1058–1064. Statement approved by the Assembly of District Branches and the Board of Trustees of the American Psychiatric Association, May 5–6, 1973, upon recommendation of the Committee on Ethics, C. H. Hardin Branch, M. D., Chairman.

243

The Relation of Christian Faith to Health. Adopted by the 172nd General Assembly of The United Presbyterian Church in the United States of America, Philadelphia, Pennsylvania, May 1960.

The Selected Writings of John Jay Chapman. Edited and with an Introduction by Jacques Barzun. New York: Farrar, Straus and Cudahy, 1957.

The Spirit of Liberty: Papers and Addresses of Learned Hand. Collected, and with an Introduction and Notes, by Irving Dilliard. New York: Vintage Books, 1959.

The *Talmud.*

Thind, Bhagat Singh. *Divine Wisdom.* Salt Lake City, Utah: Dr. Bhagat Singh Thind, 1928.

Thurber, Cleveland. Personal observations.

Thurber, Donald M.D. Prismatic Club presentation.

Titus, Harold N. *Ethics for Today.* 2nd ed. New York: American Book Co., 1947.

Tourkow, Lawrence P., M. D. Personal observations.

Tourney, Garfield, and Gottlieb, Jacques S., eds. *Lafayette Clinic Studies on Schizophrenia.* Detroit: Wayne State University Press, 1971.

Towsley, Harry A., M. D. Personal observations.

Travis, Lee Edward. *Handbook of Speech Pathology and Audiology.* New York: Appleton-Century-Crofts, 1971.

Ulveling, Ralph A. Personal observations.

Untermeyer, Louis. *A Treasury of Great Poems, English and American.* New York: Simon and Schuster, 1955.

Urban, Wilbur Marshall. *Fundamentals of Ethics.* New York: Henry Holt and Co., 1930.

Van Doren, Mark. *Autobiography of Mark Van Doren.* New York: Harcourt, Brace and Co., 1958.

Van Epps, James McCone, M. D. Personal observations.

Vidor, King W. Personal observations.

Waelder, Jenny. "Analyse eines Falles von Pavor Nocturnus." *Zeitschrift f. Psychoanalytische Paedogogic* 9 (1935): 5–70.

Waelder, R. *Progress and Revolution.* New York: International Universities Press, 1967.

_____. "The Problem of Freedom in Psychoanalysis." *Internat. J. Psycho-Analysis* 17 (1936): 89–108.

Walshe, Sir Francis. Observations in medical psychology.

Watts, Alan W. *Psychotherapy East and West.* New York: Pantheon Books, 1961.

Weeks, Solan W. Personal observations.

Weiner, L. M. Personal observations.

Weipert, William J., Jr. Personal observations.

Westman, H. *The Springs of Creativity*. New York: Atheneum, 1961.

Wheeler, Harvey. "The New Balance of Power Politics." *Center Report*, ed. Mary Kersey Harvey, Center for the Study of Democratic Institutions (June 1972): 11–14.

White, E. B. "One Man's Meat." A collection of essays first appearing in *Harper's Magazine*, July 1940.

White, Mildred R. Personal observations.

White, W. A. "The Frustration Theory of Consciousness." *Psychoanal. Rev.* 16 (1929): 143–162.

Whitehead, A. N. *An Introduction to Mathematics*. New York: Henry Holt & Co., 1911.

———. *Modes of Thought*. Cambridge: University Press, 1938.

Whittaker, Alfred H., M. D. "James T. Whittaker, M. D., of Cincinnati." *The Ohio State Medical Journal* 50 (February 1954): 142–146.

———. "Treatment of Burns by Excision and Immediate Skin Grafting." *The American Journal of Surgery* 85 (March 1953): 411–417.

———, and Sloan, Ralph E. "The Roots of Medical Writing." *Journal of the Michigan State Medical Society* 60 (1961): 195.

Wilbur, George B., M. D. Personal observations.

Wilcox, Herbert G. "Moral and Social Constraints of a Bounteous, High-Energy Technology: Can We Meet the Challenge?" Prepared for delivery and distribution at the Second Annual Environmental Law Conference, West Virginia University, June 2, 1973.

Willson, Robert F. Personal observations.

Woodroffe, J. *Shakti and Shakta*. London: Luzac, 1929.

Woolley, Paul V., Jr., M. D. Personal observations.

Wundt, Wilhelm. *Volkerpsychologie*. Vol. 1, Part 1, 1900.

Wylie, Philip. *An Essay on Morals*. New York: Holt, Rinehart & Winston, Inc., 1947.

Young, Whitney M., Jr. *To Be Equal*. New York: McGraw-Hill, 1964.

Yu-Lan. Fung. *A Short History of Chinese Philosophy*. Ed. Derk Bodde. New York: The Macmillan Co., 1950.

Yutang, Lin. *The Wisdom of Laotse*. New York: Random House, 1948.

Shepherd, George W. Jr., Editor, *"Racial Influences on American Foreign Policy,"* Basic Books, Inc., Publishers, New York, London 1970.

INDEX

NAMES

Abse, D. Wilfred, 225
Adams, Henry, 225
Adler, Felix, 54
Adler, Morris, 225
Adler, Mortimer J., 225
Alighieri, Dante (see Dante)
Allee, William Coit, 225
Anaxagoras, 34
Anderson, Ralph D., Jr., 225
Antisthenes, 34
Aquinas, St. Thomas, 133, 171
Arasteh, A. Reza, 225
Aring, Charles D., 225
Aristotle, 4, 35, 36, 40, 48, 53, 111, 113, 118
Asch, Sholem, 225
August, Harry E., 225
Augustine of Hippo, 39
Aurelius, Marcus, xvii, 37

Babcock, Allen S., 225
Babcock, Winifred, 234
Bach, Marcus, 225
Baha, Abdul, 27
Ballinger, Malcolm B., 225
Bando, H. Walter, xxvii
Banks, A. A., 225
Barksdale, L. S., 225
Barrett, Albert M., 225
Barrett, C. Waller, 225
Bartemeier, Leo H., 225
Barth, Karl, 226
Barzun, Jacques, 244
Basilius, Harold A., 43, 226
Basler, Roy P., xxvii, 226
Bean, William B., 226

Beauvoir, Simone de, 226
Bell, Martin, 226
Bell, Whitfield J., Jr., 226
Bender, Lauretta, 226
Benham, Hamilton, 226
Bentley, A. F., 229
Bergson, Henri, xxvii, 165, 226
Berkeley, George, 42
Berlien, Ivan C., 226
Bibring, Grete L., 226
Billings, Ardella M., 226
Blackhurst, J. Herbert, 227
Blain, Alexander III, 227
Bodde, Derk, 57
Boelen, Bernard J., 227
Bohm, Henry V., 227
Bosanquet, Bernard, 48
Bowen, Lem W., 227
Bowne, Borden P., 52, 227
Boyd, Julian P., xxiv, 227
Braceland, Francis J., 227
Brazier, Mary A. B., 227
Breese-Whiting, Kathryn, 227
Brennan, Thomas P., 227
Brentano, Frances, 237
Brierley, Marjorie, 227
Brightman, Edgar Sheffield, 227
Britton, Erwin E., 227
Bronowski, J., 227
Brown, N. O., 227
Buchner, Franz, 152, 227
Buckham, John Wright, 227
Bueche, Gary, 227
Buffon, Georges, 173
Buhler, Karl, 91
Buonarrote, Michelangelo, 41

247

250

253

254

255

Good will, 43, 98
Goodness, 69, 75, 91, 105, 122, 136
Grace, 38, 151
Grammar, xvi
"Growing pains," 133
Growth, 120, 131
Guilt, 94, 123, 190

Habit, 25
Happiness, 5
Hardihood, 72, 133
Hate, ix, xvi, 79, 202
Health, xi, xii, 86, 174, 192, 200, 208
Health, "physical," 65
Health trouble, 9
Heaven, 5
Help, 110
Hero, xi
Hesitation, 167
History, 58
History, of ethic, 27
Holism, 153, 162
Human form, xxv
Humanity, 100
Hurt, 110
Hypochondria, 175

I, 70
I am that I am, 30
I-world, my self-world, 105
Idea, 90
Ideal, 86
Idealism, 105
Ideality, practice of, 26
Identity, 91
Identity, in ethical and unethical, 98
Identity, in opposites, 93, 97
Identity, personal, 79
Idiolect, 1, 13, 114
Idiopsychology, 140
Illness, 192
Illusion, 9, 72, 95, 119, 175, 176, 184, 207
Illusion, helpful, 149
Illusion, of externality, 31, 159
Imagination, xix, xxi, xxiii, 7, 14, 20, 28, 41, 64, 76, 92, 101, 103, 126, 140, 153, 159, 160, 166, 174, 210
Imagination, freedom of, 209
Immorality, 115, 195
Imperfection, 63, 116
Impotence, 166
Independence, 170
Individual, 58, 89, 113, 118
Individuality, 1, 90, 95, 148, 154, 166, 193, 208, 211
Individuality, conscious, 30, 39
Individuality-consciousness, 32
Individualization, 64
Infinity, 200
Inhibition, 78, 81, 110, 157, 166, 167, 206, 207
Injustice, 45, 63
Innocence, 170
Insight, 86, 113, 134, 141, 205
Insight, political, 86
Instinct, 28, 52
Integration, 3, 19, 110
Internal, x
Intuitionism, 50
Involuntary, 210
Irresponsibility, 128

Jealousy, 77, 79, 133, 134, 212
Joy of living, 124
Justice, 5, 27, 35, 39, 44, 48, 126, 191, 195, 211

Kindness, 44, 212
Kingdom of God, xv
Know thyself, 35, 47
Knowledge, 91, 167

Labor, manual, 46
Language, 46, 66
Laughter, 210
Law, 19, 27, 36, 55, 111, 112, 132, 139, 141, 161, 173, 199
Law, my, 82
Law of laws, 88
Learn, learning how to, 187
Learning, 27
Lie, 212
Life, xi, 2, 3, 6, 28, 39, 63, 108, 124, 125, 157, 158, 161, 200, 205, 208, 209

256

257

258

259